DIARY OF AN ON-CALL GIRL

WPC E E BLOGGS

Monday Books

D0452446

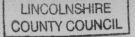

LINCOLNSHIRE
COUNTY COUNCIL

© E E Bloggs 2007

First published in Great Britain in 2007 by Monday Books

The right of E E Bloggs to be identified as the Author of this
work has been asserted by her in accordance with the
Copyrights, Designs and Patents Act 1988

All rights reserved. Apart from any use permitted under UK
copyright law no part of this publication may be reproduced,
stored in a retrieval system, or transmitted, in any form or by
any means, without the prior written permission of the
publisher, nor be otherwise circulated in any form of binding
or cover other than that in which it is published and without a
similar condition being imposed on the subsequent purchaser

A CIP catalogue record for this title is available from the
British Library

2007 ISBN : 978-0-9552854-7-9

Printed and bound by Cox and Wyman

www.mondaybooks.com
info@mondaybooks.com

CONTENTS

Foreword

*To all my colleagues, who laugh, seethe
and sometimes grieve together.*

Foreword

Before you turn to page 1, the first thing you need to do is FORGET EVERYTHING YOU THINK YOU KNOW ABOUT THE POLICE.

You know - the bits where they come out when you call 999, try to find out what's happened and arrest the guilty parties? Forget all that. While you're at it, forget all about common sense, too.

Instead, try to imagine a world where the police are run by a group of paranoid, pedantic and politically-correct accountants. On acid.

Imagine that half of the people who call the police are drunken, squabbling four-year-olds, but that the police still take their calls *really* seriously.

Imagine that half the people who work for the police spend their lives phoning officers asking them to respond to emails asking why they forgot to tick a box on the fifth in a set of a dozen forms relating to an incident where one of the drunken four-year-olds said a rude word to the other.

The modern British police is like all that, only much, much madder.

I am PC Bloggs, a 21st Century Police Officer.

I work in a place we'll call 'Blandmore', an average town somewhere in England. Unlike most coppers, I am a woman - in case you hadn't realised - and I work shifts on 'response'.

Being a police woman is very like being a police man, but with a lot more arguments.

I'm not a strident feminist, and nor am I in favour of positive discrimination. I don't think we should lower fitness standards to allow more women into the force, and I don't think anyone should get treated differently - whether better or worse - just because they have children.

I don't like kittens, but I probably do cry a bit too easily.

I wrote this book after realising, mostly from chatting to my family and friends, that people outside the job have absolutely no idea what's going on in the police.

They think we spend our days arresting criminals, cleaning up after road accidents and finding missing kids. And front line coppers like me do do all that, obviously (though we spend most of our time going to the same houses over and over again and sorting out domestic squabbles about TV remotes, rude text messages and ownership of the PlayStation). But most police officers and civilian staff are stuck in offices all day, sending emails, drawing up policy, auditing files, planning strategy, liaising with community groups, managing complaints, circulating strategy documents, setting targets and sending yet more emails. Actually laying hands on baddies? In our dreams!

Modern policing is a bizarre, twilight zone: one part George Orwell, one part Franz Kafka and one part *Trisha*.

At times, you may find it all a bit confusing. That's because it is. There are various references to police departments that sound unnecessary and pointless. That's because they are. To help you pick your way through this tragicomic minefield, there's a semi-serious glossary at the back.

It's all tremendously frustrating, though there are some satisfying moments and we have some great laughs. I do still love my job.

Everything I write about is true, though I've disguised the details and identities of those involved, obviously. If you think you've spotted yourself, trust me, you haven't! And, no, sadly that's not me on the front cover.

Finally, this book comes with a health warning: CONTAINS SATIRE, IRONY AND TRACES OF SARCASM.

If you read it and don't find yourself chuckling, congratulations: you are the Minister for Police.

1

W is for Woman

I AM A 21ST CENTURY Police Officer, a fearless and relentless crime fighter, and I'm very, very tired.

In fact, I'm dozing in a Transit van.

We're en-route to a 'domestic'. A concerned Mop - a member of the public - has called us to report that the man in the flat above may be murdering his wife.

Apparently, there has been a lot of banging around and screaming and shouting about knives.

We get a lot of calls like this, and they always mean blue lights and lots of nee-nawing. We know the couple in question, and there probably won't *be* a knife - there seldom is when you attend a report of a person with a knife, though if you attend a report of someone driving without car tax, or trying to return goods to a shop without a receipt, the odds are you're about to come face-to-face with an axe-wielding maniac. This kind of unpredictability just makes our job more exciting.

Somewhere in my dreams, the warmth of the van and the revving of the diesel engine has mutated and I feel I'm on a boat, somewhere in the middle of the sea. It might be the Med. I'll probably have a cocktail in a minute.

I jolt out of my pleasant reverie as the police carrier lurches to a halt.

Wiping the drool from my chin and unsticking my eyes, I glance around. Did anyone notice that I was asleep? The rest of the team are climbing out of the Transit, batons in their hands, so it looks as if I got away with it. I follow them, blinking in the glare of the harsh orange streetlights and shivering momentarily at the cold.

There are six of us, seven including the sergeant. We don't normally send a van load of officers to a domestic, but we're all out in the Transit tonight on 'Operation Patronise'. The aim of the Operation is to pour out of the van at strategic locations around town and Reassure the Public. So far, we have Reassured the staff in the Wild Bean Café and a few hoodied youths in McDonalds. But domestic violence is a high priority for us - perhaps the highest - so the duty inspector has ordered us to break away from the important business of Reassuring to come here.

I spend a moment or two reorientating myself, and flick open my own baton as I do so. It's a retractable metal stick, a snazzy, lightweight little thing which replaced our heavy wooden truncheons some time ago. As a means of subduing a drunk and angry male it's virtually useless, but it does hang nicely on my belt.

Everyone is milling around and whispering urgently to each other as they look for the address. Although well-known to us, the couple regularly move, and we're the first officers to visit them at this latest flat. House numbers on Britain's rougher estates seem to have been designed with the object of confusing the police: if you're outside No15, you can be sure that No39 is next door and No16 will be a quarter of a mile away. There's a lot of head-scratching going on, so I look down at the back of my hand. This is where all the important information gets recorded and there, underneath the team supper order (7 x pie and chips), is a number: 22.

Blinking, I look at the flats in front of me. A sign above the doorway says, '16-24'.

I check the back of my hand again.

Then a surge of adrenaline wakes me up.

'It's here!' I say, and move quickly towards the door. The team flocks over, elbowing and jostling each other to be first; chances to wrestle a knife-wielding man to the ground are all too few.

I open the door and dash up the concrete stairs.

Bongo is inches behind me, panting and grunting down my neck like a wild boar. As I run, I wonder whether it might be charitable to let him have first crack at the lunatic, but decide against it. He'll think I'm scared.

We arrive at the first landing, and pause. I glance at the door numbers and start up again. For some reason, incidents requiring the police always happen on the top floor.

'Do you want me to go first?' gasps Bongo.

W is for Woman

Our shoulders jam in the stairwell for a moment. I wrestle an elbow free, jab it into his heaving ribcage and surge ahead. I even find time to glance over my shoulder and give him one of my looks.

Suddenly, I find myself at the door of No22.

One by one, my colleagues arrive in various stages of panting dishevelment. We form a professional queue, backs pressed to the walls either side of the door, all gasping for air as quietly as possible. I can feel my heart thumping. I reach out a fist to knock, politely. The door isn't latched and it swings inwards.

It's gloomy inside, but I can see a man illuminated by the landing light. He's facing away, his upper half bare, his lower clad in scruffy combats. He's not wearing shoes and his hair is sticking out like straw, with sweat leaking out of it and running down his back.

It's unmistakeably Wayne Perril.

'Good evening, Wayne,' I say. He doesn't seem to have a knife. 'Is everything all right?'

I peer round him, sussing out the flat. Old takeaway containers are piled up around his feet. Beer cans litter the floor.

'Yeah,' he says. 'Everything's fine.'

'Is Lisa here?'

As if on cue, the bathroom door flies open and she staggers out. She's about twenty-three and dark-haired; her cheeks are flushed and splotchy. She is completely hysterical, gasping for breath and crying silently. Eventually, she recovers enough to start bawling.

'Look what he's fookin done to me!' she howls, pointing at her face.

I look at her. He seems to have plastered her in cheap make-up.

'I haven't done nothing, you stupid bitch,' says Wayne. 'But I fookin can if you want.' He raises a fist.

'Go on then, have it!' she shrieks back.

While it's very tempting to stand back and let them settle things with a good old-fashioned fist-fight, it probably isn't a good idea. So I step into the flat and get between them, my baton across Wayne's chest like a bar. Bongo follows me and pushes Wayne out onto the landing. I collapse my baton and turn to Lisa.

'He's beat me up,' she cries, gesturing to her face again.

I peer closer; the dark patch on her cheek is not mascara but the beginnings of a bruise, and her lower lip is puffy and bleeding. I poke my head out of the door and talk in the general direction of the rest of the team. 'He needs nicking for assault.'

This is highly magnanimous of me. Not only am I giving my team-mates the chance to grapple with a half-naked drunk - something all police officers love to do - but I am presenting one of them with a free opportunity to edge one step closer to their monthly target of eight arrests.

While police officers love to prevent crime, protect the public and keep the Queen's Peace, it's really all about 'targets' these days. One of our most important targets here in Blandmore is arrests. Our force isn't all that bothered who we arrest, or why, as long as we fill our cells with bodies, so each officer has a monthly arrests target. You can count an arrest towards your monthly target if you are the one who says the magic words (which are, believe it or not, 'You are under arrest'). Bongo is an arrest machine; he already has 15 for the month and is looking to beat the station record, set by 'Swanny' on Team 3. I'm currently on five.

I turn back to Lisa. 'I'll need to get a statement from you about what happened, and you'll have to come down and get some photographs taken of your injuries,' I say. I have a whole spiel that I give to victims of domestic violence, about bail conditions, prosecution, court and victim support, and I launch into this with a well-practised air.

Lisa listens, nodding and sniffing.

When I've finished, she says, 'You ain't gonna arrest him, are you?'

I am taken slightly aback. 'Well, of course we are. In fact, we have.'

She starts crying, and stamps a foot. 'I don't believe this. I don't want him arrested!'

'It's too late,' I tell her. 'And it's sort of what we do?'

The pitch of her wailing rises several notches - she sounds like a hare caught in a trap - and now both feet are stamping alternately, faster and faster, until the door shakes shut.

'Does this mean you're not willing to give us a statement?' I say.

There is no response, so I go on. 'Perhaps you'd sign here to confirm…?'

The proffered pocketbook is met with an even louder screech, and Lisa storms back into the bathroom, slamming the door behind her. I scratch my head. I need a signature to prove to my supervisors that

W is for Woman

Lisa has refused to give a statement. Otherwise they might even have to take my word for it, and they don't like having to do that.

I tap hopefully on the bathroom door. 'Er… Lisa?'

'Go away!'

'Um, unfortunately, we *are* still going to be arresting Wayne, so you may as well talk to us. You see, we can't leave him here with you both so angry, and at the end of the day he has smacked you and should answer some questions about it...'

Before I can listen for a response, I feel a nudging on my back. It is Lloyd bending down from his six foot four tower to murmur in my ear, 'Did you say we're arresting Wayne?'

I turn my head. 'Yes… I said he needed nicking?'

'Ah,' he says. 'I didn't hear you. So where is he?'

'He's just out there.'

'Out where?'

'Out there, on the landing. The half-naked drunk guy covered in sweat… you know, the one who looks exactly like Wayne Perril?'

'He's not out there, Bloggsy.'

I look at him, and then I go to check. He's quite right. Wayne's nowhere to be seen.

'But,' I say. 'But Bongo sent him out there.'

All eyes turn to Bongo. 'Well, I just pushed him out of the way, really,' he says. 'Didn't anybody think to stop him?'

We all freeze, and then run to the nearest window. Through the smeared, greasy glass I can just make out a dishevelled figure staggering at some speed between the blocks of flats.

'There he is!'

We charge down the stairs in a flurry of elbows and clanking batons, half-climbing over each other in the race to get after him.

Outside, Wayne is nowhere to be seen: he must have ducked for cover. Somebody calls up on their radio to alert the rest of the police in Blandmore, and we break off into pairs to look for him.

I fall in with Becks, half-jogging, half-walking in the direction we saw him last.

'What's he done this time?' she asks.

'Smacked her about a bit,' I say. 'She doesn't want him arrested, again.'

Becks sighs. 'She's just as bad as him.'

'Well, that's not very feminist,' I say.

'Yes it is,' she says. 'Women are just as capable of committing crime as men. She's just weaker, so she always loses the fights. What's not feminist about that?'

We have now circled two of the neighbouring buildings, checking all doorways and bins, and are emerging onto the main road. Still no sign of Wayne.

I hear on the radio that the force helicopter and a pair of dogs are on the way to assist. The chopper costs about £2,000 for every minute it's airborne, and is rarely deployed for anything less serious than a fleeing drink driver, so this is really quite thrilling.

We're instructed to take up static points to contain the area. This means we stand still at strategic locations to avoid running all over the track that the dogs are about to follow. Unfortunately, we've been running all over it for a good ten minutes.

Becks and I come to a halt by the edge of Wayne's block and fix our gazes on the various paths threading between the buildings. We wait fifteen minutes and then finally hear the whap-whap-whap of the helicopter above us. Shortly afterwards, the dog handlers arrive and deploy their wet-nosed charges on long rope leashes. A small crowd of Mops is gathering on the pavement.

The nearest dog has latched onto a strong scent and is straining to pull his handler along behind.

Becks clears her throat. 'Do you think we should tell him that he's following the trail we just left?'

The handler in question is Trevor. I first met him when I was new in the job and had accidentally wandered through an area he was about to search for a burglar. He called me names I'd never even heard of and he wasn't even sorry when I burst into tears.

'What he doesn't know won't hurt him,' I say.

Trevor is getting increasingly frustrated as his German Shepherd keeps trying to run over to us. 'Get back here, you daft hound,' he says. 'Those are police officers.' After half an hour or so, he calls it a day. 'No dinner for you,' he says to his dog, and they disappear off back to his van.

Becks and I giggle discreetly.

The helicopter peels off, and the other dog van leaves, too. Defeated, we traipse back to the Transit. Sergeant Woodcock arrives last, lathered in sweat and about as annoyed as he ever gets.

'Well, that was professional,' he says.

'Sorry, sarge,' we all mumble.

'Down to Bongo, so he can buy the doughnuts,' he says.

If you're late for work, fall asleep in the passenger seat of a police car or lose a prisoner, you have to buy doughnuts for the whole shift. As losing a prisoner is a disciplinary offence for which you could be fined, demoted or even fired (if you kept doing it), no-one complains much about the doughnut rule.

Lloyd fires up the engine and we head out of Corinthian Way in the direction of the late night Tesco. A couple of minutes later, we park up in the bus stop and Bongo gets out, heading for the bakery counter. Becks gets out to have a cigarette, and I follow to chat with her while we wait.

'Trev wasn't amused,' she chuckles, blowing smoke out of the corner of her mouth.

'I know, he…'

I break off, staring at the entrance to the supermarket.

There, still shoeless and shirtless, and remonstrating with a security guard, is a familiar figure.

'Look,' I say. 'There's bloody Wayne .'

Becks stubs out her cigarette and we go across together to address the runaway. He waves a laden carrier bag and throws us a cheerful grin.

'Hello, girls,' he says, his attempt at flirting rather spoiled by a large belch that almost over-balances him.

'Hello, Wayne,' says Becks. 'We've been looking for you.'

'And I've been looking for you,' he leers.

She rolls her eyes, and then lays both hands on his right arm. He swings round in surprise, the carrier bag flying up and hitting me in the chest with a thud. I pull it from his hand and take his other arm, and together we handcuff him.

'You're under arrest for assault,' I tell him. This moves me onto six arrests for the month. Result!

He puts up no resistance as I caution him and lead him over to the Transit. I know Sergeant Woodcock is elated because he goes so far as to raise his eyebrows. We open the cage doors and insert our prisoner.

Becks is peering into the carrier bag.

'What is it?' I ask.

She reaches in and withdraws a six-pack of Carlsberg.

It turns out Wayne wasn't running away; he just went to buy some more beer.

Bongo returns, armed with doughnuts, and we all clamber back into the van. He sits down at the back and rubs his head, clearly embarrassed at the fiasco he's created. To make himself feel better, he inserts an entire doughnut into his mouth.

'Here,' says Wayne, through the mesh of the cage. 'Can I have one?'

Bongo's eyes open wide in amazement, and he starts to choke. Eventually he recovers and points at Wayne. 'H-h-how the bloody...?' he stutters.

'Oh yes,' says Becks. 'Funny story, actually...'

She fills him in while we drive to the police station and I am deposited with my prisoner, Bongo staying to help me go through the booking-in procedure.

The rest of the shift pile back into the van and head off to the next family crisis.

* * * * *

I should probably mention at this stage, in case you have not gathered, that I am a woman Police Constable. WOMAN. I have been doing this job for several years and if I wasn't a moody, bossy cow before (which I was), then I am now.

Being a WPC means I'm a member of a special club. I get invited to special seminars. People phone me at home with offers of promotion. When I joined, I was permitted to ask for a skirt (although this privilege has now sadly been stripped away) along with the 'tight allowance' - not just a description of my salary, but a special bonus to pay for tights. I also get to put 'W' before my title to pre-warn members of public that they have the privilege of being served by a Woman. This 'W' also appears on my personnel screen, next to 'R' for Response driver and 'L' for Languages (apparently, I once said I could speak French), so that the bods in the control room can search for officers with the correct Woman training required for certain jobs.

All in all, being a WOMAN POLICE CONSTABLE is pretty special. Lucky me.

W is for Woman

I am one of two females out of eight officers on my Shift, a Shift being a team of Response officers whose main job is to race out to crimes in-progress, crimes just happened, or crimes which 'happened last week but I only decided to call the police today because my partner called the police on me first'.

In case you were unaware, 21st Century Women are EQUAL to men. It's taken us a few millennia to catch up, but at last we've done it and the view from up top is pretty fab. Where once we were only allowed out with a male officer, I am now permitted to be crewed with another female, which makes for lots of girly chatting. I am also permitted to be single-crewed, which gives me lots of chances to fight men and show how equal I am. For the first time, not all female police officers are lesbians, so that makes for a much happier atmosphere of flirting and inter-colleague affairs, rather than all the nasty insults about 'dykes', which are now just reserved for those women officers with really short hair or who don't flirt enough.

Occasionally, you hear a gobby female mouthing off about how 'we still have a long way to go', about 'sexism in the workplace' and such clichés. These females need to have it pointed out to them just how far we have come. Over just a few months in 2005/06, no fewer than three Woman Police Constables were shot, SHOT, in the line of duty. One even died. How much more equal can we get?

Because women have found it so hard to become equal, there is a lot of help out there for the Woman Police Constable. Take the police fitness test. In 2004, the pass standard was lowered to ensure applicants would not actually have to break sweat. This was because of campaigns by various Friends of Women societies making the point that women simply cannot run faster than a slow jog, it is JUST NOT POSSIBLE. Anyway, you don't need to run quick to be a police officer, male or female. We're all equally unlikely to get out of our station or car on any given day, and on the few days per year where a chase occurs I've found it's better to let the men win anyway, as they really do love catching baddies more than we do.

Bongo, whose 'real' name is Paul, is a prime example of a man who loves catching baddies. He has very little interest in victims, witnesses, decaying bodies or speeding cars. But put him in sight of a running man and a recently-robbed old woman, he will chase the offender down until he nails him, whether it takes a minute or an hour.

This might have something to do with his enormous arrest rate. How many of his arrests actually make it to court is another matter.

Bongo leans on the counter as I fill out the search forms and then he takes Wayne's handcuffs off and pats him down. It's impossible to carry out a full search on the street, so we have to wait until we get them to the nick. Custody law dictates that a search must be same-sex, which is a relief. A surprising number of male criminals hide weaponry and stolen goods in their underwear, and, odd as this may seem, I have no desire to prod around in the underwear of our male customers. I should add that I don't especially desire to prod around in female underwear, either, though sadly, from time to time, I have to.

I watch my colleague carry out the search, impressed, as always, with his thoroughness. Despite banter to the contrary, it is a remarkably uncomfortable feeling having to run your hands over a stranger's body. When I first joined, I was intensely squeamish about it and it took an incident where I overlooked a syringe in a woman's bra before I got my act together. Nowadays, if arrested by yours truly, you are going to feel searched good and proper by the time I'm finished with you. Oh, and no matter what offence you've been arrested for, you WILL have your shoelaces, jewellery and belts taken off you. The gaolers really don't want any of these items plunged into or wrapped around their necks as they walk past later on.

Unsurprisingly, Bongo finds no knife secreted within Wayne's clothing.

It takes forty minutes to book him into custody, take his fingerprints, photograph him and thrust him into a cell. We then consider our options and come to the conclusion that we should at least pay Lisa another visit to see whether she has changed her mind about prosecuting.

Sadly, she hasn't. She just wants Wayne Back Home Now.

There are some incidents which can be written off with the words, 'This is not a police matter.'

These include: Cars parked on the kerb, someone you lent a mobile to not returning it, your divorce, being locked out of your house, needing a lift home, spending all your benefit money and pretending it was stolen to get a crime reference so they'll issue it again, and wanting to trace a long-lost relative. Believe it or not, some people do contact us for help with these matters. Some of them even dial 999 and then they make a complaint when we tell them they need to call a taxi/locksmith/lawyer.

There are some things, however, which are *always* police matters. One of these is DOMESTIC VIOLENCE. If you learn nothing else as a 21st Century Police Officer, you learn that your sole aim in life is to prevent Domestic Violence. To prevent people from living in fear. To help victims make 'good choices'. To help women who are with 'the wrong guy'. To arrest 'the wrong guy'.

It can only be a matter of time before the police are called on to vet all relationships at an early stage to prevent women from getting hooked up with 'the wrong guy' in the first place.

For now, though, we must fall back on our training and our powers of arrest.

It is impressed upon us, in computer-delivered training sessions sent to us by email, that as soon as we discover that the person who has called the police is in a relationship, we should look to arrest their partner. If it isn't clear which party is the offender, both should come in. This is because every arrest for Domestic Violence should be thought of as preventing a potential future murder, and thus keeping the name of Blandshire Constabulary out of the papers. You might imagine that most police officers don't actually want Members of the Public to die horribly at the hands of their maniac partners. Further, you might assume that, given that we have vast experience of visiting domestics, we ought to be trusted to decide who really needs arresting and who can be let off with a stern talking-to. This is because you are Naïve. Blandshire Constabulary is not Naïve: hence the training.

I first saw our training put into practice by none other than Bongo himself. It was in my first few weeks on Response, and I was paired with him on a night shift.

The call came in, 'Male is being hit by his partner.'

As we drove, blue lights a-flaring, the crucial information was added: 'A crime report for assault has already been created.'

The golden rule of modern policing is that a crime report, once created, cannot be deleted, altered or removed without the use of deep magicks beyond our ken (involving dozens of forms and emails between officers and our Auditors). This unalienable truth guided our actions for the next minute or two.

We pulled up outside the address. Bongo was first in to the house. I paused to lock the panda and, as I got to the front door I met him coming the other way with a handcuffed woman, uttering the words, 'You do not have to say anything, but it may harm your defence if you do not mention when questioned something you later rely on in court. Anything you do say may be given in evidence.'

These are the words of the police Caution, said whenever someone is arrested. Without these hallowed phrases, any instantaneous confession offered by your prisoner is invalidated and you run the risk of being labelled 'oppressive'.

As he marched past, he said over his shoulder, 'Find out what she's meant to have done, won't you?'

I looked at him, blankly. Surely *he* must know what she had done, in order to have arrested her? You see, at that stage of my career, I was still Naïve.

I located the caller at the back of the lounge, still on the phone to the police operator. He hung up when he saw me.

'What happened?' I said.

'She punched me in the mouth,' he said.

I saw a red spot on his lip and relayed this fact via radio to Bongo.

'Come on then,' he radioed back.

And that was it. We carted the female, whose name I still do not know, to custody, and other officers went to the address to take a statement from the victim.

As we drove, I cleared my throat tentatively and raised the issue. 'So,' I said. 'That was… efficient.'

Bongo shrugged. 'If there's already a crime report with the Domestic Violence box ticked, you know we're going to have to arrest her at some point,' he said. 'It will either be tonight, or next week after ten emails from the Auditors. Why waste time talking to the victim? If it turns out the assault isn't serious or can't be proved, she'll just be released. Just like she will if it is serious, actually.'

I nodded slowly. 'What if there isn't a crime report?'

'Well, then it's up to us to decide whether there's actually been an assault or not.'

Crime reports. Auditors. Boxes ticked. Back then this was all desperately confusing to an idealistic young girl like myself, who had joined the police with the vague notion that I would arrest people when I had proper evidence that they had committed a crime.

But the beauty of Bongo's approach soon became clear. Not only would we end up spending less than ten seconds inside often unpleasant homes, our actions would actually be supported by force policy. Nowadays, I'm equally efficient when I attend these incidents. If I see a bruise, a cut or even a slight reddening of the skin, my handcuffs are out of their pouch before the victim has even opened his or her mouth, never mind the suspect. In this way, I can feel I am achieving great things for Blandshire Constabulary. Soon we will be able to declare ourselves the Top Force for Domestic Violence Arrests with the least amount of time spent on them. And look at the money we save. Rather than training police officers to be sensitive, flexible and compassionate, we merely need to teach them the words of the Caution.

There are people out there who live in desperate hope that the police will swoop to their door and rescue them in their time of need, that we will comfort and advise them, and then make an informed decision about what to do. I can give you my advice without needing to swoop anywhere: if you don't want him arrested, don't call.

* * * * *

By now you may be thinking I am some sort of cynical, hard-nosed bitch, and possibly a 'dyke' to boot. You probably have an image of a ginger-haired, lean, mean fighting girl who attends a rifle club on her days off and owns an Alsatian with a studded collar.

If this is the case, please indulge yourself.

There are women like that in the police. And there are also girls like Joanna from Team 1.

Jo is in the report room when Bongo and I return from seeing Lisa again. She is leaning over Lloyd as he scans a website for holiday destinations; one delicately-manicured fingernail is tapping the desk. Her shirt is undone to the third button and she's wearing her warrant card on a red cord around her neck as the next best thing to a necklace.

But Lloyd is a through-and-through family man whose only quirk is an unnatural interest in flatulence (bizarrely shared by the rest of the blokes on my team) so he is oblivious to Jo's blond-streaked, straightened hair and her teeny weeny turned-up nosey. That doesn't stop her from strategically deploying these attributes and she is equally oblivious to his obliviousness.

Guy, another bloke on my shift, is watching Jo's antics wistfully from the other side of the room, and trying to get her attention by stapling pieces of paper together.

Bongo wishes to get past me, so - as usual - he grasps the scruff of my stab vest and lifts me bodily to the left. I consider lodging a complaint of sexual harassment, but instead take my revenge by filling an envelope with hole-punch circles and putting it in his post tray. That will give us a moment of hilarity next week when he sprays them across the room. Unless it's one of the many envelopes that he bins without opening.

I sit down to log onto a computer. It's always worth logging onto a computer if there's one free, as you never know when it will happen again and there's always some pre-emptive paperwork you can do. Beside me, Rich is playing an Internet game where you fire cats into the air in order to kill moles and across the desk Becks is 'surfing' the Incident Control System to read transcripts of incidents where people have died. This hum of inactivity isn't down to laziness; it's merely evidence of the important police skill of Email Avoidance. Most police officers receive around 100 emails a week. Most of them are completely pointless and sent by someone in an office somewhere who is paid solely for this purpose. The best thing is just to delete them without reading them.

I produce a report on Wayne Perril so that someone can interview him when he's sober. We have this time-wasting attitude that if someone has whacked his partner, at the very least he should have to answer some questions about it. The report contains the words 'as bad as' and 'each other' to reflect past occasions when Lisa has thumped Wayne, but in the interests of fairness also the words 'abusive', 'drunken' and 'thug' to highlight his possibilities as a prosecution candidate. I then pass it to the sergeant to sign.

Sergeant Chris Woodcock has twelve years' service and is therefore considered competent to sign a large number of forms every day. Chris has wanted to be in charge of signing things since he was a little boy, and it's wonderful to see him achieve his ambition. Bear in mind that only two other people check the work he's signed afterwards to make sure he hasn't lied or cocked up. Now *that's* trust.

He shakes his head wearily as he reads the paperwork. 'Those two *both* need locking up,' he says, 'We're called out to them at least once a month.'

'I know, sarge.'

I take back the signed document ready for dispatch to the Domestic Violence Unit (DVU). 'Do you think DVU will deal with him this time?'

'Only if there are no Strategy Conferences going on in the entire country.'

DVU staff *do* seem to attend a lot of conferences. There's a momentary pause.

'What do DVU *do*, sarge?'

'They support shift officers, Bloggs, as do all support departments.'

'*How* do they support us, sarge?'

'Well, we send them completed risk assessments and they support us by reading these and further assessing the risk to that victim.'

'Hmmm,' I say. 'Is that *it*?'

'Don't forget that they then ring up the victim and fill out another, longer risk assessment.'

'And...?'

'They then set up a meeting with the local Council to compare risk assessments and decide on a new and final level of risk which will be reassessed and agreed by their supervisors.'

'I see,' I say, my eyes glazing over slightly. 'Sorry, *how* do they support us again?'

'Well, with all that risk-assessing, they are then fully equipped to send us emails telling us where we went wrong and what we need to do next to put it right. That's where the support comes in.'

Sergeant Woodcock is *so* wise.

I take the information on Wayne Perril up to DVU. One baffled officer is working the late shift. This is due to an administrative error: there shouldn't be any, as DVU is strictly a 9-5 sort of thing.

I discuss the case with him. He explains that if there'd been airtight evidence proving the crime, his unit might have been able to help. But since there isn't, the incident is better investigated by someone with less specialist training, who doesn't have so much risk-assessing to do. That is, an ordinary response officer like me.

The night shift of response officers are delighted to take over the job from me, and I sign off-duty at 11pm sharp with the pride of someone who has just saved her force from paying her any overtime. I can now afford to forget about the mad, sad plight of the Perrils, although something tells me that I will be hearing from them again soon.

On arriving home I am confronted by a naked white mattress and duvet. I just about remember putting every sheet I own into the wash at lunchtime in a fit of anger over an offhand remark made by my boyfriend, Luke, which may or may not have been to do with women and housework. I don't remember taking them out again. This oversight is known as Policeman's Fog and you should bear in mind that any police officer attending your house might be suffering from it at the time he or she inserts your complaint into a bin. I said 'might'.

It will take half an hour to dry a sheet, so I give up and lie down on the mattress with a towel for a blanket.

I dream that I have received emails regarding my lack of laundry expertise and suggesting that some re-training is in order.

2

Crap Car

BELIEVE IT OR NOT, I do sometimes patrol alone. Health and Safety don't like it and, yes, it is dangerous and, yes, I am taking risks. I guess I'm just one crazy gal.

The terrors of stepping out into the darkness without male support are allayed by the cheering remarks I receive from concerned Mops.

Wrinkled old ladies stop me and say, 'Should you be out on your own?'

Housewives turn back from pouring me a cuppa and ask, 'Don't they put you with a man, normally?'

The occasional chap will give me a flirty grin and say, 'Gosh, you're too pretty to be a police officer.' (As a professional woman, I can never hear that one enough.)

Then there are my regulars. They tend to be slightly more direct. Like, 'Oi, Bloggs, you pig bitch.'

(When I'm crewed with Becks, the above comments will double or treble and also change in nature. For many Mops, two female officers fighting crime on their own is quite the most exciting thing they've ever seen; for some, it's second only to watching lesbian porn movies. And we like being crewed together, as it gives us a chance to bitch about the boys and discuss handbags, jewellery and fluffy animals. Our sergeant understands the womanly need for chats like this, and so he sends us out together at least once a week - and damned be the consequences! I respect him for that.)

I'm on my own today, in a panda, heading to the outskirts of town, but I'm not patrolling. I'm on my own because I have been designated today's 'Crap Car.'

CRAP is a police acronym which stands for Quality Service Department. This is a Department set up for the purpose of pacifying people who have been treated badly by the police, and it's well worth the cost of the staff who have been taken away from serving the public to man it.

When people call the police, they are immediately classified as one of three kinds of caller:

1) Someone who needs the police.

2) Someone who will need the police soon.

3) Someone who doesn't actually need the police but still wants them and will keep calling until they come.

The first two kinds are seen to by the response units, but the third category is the most important. These are the grassroots callers where we get most of our custom. As you'll have gathered, it can be a difficult task to identify exactly why some of these people have actually called the police, or what crime is meant to have been committed. But it is always worth the hour-long discussion to find out.

Calls from this category can number up to twenty a day in Blandmore, so one car containing one officer is assigned to deal with jobs like this which have stacked up over the days and weeks; this is the Crap Car.

One of the main duties of the Crap Car is to apologise to as many people as possible for taking a week to get to them.

In briefing, when Chris read out the assignments for the day, I might have let out a quiet moan.

'I know you've been Crap Car twice this week, Bloggsy, but if you will keep turning up to work every day…'

I accepted the sergeant's sympathy with my usual maturity: 'But, sarge, it's not fair. Can't we just tell the Quality Service Department that we don't have enough people on duty to provide a Crap Car?'

He looked up in surprise. 'But, Bloggsy, we have nine officers working today.'

I shared some baffled expressions with my team-mates. With Lloyd in court, Nick still off sick and Guy on a Transit-driving course, I counted five heads in the briefing room.

'Nine, sarge?'

'According to the email I got yesterday,' he elaborated. 'There's you five, then there's Frances, Woody, George and Louise.'

Some of the names evoked a pang of nostalgia. Frances disappeared over eighteen months ago when she fell pregnant. Woody was the team's serious crime guru until he took an attachment with CID and never came back.

'Who are George and Louise?' demanded Becks.

'George is our new probationer,' Chris scanned his sheet again, 'Due to start in a month's time. Except that he's come down with glandular fever and will likely be off until the summer. Louise was before your time, most of you, but she was on our Team until she got made Acting Sergeant in Charl. She keeps failing her promotion interview, but they keep her on as an Acting Sergeant because there isn't anyone else.'

I vaguely recalled a slim, red-haired woman who worked at Blandmore when I started. Back then, I really do remember having nine heads in briefing. I even recall a day when someone had to stand, due to lack of chairs.

'But how can all of them be counted in our manning levels?' Becks went on. 'Most of them aren't coming back.'

'No, but technically they're on temporary absences. We're actually one of the flushest shifts at Blandmore.'

I took in my colleagues' faces with new eyes, not having realised quite how good the situation was. With all that manpower, our arrest and detection rates will no doubt start to soar. Any day now.

*****

Today, I have been assigned five Crap jobs. I scan through them quickly and pick off the easy ones: a mini-motorbike to collect and a photograph to return to a found child's parents.

The mini-motorbike has been stolen again and the found child's family have moved house, so with the first two tasks complete I reluctantly pick up the third.

'Caller Mr Grahams from Flat 18, 38 Biffenden Road is reporting Harassment by his ex-partner's new partner's ex-partner.'

I feel a sense of dread.

Harassments are perhaps the worst of all offences.

This is not because police officers do not have a fervent desire to nab and lock up the genuinely twisted stalkers of this world. We do.

It is because of the vast gulf which exists between the police definition of 'stalking' and the average Blandmore resident's definition.

Police definition: following a rejected pass, he follows me home, appears outside my workplace, sends bizarre and creepy gifts involving dead animals, moves things around in my house while I'm sleeping, threatens my partner with a pickaxe and phones me during the night to say, 'You're wearing a blue nightdress' when I am.

Blandmore resident's definition: following a relationship which has been off-and-on until this morning, he has texted me five times and one of the texts says I am a meanie.

As a display of police impartiality, our response to these two incidents will be identical. A statement will be taken, the unsolicited texts or gifts viewed, and a crime report generated on the system. Each harasser will then be arrested, will probably deny it and the Crown Prosecution Service will then advise a charge, in order to protect themselves should he pop up and kill the victim later. It's called Arse-Covering.

The case of the text messages will likely result in a guilty plea and conviction at court due to the irrefutable evidence of the messages coming from the suspect's mobile number.

The case of violent stalking will eventually result in no evidence being offered as the victim is the only person who has witnessed it and she is legally Mad.

I take a quick look at the other two jobs I've been given. One is a summons to serve, which just means knocking on someone's door and telling them to attend court on Monday. The other is a complicated eBay fraud involving a fax to another force and enquiries with banks. It's a difficult choice between the summons, the fraud and the harassment, but after a moment's thought, maybe less, the summons wins out.

My route takes me through Upper Blandmore. Its real name is the Porle estate, but Upper Blandmore is the next parish over and is where all the rich people live, so many Porle residents like to pretend they live there, too. They seem to think that if they say they live in Upper Blandmore their house will suddenly grow a conservatory and their children will magically be called James and Sophie.

I find the street I'm looking for and look up and down the road. It's often easiest to find the house you need by its appearance, as the door numbers are usually missing. I narrow my choice down to two: one has blackened mulch covering the insides of all the downstairs windows, the other a broken washing machine in the front garden. Either could well be the home of someone due in court on Monday.

It turns out that my instinct has failed me, and I'm actually supposed to be attending the large corner house behind a high, red brick wall. There is a garden gate set into the wall with a keypad beside it.

I press the buzzer and wait. Then I press it again. Finally, I press it several times in a sort of irritated rhythm. At last, a voice comes out of the speaker.

'Yes?'

'It's the police.'

'I know. I can see your car.'

I squint through the gaps in the gate and see a woman at the upstairs window, staring down at me.

'Could you let me in?'

'I know why you're here. You've come about my son. He doesn't live here any more.'

There's a click, and I assume that means the woman thinks our conversation is at an end.

I look through the gate; there are two cars parked on the driveway outside. A quick computer check reveals that one of them is indeed registered to her son. I press the buzzer again.

'Yes?'

'His car's outside,' I say.

There is a silence. 'Well, you can't come in.'

'If you could just tell him to attend court...'

She cuts me off by hanging up with another click. I remain stumped for a few minutes. A summons has to be handed physically to the named person to be legally binding. I lean on the gate, and to my surprise it swings inwards.

I take a few tentative steps into the garden, and stop: the front door is opening, and a man is standing in the doorway.

'Mr Lawson?' I say, loudly. He is holding a large pit bull by its studded collar; the dog is growling ominously in my direction.

'Yes,' he says. 'Piss off. You can't come in.'

'That's fine. I just need to tell you about court.'

'Well, I'm letting the dog out for a walk.' He lets go of the dog's collar and makes to go back in. The pit bull starts charging towards me, fangs snapping together.

I have about a second to react: I ball up the summons in my right hand and lob it as hard as I can in his direction, racing through the gate and slamming it behind me as I do so. The dog barrels into it, yapping and growling, and I peer back through. The summons has bounced off the wooden pillar holding up the porch and rolled onto the grass. The dog pounces on it gleefully.

Panting slightly, I phone up the guy in the Quality Service Department and inform him that the summons has been served. It's a dangerous world out there for a 21st Century Police Officer.

I head back to my panda. As I drive away, my radio crackles into life.

'PC Bloggs, control, over?'

As the Crap Car, I shouldn't really be getting calls from control. Being alone, I am no use to anyone, because I'm not supposed to make arrests or attend fights and car crashes in case I trip over and break a bootlace whilst doing so. Of course, you frequently end up at these incidents anyway, either by bad luck or over enthusiasm, but at least then your sergeant can say he didn't send you.

'PC Bloggs receiving, go ahead.'

'PC Bloggs, the sergeant is asking if you can return your panda to the nick so that a double-crewed unit can go out in it. There are a couple of pandas at the station but no-one can find the keys.'

'Yes, copied.'

It's my fault, really, for thinking it was a good idea to get out and do some work when I could have been sitting at the police station Waiting For A Car. A good hour or two at the start of every shift in Blandmore is spent Waiting For A Car. We might have six pandas for our shift, but only four sets of keys - the number of people who accidentally take them home is astonishing. Or our cars might just have been filched by other departments.

I return to the station and Becks holds her hand out as I enter. I drop the keys into it.

'Enjoy.'

She stands up and grins. 'Sorry, Bloggsy, but at least you can't do any Crap jobs while you're sitting here Waiting For A Car.'

'I can,' I say gloomily. 'The sarge might make me take a bus.'

We both agree that would be disastrous.

'Who are you with today?'

'Will. His plane landed late and he's come straight in.'

I stifle the foolish grin that always comes to me when Will is mentioned. He isn't cute, or anything, and I definitely, definitely don't fancy him. We just get along, that's all.

'Is he disgustingly tanned?' I ask. He's been skiing for two weeks.

'Unfortunately so.'

The subject of our discussion enters and I ping an elastic band at him across the room.

'Ow. Nice to know I've been missed.' He rubs his arm furiously, and goes straight for his docket. 'Becks, I've got loads to do, so I hope you don't mind being dragged round dozens of witnesses' houses?'

'As long as you're doing the work,' she says.

'Shall we go, then, before the control room realises we've got a car? Catch you later, Bloggsy.'

I watch despondently as they drive off in my car.

There is, indeed, a brace of forlorn-looking and thoroughly keyless pandas sitting in the car park, along with numerous vehicles belonging to officers who almost never leave the station except to go to the sandwich shop across the road. Three of them are parked, brazenly, in bays under a sign reading 'Operational Officers Only', despite the fact that their owners all work in the Being Nice to Criminals Department. These are Monday to Friday, nine-to-fivers who will never, ever come out to assist you if you are burgled, robbed or raped; instead, they spend their days phoning up the parents of reprobates and encouraging them to bring them to meetings where they can apologise to the people they beat up the week before.

My radio crackles. The control room are trying to send me to a report of a male defecating in Cart Street. Fortunately, I have no vehicle and therefore no way to get to Cart Street, so I politely decline and to my great glee I hear Will and Becks being sent instead.

I spend the next 10 minutes visiting every office in the police station to ask if anyone has the missing keys to our pandas. Mostly I'm met with the blank faces of plainclothesers who have not used their own locker key in years, let alone the key to a marked police car.

Finally, I find myself back out in the car park, standing next to the smoking room and quietly fuming. I put a call out on the radio. 'PC Bloggs... Does anyone know where the keys are to the two shift pandas in the car park?'

As I release the transmit button, I see one of our vehicles slide in through the gates. It's my favourite, the brand new Ford, nippier than and not as battered as the older ones. I see the driver glance sheepishly in my direction as he drifts by. It's Phil Cox, one of our Friendly Neighbourhood Officers. What the hell is he doing out in one of our cars?

I press my send button. 'Cancel my last, I'm sorted.'

Friendly Neighbourhood Officers allow the 21st Century public to have their policing cake and eat it, only to find that it is past its sell-by date and contains unexpected nuts. One FNO is allocated to each area; this means the local residents get a better service, as one police officer will respond personally to their calls instead of seven or eight.

The government loves FNOs and it won't be long before they completely replace ordinary officers who lack the requisite Friendliness. Plain old beat bobbies are already being replaced by civilian Police Community Support Officers, who are specially trained in walking the walk and talking the talk of beat bobbies. However, PCSOs cannot actually record crime or investigate it, which should help the figures dramatically. I foresee a glorious age whereby PCSOs gradually learn to do everything done currently by police officers. When they get powers of arrest they will receive a warrant card, and will then be unable to strike or complain about their working conditions. They will no longer be called PCSOs, but will be given a sparkly new title like, 'Police Officers'. They will then do all the work that people like me are currently doing, whereupon they will demand a pay rise. If that's not an economy, I don't know what is.

I ruthlessly take the car from Phil, who goes in search of a bicycle helmet, and throw open the boot. I always do a cursory check of what equipment I have, and I'm gratified to see three out of the five cones that should be there, one 'Police Slow' sign out of two and half a broom (the handle half). There is also a fire extinguisher which is wedged into one of the cones. I prop it back in its holder, shove my massive bag of Crap Car paper in on top of it and hop up and down on the boot latch until it shuts.

There's an ominous hissing sound. Gingerly, I reopen the boot and discover why the fire extinguisher had been stuck into a cone. The holder is faulty and has allowed the extinguisher to fall out, whereupon it has 'gone off'. My kit bag is now a powdery beige foam mountain and the car will have to be sent for specialist cleaning.

Sod.

I hose down my kit bag and return to the report writing room. Even the Department of Critical Emailing has not managed to get up early enough to send me anything new in the last half hour, so I put my feet up and relax into some more Waiting For A Car.

* * * * *

It is 10.30am before I finally locate a useable panda - one which has been returned from the workshop following repair after Alex on Team 5 reversed into it last week. By this time I am actually looking forward to going out to Biffenden Road and meeting my harassment victim.

Unfortunately, this is the oldest of our vehicles. It has done 120,000 miles and makes a multitude of tuneful noises when performing simple tasks such as gear changes and braking. Worst of all, it's a three-door model, which is an absolute nightmare. Male readers have probably never noticed, but the driver's door in a three-door is about a foot longer than a five-door, to leave room for people to get into the back. Being female, I am naturally particularly short (5ft 7¼in, and don't forget the quarter), so I have to sit underneath the steering wheel to reach the pedals. To put on my seatbelt, I therefore have to perform an ape-like motion involving reaching back with both arms and severely twisting my back. Trust me, with a stabbie on it's not easy.

Additionally, the seatbelt always attaches itself to the slider underneath the driver's seat and acts as a tripwire every time I get in or out of the vehicle. Worse still, it has been known to attach itself to my baton and prevent me from getting out at all. Then again, that is no bad thing.

Finally, the vehicle's immobiliser has a dodgy connection, so I have to insert my key fob into it - to register myself as the driver - three times. Then it beeps at me for five minutes before finally agreeing to let me start the engine. Good job I'm not working for one of the emergency services, eh?

Once the spasm in my back has died down, I lurch out of the station in my new wagon and hit the road.

As you know, the house numbers in our area work on the Fibonacci sequence, so I spiral round in despair for eighteen minutes in an attempt to locate my target. It turns out that No38 is actually on Mule Lane, which does not adjoin Biffenden Road at any point. If Blandshire Constabulary could use one more administrative form-creating department - and I think you will agree it could - I am bidding for the Address Location Unit.

I squeeze through the communal door, keeping a few inches of air between my shoulders and any solid surface and trying not to inhale as I climb the stairs to Flat 18. My rubber soles slurp as I prise them off each step and put them down again. Naturally, my destination is the top floor. This means that I have to pause for breath half way, having lugged my 5kg body armour and 10kg of paperwork up there with me.

Eventually, I arrive, and knock tentatively on the door. I'm rather hoping that the occupant won't hear me so I can leave a calling card with an illegible signature in his letterbox. Sadly, he is poised by the handle and flings it open mid-knock.

'About bloody time,' he says. 'I could be dead by now.'

Call me irritable, but I take offence at being greeted like this, particularly when I've put myself out considerably just to reach the door. My gaze is probably cooler than is professional as I reply, 'Well, luckily you're not.'

Mr Grahams lets me in and jabs a finger at the hall mantle. 'What do you think of that?'

I nod slowly. 'Very nice. Art deco?'

'No.' He turns on the light, a single grubby bulb which makes the bags under his eyes glow orange, and picks up a stack of mail. He thrusts it at me, 'What do you think of THAT?'

I take the post and sort through it quickly. 'Yes,' I say. 'It seems you've received some junk mail.'

'Precisely. Rather a lot, don't you think?'

'Well, I get a lot myself,' I say, slightly hesitantly.

We head through to the living room where Mr Grahams clears a space for me on his sofa. It looks rather unclean. I shake my head. 'I've been sitting all day. But thanks.'

He takes up his own perch and I rest the tips of my shoulder-blades against a cleanish patch of wallpaper.

Crap Car

As Mr Grahams begins describing the horrendous harassment he is receiving from his ex-girlfriend's boyfriend's ex-partner, I feel my trouser leg press against my skin and my eyes swerve downwards. A tabby cat is rubbing himself against me. I have nothing against people owning a cat or two, or even cat-lovers *per se*; I just don't particularly share their affection. I hand the post back to Mr Grahams and deliberately drop it on the floor in front of him. As he bends down to pick it up, I boot the cat in the chops and it runs out, yowling.

'What was that?' says Mr Grahams, sharply.

'What?' I say.

He looks suspiciously at me for a moment or two. I can see the cat glaring at me from the hallway.

'Anyway,' I say. 'About this harassment.'

We to-and-fro for a few minutes. Mr Grahams tells me that he's had a car parking in his space downstairs, the compulsory five text messages telling him he isn't a very nice man and this blessed junk mail. I conclude that he is suffering from the local definition of Harassment, as opposed to the statutory version.

'Have you actually seen the driver parking this car?' I ask.

'No.'

'Have you had any actually threatening texts?'

'Not threatening, exactly, no.'

'Why do you think she's behind the junk mail?'

'Why do I… Well, who else would it be?'

I glance at the topmost envelope. 'Er… Pizzas-R-Us?'

'Have I signed up for mail from Pizzas-R-Us?'

'Well, I don't know. Have you?'

'No.'

I glance at the next.

'A NatWest credit card application letter,' he says, with the triumphant air of a man who believes he has proved something. 'I haven't asked for that, either.'

'So, Mr Grahams,' I say, 'are you suggesting that your ex has signed you up for all this stuff?'

'No,' he says.

I blink at him.

'I'm suggesting my ex's new bloke's ex has done it. We had a row a month or so back. She drinks in the Golden Lion. We'd all got drunk together one night and she accused me of… well, there's no point going into that. Anyway, I know it's her.'

'Hmmm,' I say. 'The thing is, I get lots of this sort of stuff myself, and as far as I know I've never met your ex's new bloke's ex. And anyway, without proof…' I allow my voice to tail off.

He doesn't look happy, and why should he be? He pays his taxes, except that he doesn't because he's on long-term sick and hasn't worked for 15 years. But be that as it may, he surely has as much right as the next man to expect the police to monitor his parking space, vet his text messages and chuck his junk mail in the bin for him each morning?

I sigh. Mr Grahams is a Complainer, and the prognosis for this is not good. As the condition takes hold, he will start appearing at the police station and demanding to see my inspector. To prevent things deteriorating into a letter to the local MP, my inspector will put him on a course of placation: PC Bloggs must call him once a day to assure him that she is taking the actions Mr Grahams deems appropriate. This is known as Complaint Managing and is an example of how the police can best use their skills to let the public guide their investigations.

As a result of my diagnosis I take out my file.

'I'm going to take a statement of everything you have told me, and create a crime report.' I pause. 'It will take up to an hour.'

Sadly, this doesn't put him off.

I dial up for the crime reporting centre on my mobile and hum to myself as I go through the touch-tone options. Policing has finally caught up with other businesses, and we now have an automated switchboard and queuing system before officers can get through to a civilian in the Crime Centre who will create an electronic crime report for them. This is far quicker than just filling out a report yourself, and has the added benefit that all the victim's details are instantly entered onto a computer back at the nick, so that when you require them again for the rear of the statement form you are compiling in Mr Grahams' flat you have to ask the same questions a second time instead of just reading them off the front. You therefore spend twice as long with the person in question. This is called Efficiency and will result in Victim Satisfaction.

Eventually, I get through and begin to update the operator with the facts of the case. This includes a series of mandatory questions which he asks me and I, in turn, ask Mr Grahams.

'How would you identify your ethnic group?'

'Well I'm bloody British, aren't I? Isn't it obvious?'

I hold out a list of options.

He snorts in contempt, 'Just put British.' All of the options include British as a subtitle, but he doesn't seem to have noticed this. I record him as White-British and continue. 'Do you require Victim Support?'

'What's that?'

'They can offer counselling and advice if you are distressed by your crime.'

Mr Grahams chokes on his own gritted teeth. 'Do I look like I need counselling?'

I refrain from answering that one, and tell the operator, 'No.'

The next question is, 'Are you happy for us to send letters to your home address?'

My eyes fall on the stack of junk mail sitting between us; from the mottled purple appearing round Mr Grahams' eyes, I can tell he's not amused.

In the end, it takes me two hours to write up his complaint, by which time it's after noon; in half an hour, the canteen will be closing. I therefore head back towards the nick with food on my brain.

My mobile rings as I'm driving and by squeezing it out of my pocket I can see that it's Luke, my other half. I press the red button to cut off the call.

Despite the natural limitations brought on by being female, I manage to reverse the panda into a space without scratching anything, and carry the non-harassment papers inside to re-type their contents onto a computer. I have taken the junk mail on Mr Grahams' instructions to 'fingerprint them or something', so they need booking into the property store for safekeeping. With all that done, I can then lie low and try to eat before being sent to another non-harassment. As I enter the property store, Luke rings back and this time I answer it, balancing the mobile between my ear and shoulder as I record details of Mr Grahams' junk mail in the property book.

'You cut me off before,' he says, sounding slightly hurt.

I sigh. 'Well, I was driving.'

'You never talk to me at work.'

'Sometimes I just can't.' The truth is, sometimes I literally do have to say to friends and family, 'got to go' and hang up on them without preamble.

'Are we still going out tonight?' he asks.

I picture myself at the end of the day. 'I could do with going straight to bed to be honest,' I say. 'I'm knackered.'

'You're always knackered.'

'Well, it's the shifts.'

'Tomorrow?'

'I'm working a late shift tomorrow.'

Luke's tone takes a turn for the worse. 'How convenient.'

As if he thinks I might use the unpredictable nature of my shift pattern as a cover for not seeing him. As if.

The property manager is trying to slide out of the store past me.

'Luke,' I say. 'I'll have to call you back.'

'You know what, Ellie?' he says. 'Don't bother.'

The phone cuts off and I drop it onto the desk. All this without stopping writing for a moment.

It's only after I tear out the receipt slip from the Crime Property Book that I realise I've picked up the wrong book and accidentally listed the junk mail in the Lost Dog Book. I now have a choice: delete the entry, which will involve a complicated procedure including two supervisory signatures, or file the property in the dog kennel. Opting for the former, it takes me half an hour to sort the problem out and get the items stashed away in the locked store.

The canteen has now shut so I mooch down to the kitchen where I plan to review the paperwork whilst eating a chocolate bar. The chocolate machine eats my £1 coin and gives me a packet of fruit Polos. I am shaking it and screaming when Sergeant Charles Hammond comes in to the room and sees me.

Charles is Blandmore's Crime Management, Investigation and Detections Supervisor.

He and his colleagues spend their lives trawling through mountains of paperwork, emails, print-outs and crime files to find boxes which bobbies have accidentally left unticked (thereby negating a detection). Then they get us to tick them and follow that up with emails warning us not to forget to tick them again.

Crap Car

Then, every Wednesday, we have Detection Night, a weekly ritual in which Charles tots up our figures and produces the all-important news bulletin: Yes! We have this week Met Our Target of One Hundred Detections.

It's been a while since he has been able to announce this news. For the last five weeks the bulletin has been: No! We have this week Just Missed Our Target by Ten Detections. But he is Sure We Can Do Better.

You may be thinking that this whole thing is confusing, and mad, and a million miles away from what a police force should be trying to do i.e. catch bad people and lock them up. If so, you have misunderstood the purpose of a modern police force.

And there's more.

To understand where Charles is coming from, you need to be aware of his nemesis: the force's Crime Compliance Department.

Crime Compliance is staffed by civilians or ex-police officers who are experts in the National Crime Recording Standards; their whole raison d'être is to go through all of the same paperwork, look for the same errors as Charles and use them to trip us up and take away our detections.

You may be wondering why a police force would employ people whose job it is to cast a negative light on its own performance. Me too.

You may also be wondering how much this all costs, and whether the money might be better spent on more frontline cops catching bad people and locking them up. Me too.

Anyway, Charles' job is to find ways of increasing the number of detections we get to counterbalance the ones they take away. Got it?

As I start to weep for my lost Mars bar, Charles raises an ominous piece of paper and addresses me. 'Ah, PC Bloggs. You're on my List.' For some reason I'm always on Charles' List. 'Have you got a minute?'

My arm is stuck halfway up the vending machine, with my fingers scrabbling at the tip of the chocolate bar, so I can hardly say no. We go to the report writing room and Charles opens up the computer system.

'It's this one,' he says, typing in a reference number. An Assault flashes up.

I view it with a half-frown, still thinking bitterly about my Mars. I offer Charles a Polo.

'I don't think that's one of mine,' I say.

Charles points out my name. 'Flat 22, Corinthian Way.'

The Perrils' latest address.

'Oh, that one,' I say. 'I just handed the job over to night shift. Perril was too drunk to interview.'

'And what happened when he was interviewed?'

'I don't know, I was at home dreaming about laundry.'

Charles is horrified. 'Let me show you.' He opens up the Outcome field. 'What do you notice about that?'

'Er... nothing.'

'Precisely. It has not been filled in.'

'So we'll never know.'

'It MUST be filled in!'

'Oh, right. I guess we should tell whoever interviewed him?'

'It's in your name. That means it's *your* job.'

'But I have no idea what happened, Charles. I went off-duty and no one has said anything to me since.'

'Have you tried to find out? Have you located the paperwork?'

'Well, no.'

Charles coerces me into searching through the trays of every PC who was on night shift on the relevant night. Eventually, we find the paperwork. The statement of the interviewing officer says that Wayne Perril denied hitting Lisa and that, as she refused to give a statement, the assault charge was dropped.

'Looks like it's going nowhere,' I say.

Charles' eyes gleam. 'Read on,' he says.

I read on. 'Blah... blah... Wayne this... Lisa that... Here we go, Wayne admits to throwing Lisa's mobile phone across the room and breaking it, and was consequently charged with criminal damage.'

'Ah ha!' Charles is absolutely ecstatic. 'I *knew* it! You see, this is how we lose detections through bad management.'

I nod as if I'm following him, but I'm not so I drop the pretence. 'Er... how is it lost? He's been charged, hasn't he?'

'Yes, but you can't claim a detection for assault when he was charged with criminal damage.'

'So we'll change the crime report to criminal damage.'

'Crime Compliance won't let us do that!' He is aghast at the suggestion. 'We can't just lie and say no assault happened. That. Is.

How. We. Lose. Detections.' He stabs the desk with his finger to emphasise each word.

'But we won't be lying. We'll just say we couldn't prove the assault and he was charged with something else.'

Charles tuts for, ooh, at least eleven seconds. 'Dear, oh dear, these bad practices... No, no. The only thing we can do is to file that one and create a new crime report for criminal damage.'

'OK... so we'll do that.'

Charles looks at me.

'Oh, you want *me* to do that?' I say, as the penny drops.

'You'll have to ring the Crime Centre.'

'But I'm not even the officer dealing with that case any more.'

'I know, but PC Chievely isn't on duty until tomorrow and if we don't get it in today it won't count towards the weekly target.'

I ring the Crime Centre while Charles watches me. He's almost salivating in anticipation; clearly his battles with Crime Compliance have become personal.

As the phone on the other end rings out, I wonder whether it might make more sense for him to make this phone-call, rather than both of us sitting there for fifteen minutes while members of public somewhere are ringing in on another line to complain that no one has yet responded to their calls for help. It's just that it seems a bit of a waste, Charles Hammond, a full police sergeant, trained in all kinds of law, with ten years' experience of frontline policing and paid in excess of £32,000pa, sitting there watching a PC make a phone-call.

My mind idles and somewhere, far away, a telephone rings plaintively. Will and Becks erupt into the report room. They are swearing in raised voices and holding their arms away from their bodies as if they have just been rolling in excrement.

'We've just been rolling in bloody excrement,' Becks curses. 'I'm never arresting someone for Public Nuisance again! Will, have I got any on my back?'

She pirouettes, and he brushes down the back of her stabbie with gloved hands. She proceeds to do the same for him, and I catch his eye as she flicks a speck of indeterminate matter off the inside of his trouser leg.

I've known Will since I joined the police, although we've worked on different teams for most of our service. I find myself wondering whether he's always secretly wanted Becks to brush down his inner thigh. His face, wrinkled in disgust, doesn't give much away.

'Oh yuck… Will, you've got it on your shirt.'

He cranes his neck and gingerly holds out the edge of one shirt-sleeve, before his gaze falls on Becks' head. 'Er, Becks? You might want to wash your hair,' he says.

She screams in horror, flapping frantically at the top of her head, and they depart in the direction of the locker rooms.

At last, the woman at the Crime Centre picks up. I quickly outline the problem. If it's possible to send a withering glance by telephone, she does so. In fact, she sounds literally appalled by my request, as though I'd just asked if I could pop home and sleep with her husband. 'I'm sorry,' she says. 'Did you say you want TWO crime reports for ONE incident?'

'Er, yes. One is assault and one is criminal damage.'

'Oh, you can't do that. National Crime Recording Standards say that you may only have one crime report for one victim.'

'What if she was assaulted every day for a week?'

'One crime report.'

Otherwise people might start to think the police are actually solving crimes, I suppose.

I put on the speaker-phone and Charles talks to the woman. Eventually he persuades her that the request is legitimate and PC Bloggs is not trying to claim two detections for one incident. Apparently, she's right about the one crime report thing, but he puts his hand over the receiver and mouths to me that he has a plan to evade this issue with some clever manoeuvres later on. I can't wait.

The phone goes down. I get up, 50p at the ready, determined to get my chocolate if I do nothing else for the rest of the shift.

But he grabs my wrist and pulls me back to my seat.

'Wait, it isn't over.'

'It isn't?'

'First we'll claim this detection…' He updates the criminal damage charge. 'But now, we have this assault crime report, which is undetected and therefore counting against you at the moment.'

'Oh well, I don't mind.'

'No no, we must link it to the criminal damage and then file it as part of the criminal damage and therefore all one job.'

'And we couldn't just do all that with the crime report that was already there?'

'Of course not! That would be deceitful.'

I begin to despair and I feel my pulse throbbing in my temples. No wonder Charles' hair is grey.

'So now we'll just put this all in PC Chievely's name...'

'Do you need me for that?'

'Well, no, but you might be interested…'

I am not.

I leave Charles prowling the corridors of Blandmore nick for the next person on his List.

I find out by email later on that my attitude towards Crime Management needs 'adjusting'.

3

Over-reactive Policing

I'VE BEEN AWAY for the weekend finalising the break-up with my boyfriend, and yesterday I was in court. So Mr Grahams and his vast mountain of junk post are far from my mind.

Luckily for law and order, however, other minds are working away at the problem with a relentless dedication.

I received a couple of emails on Friday asking me why I had not yet arrested Mr Grahams' harasser. I replied that I did not consider that the offence was serious enough to warrant an arrest. There I hoped the matter would lie.

Sadly, and unsurprisingly, I was mistaken.

Today, I turn on my computer to find a further five emails blinking at me from my inbox. They represent a conversation between three departments within my force who have reviewed both the case and my performance in respect of it; thoughtfully, they have cc-d me in. In their emails, they agree that, on the one hand, it would be unlawful to order a PC to make an arrest she was unhappy with. However, on the other hand, they also agree that my unhappiness is in direct contravention of force policy. I might, therefore, want to reconsider it and become happier?

As it's a Tuesday, I will most likely only be attending incidents which are not police matters and will therefore not be able to make any arrests even if I wanted to. One of the first things you learn in the police is that every day of the week comes with its own expectations. Friday, for example, is Fight Day. Saturday is Wife-beater Day. Tuesday is Nothing Day.

There are six of us on duty, which is pretty good going out of eight. I won't count the sergeant because, for him, Tuesday is Complaints Day. On any given Tuesday, he will receive at least two complaints at the front counter and disposing of them will require all his tact, patience and attention; he will then be tucked up for the remainder of the day writing up the reports explaining why he disposed of the complaints in the way he did.

I am on my own again today, as I'm supposed to be sorting out my paperwork. However, the night shift had an attempted stabbing taking up all their resources all night, so there was a glut of unattended incidents out there waiting to be attended when we clocked on. I have therefore been removed from paperwork-sorting and instead dispatched to sort out as many of the simple complaints as I can.

To this end, I have already attended two 'neighbour' disputes and a 'dangerous dog'. All three victims just wanted some advice, and were blissfully unaware of the crime-generation processes they had sparked with their phone-calls. They will now experience the joys of the Victim's Charter as I rigidly update them as to my lack of progress every seven days, no matter what hours I am working.

For my fourth port of call I am to attend an Abandoned Vehicle. As usual, the radio controller has tried to con me by beginning with the words, 'PC Bloggs, you couldn't take a quick drive down Wigmore Road, could you?'

In the police, there is no such thing as a 'quick' anything.

'Er... maybe,' I say.

'A caller is reporting an abandoned vehicle. There's no registration given, just that it is a green Fiat Punto. Or possibly a red Ford Fiesta.'

You might think this is an example of the irony I warned you about earlier but, no, we really do get information as vague, unspecific and apparently contradictory as this. I'm never sure whether it indicates that the callers are blind, the call-takers can't type or the controllers can't read. Or possibly all three. I head to Wigmore Road in the certain knowledge that the vehicle will be a blue Saxo.

It takes me several minutes of three-point-turns and neck-craning to work out that the white Range Rover parked half on the kerb blocking the trades entrance to a Chinese takeaway is the vehicle I'm after. Running the registration through the Police National Computer prompts the worst possible response.

'It's coming back as an unconfirmed stolen vehicle... reported this morning by a Petra James of 14 Cook Gardens, Derberry.'

I have a headache. It's cold. It's raining. I'm feeling a bit sorry for myself and I still haven't made up my mind whether to arrest Mr Grahams' ex-girlfriend's new boyfriend's ex-wife. Now I'll have to get this thing towed away for Scenes of Crime to look at. What's more, because it's 'unconfirmed' stolen, I will also have to obtain a statement from Petra James confirming that no one had permission to steal her car and dump it in a town fifteen miles from where she lives. Worst of all, Derberry is not covered by Blandshire Constabulary and that means requesting the statement from another force. I think it's the fact that I'll have to use the fax machine that's the final straw. I don't like using fax machines and they don't like me; I almost commit a Section Five Public Order offence - luckily, someone else has to hear you swearing, so I don't - as I park up behind the vehicle and await Recovery.

There's nothing happening, so I try to doze off to the sound of the rain drumming on the roof of the panda. You know you've spread your wings as an experienced officer when you master the 21st Century art of Waiting. Few outside the police appreciate the importance of this transferable skill and, if I'm honest, few inside the job ever really achieve true competence at it. Being female, I am particularly poor at Waiting. Sure enough, within a few moments, I open my eyes. My finger toys with the radio controls. I'm itching to chase up the tow-truck. No point. I close my eyes again, irritated, and console myself with the knowledge that, if I can't Wait properly, at least I compensate by being a fine Rusher. I'm exceptionally good at Rushing. Once the tow truck arrives, I can guarantee presenting the driver with ready-filled-out paperwork and a running engine. My reward for this speed is that I am able to attend twice the amount of incidents as my more patient colleagues.

I open my eyes again. The world outside is grey and boring and the rain is sheeting down. I watch the raindrops as they splat onto my windscreen. I put the wipers on. I don't know why. I'm stationary, for goodness' sake! All I've got is a better view of a maybe-stolen Range Rover. I sigh and move around in my seat. It's very quiet. I move the indicator stem up and down. Then I drum on the steering wheel. I look at my watch. Three minutes since I pulled up and stopped.

I could die here and hardly anyone would notice.

I am interrupted by a squawk on the radio.

'Reports of ten males fighting with baseball bats on Green Path. Any unit to respond.'

Over-reactive Policing

I listen as Lloyd and Rich call up and dispatch themselves to the incident. I feel mildly jealous of them. I have no doubt that the ten men will actually turn out to be two and the baseball bats a mere trick of the light, but for a Tuesday this is good stuff.

Will and Becks follow after the other two as back-up, and then I hear Guy departing the scene of a vicious egg-throwing to do likewise.

I do not offer my services. Knowing my luck, the Range Rover will be re-stolen as soon as I turn my back. But I listen with half an ear, hearing all units circling the area in an attempt to locate the unmissable brawl. As I sit, I catch a movement in my rear-view mirror. No sooner have I turned my head than two males turn to jog away, back wherever they came from.

There are a number of ways in which you can recognise someone who is 'known' to the police. They are skinny and usually pale. Their arms are like sticks. They can do nonchalance better than Robert de Niro. They balance on the balls of their feet, like athletes, while they wait to see if you're going to pull over. They are always up to 'nuttin'.

I hop out, pulling my collar up to keep the rain out, and stop the two guys. My womanly brain being especially skilled at face-recognition (though admittedly poorer on the map-reading front), I quickly identify them from the rogues photo gallery at the police station as 'Big G' and 'Goldie', aka Lee Hornby and Martin Bradshaw. I used to think that these nicknames only appeared in films like *Snatch* and *Donnie Brasco*, but I now know that there really are such people. It is a rare privilege for a lowly response officer such as myself to meet them.

'Can you wait there a sec for me, chaps?' I say.

They come to a reluctant halt and turn to face me. Big G is a chunky Jamaican guy with dreads to his waist and eyes which look in different directions; Goldie is a scrawny white guy. They are drug dealers.

'Where are you off to in such a hurry?' I say.

'Nowhere, lady,' says Big G. The rainwater drips off his nose.

'Well, you just came down here and turned around when you saw me. Either I'm dreadfully ugly, or you don't want to talk to me for some other reason.'

'We's talking to you, isn't we, girl?'

If there's one thing I object to - and I assure you there isn't just one - it is being called 'girl' by a drug dealer. I'm just sensitive that way. But I let it go for now.

'Maybe you're here to pick up your ride?' I nod at the Range Rover.

'No way, mon! Nuttin' to do wid us.'

I have now gone from 'lady' to 'girl' to 'mon' in the space of 60 seconds. I consider searching them for the keys to the stolen car. Out on the street, cross-gender searches are permitted but they aren't really advised if you're a lone officer. There's always the chance that Goldie will leg it, for instance, or cosh me while I'm engrossed in patting down Big G's groinal area. I decide to request a male officer to carry out the search. As my entire team is currently at Green Path, that means trying to raise a Friendly Neighbourhood Officer from the nick.

My finger is halfway to the transmit button when I hear, 'We've found the fight - ten males... one on the floor... need an ambulance. They're making off!'

I thought it was Tuesday today. Any male officers I might have summoned will now be racing out madly to join in the chase. If there's one thing that will dredge up even the laziest of the lazy from the police station, it's the sound of someone out of breath on the radio and the chance to lay hands on a fleeing suspect.

'Can you just wait here a second, please?' I say to the pair of ne'er-do-wells hopping from foot to foot in front of me.

There's a lot of ostentatious sighing and teeth-sucking, but they do as they're told; Goldie hops up onto someone's garden wall, legs dangling like an overgrown kid, and Big G starts pacing up and down like a mental polar bear. A few minutes pass. The rain has eased off. I listen to my radio. Somebody appears to have been caught. Then the controller interrupts proceeding. Her voice is urgent. 'I need a unit to re-deploy to Park Street, where our caller says a shot has been fired at his car.'

It *is* Tuesday, isn't it?

That's it; I give up on the idea of the search and content myself with recording the drug dealers' details. I watch them walk away, wistfully imagining a car-key-shaped bulge in Goldie's right pocket. On the radio, all hell is now breaking loose, with the sergeant attempting to find resources for a simultaneous ten-man fight and firearms incident. I make the executive decision to join in with the fun and power up my panda. Using the man-side of my brain, I begin a reversing-type manoeuvre. I miss crashing into the tow-truck by about three inches.

I leap out. 'I've got to get off to another job, mate. That's the Range Rover there. Just take it in for Scenes of Crime.'

The recovery driver climbs down from his vehicle and scratches his head in the slowest way imaginable. I hurry over, planning to repeat what I've just said, only louder. But then I see where he's coming from; the road narrows ahead, so he'll have to reverse out, and that's going to be tricky in a big flatbed with cars parked either side.

'I'll watch you back,' I say.

Fortunately, police officers are endowed with eight ears, so I assist the driver in reversing whilst keeping an eye on the Range Rover and monitoring two emergencies in my earpiece. Somewhere in the back of my brain, I vaguely catch the fact that the Tactical Inspector is now ordering all units to break away from wherever they are and set up a 'containment' on the firearms incident. What the Tactical Inspector wants, he gets.

I run over to the truck driver. 'I'm sorry mate,' I say. 'I've really got to go.'

He's not best pleased. I announce my presence to the radio controller and tell her to dispatch me where she sees fit.

'Erm... you'd better go to Green Path and see if the fight is still going on.'

In my experience, most fights last about four minutes and tend to cease just prior to police arrival, so I cruise over there without any great urgency. I am astonished, therefore, to turn down Green Path to find a large group of people milling around.

Nobody is actually fighting any more; it's been downgraded into more of an agitated gathering. I get out and shoot a look up and down the road. There's an ambulance blocking the entire street a hundred yards away. Another ambulance is parked at a T-junction fifty yards the other way. Despite this glut of medical aid, I can't see a single paramedic.

I bend down slightly and look through the mass of legs in the direction of the first ambulance. I glimpse a figure lying on the pavement. I turn and bend to my right, and see a second figure likewise stretched out. The mob spots me, and I'm surrounded by gesticulating locals, all talking at once, mostly wondering why on earth four police cars turned up and then shot away again to be replaced by just one containing a rather bemused girl?

At least, I think that's what they're saying. The rain is back with a vengeance, now so heavy that I only make out one word in five. I ponder my position as the water trickles down the back of my neck. There's little point trying to call for assistance; the firearms incident is just too exciting for anyone even to stop talking about it on the radio, so I've got no chance of getting the air-time just to describe my situation. The wonders of modern technology, and our gleaming new digital 'Airwave' radios, mean that only one person can talk at once. Thank goodness our incidents only ever happen one at a time! Accepting that I'm here on my own for now, I head for the nearest fallen person.

It is a large, round Asian woman in floral skirts and a turquoise cardie. She is lying on her back with her eyes wide open. At least seven family members are sobbing and kissing parts of her body, so I muscle my way through them and come up with a professional analysis: she's blinking, therefore she's probably not dead.

I walk briskly down to the other casualty. He, too, is lying on his back, but this time an ominous pool of blood is spreading around his head. A couple of women are leaning over him. One is crying. I kneel in a puddle and check for a pulse. Oh my God! This one *is* dead! What do I? No... no... my mistake, there it is!

As if to confirm his status, the man opens his eyes and says, 'My bloody head's killing me.'

I turn round and find myself confronted by two enormous green overalls.

'We've been wondering when you'd arrive,' the first paramedic says. 'They said the police were on the scene but when we got here they'd gone.'

His bronze badge, which is at the height of my eyes, says his name is Andy. If the paramedics were to hold an annual gurney-lifting tournament, and I believe they should, Andy would surely win it hands down, I think. That's until I notice Bill, his colleague. Bill's name-badge is in line with my forehead and his Lincoln green suit stretches taut over his biceps in a fashion that would make Simon Cowell weep.

The two of them standing shoulder to shoulder are wider than I am tall.

'How long has he been there?' I ask.

'About fifteen minutes,' says Andy. Bill must be the strong silent type. 'I think he's OK. But we were told to Wait Out.'

I say nothing, but the Bloggs eyebrows must be skittering skywards, for he adds, slightly defensively, 'It isn't our job to go into violent situations. If they tell us to wait out, we wait out.'

Waiting Out, not to be confused with Waiting, is yet another tool in the kit of the 21st Century response officer. It applies to ambulance services and police alike, as well as gasmen, mental health workers and the guy who checks the electricity meter. (You will notice the omission of the fire brigade, who have a strict and laudable policy against Waiting of any kind.) The basic premise behind this skill is that our role is not to go the aid of people who need us, but to carry out Dynamic Risk Assessments, preferably of a kind that can be recorded on paper and turned into statistics. To this end, the above services do not like to send officers to the scene of an incident until somebody has written on a piece of paper that that is what should happen and transmitted it to them by radio or mobile phone. If you do decide to throw caution to the wind and rush to the side of a prone body before authorisation, you have no one but yourself to blame if you are brutally shot or twist your ankle.

'Anyway, you're here now,' says Andy. He gets down to the business of poking and prodding at the man while I tell Bill about the woman round the corner.

'That's my van round there,' he says, nodding.

'They send you guys out alone?'

It's his turn to raise his eyebrows, as he looks at all nine, feisty stones of me.

I hurry onto the pavement and shelter in a porch, where I can question the throng of anguished relatives without getting any wetter. A woman bustles over, the elder of the two leaning over Andy's victim. 'This is a disgrace,' she says, angrily. 'First the police arrive, then they leave. He's been lying there for 15 minutes now. My daughter's over there crying. There's blood everywhere.'

'You're right,' I say, with a shrug. 'It just isn't good enough. I would encourage you to go to the police station in the morning when the inspector is working and make a formal complaint.'

This takes the wind out of her sails. As she calms down, I'm able to find out what has happened. She's Battered Bloke's mother-in-law. The gist is that her daughter tried to squeeze her Volvo past a souped-up Golf GTI, which then chased her for half a mile round the estate and finally blocked her way on Green Path. The driver and his mates then got out and - in inimitable Blandmore fashion - decided that the best punishment for a cheeky girl driving in an unbecoming manner was to give her husband a pounding. Battered Bloke had taken a few hits, then staggered to his feet and made it about a hundred yards before collapsing in someone's front drive.

'And what about her?' I gesture at the Blinking Female.

'I don't know who she is.'

A little more investigation establishes that when Lloyd and Rich first arrived at the scene they managed to nab one of the attackers, who had been pointed out to them by a witness. Unfortunately, half the street came out from their houses to see what was happening and Blinking Female was one of them. The arrested man was her husband and the sight of him being manhandled into the rear of a police van had sent her into a dead faint. Other officers attended, so Lloyd and Rich left with their prisoner. But then the gunfight at the OK Corral broke out across town and everyone left, forgetting the victim in the process.

The paramedics do whatever it is they do in the background. I speak to more witnesses, take more details. Three hours later, having single-handedly carried out a major investigation, I get back to the nick and sit down to complete a report of my actions. This does not mean there is no time to read a few amusing emails, and I am busy forwarding them to external parties when the rest of the team returns.

Will and Becks enter first, once again blasting into the silent room with voices raised in conversation. This time, they are discussing guns, and their vast knowledge and experience in the field puts me to shame.

'*Walther PPK* sounds so much cooler,' says Becks.

'Nah…it's *Colt* every time,' says Will.

Becks lets out a snort. 'I'm off to make tea,' she says, 'but this conversation is not over.'

Will sits down beside me with a shake of his head. He's looking a little mussed, which is no bad thing. For some reason, I find myself in a dreadful mood.

'So, you and Becks are working together again?' I ask him.

'Um, yes, that's what the sergeant...' He seems confused. 'Is there a problem, Bloggsy?'

'No. It's fine. Why would you think there was a problem?'

'You just sound...'

'No.'

'But it's just that...'

Does the man not know when to shut up? 'Look,' I say, 'There's no problem, OK?'

I snatch my report on the Green Path assault from the printer and stomp down to the door of the sergeant's office.

Chris Woodcock stares at me in surprise. 'Bloggs, where've you been? We've been handling a firearms incident.'

'Yes, sarge, I know. I've been at the GBH on Green Path.'

Grievous Bodily Harm, or GBH, is about as bad as it gets before Murder. That is, if 'as bad as it gets' can be construed to mean a bit of a bump on the head.

'GBH?'

'The men fighting with baseball bats?'

Chris nods vaguely. 'Oh, yes... do CID know?'

'Yes, sarge.'

CID is the Criminal Investigation Department. We are required to inform them whenever a worthy crime occurs such as a serious assault, sexual offence or kidnapping, so that they can take on the role of sitting in an office and giving us directions. Quite often, the only thing an officer needs to do at the scene of such a crime is to tell the controller to inform the Duty DS, or Detective Sergeant. He or she will be asleep somewhere, just desperate to be awakened with the news that some guy's life depends on his or her next words. The DS should tell the officers on the scene to find out the condition of the victim, record details of all witnesses and 'preserve the scene'. This includes, among other things, avoiding cross-contamination, which occurs when an officer fondles the bloody wound of a dying man and then rushes off to spread this DNA all over the potential suspect. This allows the suspect to claim later that he did not have the victim's blood on him until the officer put it there.

The call to CID was just one of the eight phone-calls I made whilst guarding the crime scene. By 'guarding', I mean watching as hordes of local residents swarmed back and forth across the evidence. For some, 'Police Line Do Not Cross' is easily confused with, 'Please Enter And Enjoy'.

Relieved, Chris takes my report and turns back to his computer to catch up on the paperwork that will have arrived during the three minutes we were talking. He looks harassed. I'm not surprised. Trying to juggle the number of jobs he's had today with the number of officers available would test anyone. The numbers of police in Blandmore - police, that is, who are available to go out to deal with Mops - is at an all-time low. But I can let you in on a little secret: the Blandshire Senior Management Team have developed an exciting 12-point solution to the problem, which is about to be implemented force-wide. Someone emailed a memo about it to me in error*, which has enabled me to share it with you.

From: Chief of Personnel Directorate, Blandshire Constabulary
To: Chief Constable, Blandshire Constabulary
Subject: Staffing
Dear Chief Constable
As discussed at our last Personnel and Staffing Planning Issues Meeting, we need to address the problems caused by Shift (as I explained above, a shift is made up of response officers who drive out to see you when your ex-partner comes round for a drink. It is fundamentally agreed that 'Shift' is the problem).

To that end, we agreed the following action plan, in which we will:

1. Stop putting two officers in a unit. This is simple mathematics. If we split up a crew of two, we will then have two units.

2. Merge all our little police areas into a single giant one. Then we'll only need one Area Commander, one Chief Inspector and one Detective Inspector.

3. Decrease the official minimum manning levels. If a Shift is currently supposed to run at a minimum of six, we'll just decrease this to four. That way we can truthfully say that we're not running below minimum. They can't touch us for it! It's genius!

4. Stop PCs moving away from shifts. Except to go to Neighbourhood. As discussed, it is always good to be able to announce to the press that we're increasing numbers of officers in neighbourhoods. Note: of course, on no account should neighbourhood officers do any of the work currently done by shift officers.

5. Stop PCs taking leave.

6. Stop PCs being promoted.

7. Staff our special operations, especially those paid for by the Home Office, by making PCs work on their rest days rather than taking them off Shift.

8. Employ a lot more people to audit things and send emails. Sending emails is a good solution to most problems.

9. Send all our officers a form to opt out of Working Time Regulations. Most of them will sign it without realising. Then we can make them work any amount of hours we want.

10. Sterilise all the woman police officers. That will teach them to disappear with a baby and leave us in the lurch.

11. Neuter all the males. Most of their problems at work stem from women. They will work harder and be happier if they aren't distracted.

12. Shoot deserters. If they don't care enough for their country to work under-staffed, in dangerous conditions and in a state of blind exhaustion, they are traitors. Harsh, but fair.

*They didn't really. I'm making this bit up. It's *satire*. But it's quite realistic, if I say so myself.

* * * * *

The caller who reported being shot at has arrived at the front counter to be 'debriefed'. The word 'debriefing' suggests a short, verbal encounter, in which we check on the welfare of someone involved in an incident. This is misleading. It's an interminable bore which involves the creation of a ten-page, hand-written statement - the sort of tedious ordeal which ends up with even the victim wishing the gunman had been a bit more accurate. The Inspector Responsible for Being Responsible has decreed that all officers attending the shooting are to write out a statement of their actions. As the only person not involved and still around - Lloyd and Rich have still not returned from inserting the baseball-batter into a cell somewhere - I am therefore dispatched to carry out the debrief.

I pop to the report room with a vague notion of apologising to Will for my bizarre outburst before, but he and Becks are back in mid-handgun-discussion and the sight of them just makes me feel annoyed again. I send him a remorseful text message, and go to have my own discussion about guns.

It takes three minutes, and the repetition of the words, 'Huh', 'Yes' and 'Urdu' to establish that the victim of the shooting requires a translator. The directory of approved interpreters is yet again missing, so I risk the wrath of the Finance Department and telephone the lady who lives up the road. She always arrives within twenty minutes, but today she has unfortunately been called to London, so I phone a colleague of hers and discover that he is already in Blandmore Police Station interpreting for a shoplifter.

This breathtaking display of efficiency results in myself, the shooting victim and Mr Ibrar Haseem sitting down to business less than an hour later.

Mr Haseem is a small Asian man with a bald head and glasses, who wears a suit and produces a paper-thin laptop which he lays out on the desk with a flourish.

'Are you going to write the statement on that?' I demand.

'Of course.'

'You won't be able to print it. You can't use disks in our computers.'

'I have my own printer.' Mr Haseem points to a slot in the back of his laptop.

Pacified, I anticipate the speediest interpreting I have ever experienced.

The marvellous thing about interpreters is that they will often take it upon themselves to say the things that we police officers cannot, such as, 'You're lying, aren't you?', 'He is going to come back and kill you,' and 'Make the officer a cup of tea'.

Of course, some interpreters are a pain and make you say the actual words you want translated but plenty are more than happy just to get on with it. I've been present during interviews where I've not actually needed to say more than a few words. I just set the interpreter loose and wait while they produce either a perfect written statement or a confession.

Mr Haseem, however, turns out to be somewhat slower than I've previously experienced. He does not have a problem communicating with the victim, nor translating the questions I ask. But somewhere between the words coming out of his mouth and them appearing on the screen of his laptop, an anomaly requires him to repeat every question and answer three or four times. I am sure this has nothing to do with him being paid over £50 per hour.

After about an hour and a half, I am running into overtime and we've still only just got to the point when the victim thinks he's just seen a firearm. Both mine and the victim's eyes are drooping, but Mr Haseem is brightly tapping away at his little keyboard with no sign of fatigue.

'Right, let me read back what we have so far,' says the interpreter.

Expecting him to address the victim, I am surprised to hear instead the account being read out in fluent English in my direction. 'Oh,' I say. 'Are you interpreting that as you go? You're very quick.'

'No, no,' he says. 'I'm reading it to you. It's in English.'

Confused, I peer over his shoulder and find that, as he says, he has typed the statement up in English. The thing is, I need it in Urdu because the whole point is that the victim will have to sign it to ensure it's an accurate record of our little chat. And he can't read English.

'But...' I get that far and stop. Maybe it is the time of night or my headache, but part of me wants to throttle Mr Haseem. I take a deep breath. 'But Mr Khan won't be able to read that,' I say.

'Yes, yes,' he replied. 'He will. He knows enough. I will translate it into Urdu next.'

I gawp at him. Before I can reply, my mobile rings. It's a detective constable. He's complaining that the rain has washed away all the blood on Green Path before Scenes of Crime could stare at it and swab it up. I apologise for this unreservedly, though I'm not quite sure why. As I hang up, I sneak a look at Will's reply to my text, and am relieved to find myself forgiven for screaming at him earlier. I'm about to readdress Mr Haseem when the detective rings back. I have not provided him with any paperwork accounting for the behaviour of the rain and will now have to do a statement. I fend him off for an hour at least and turn back to my interpreter.

'It's just that I was expecting an Urdu statement for Mr Khan to sign. I mean, I could have written it out in English myself.'

'Ah, but how would you translate it into Urdu?'

'Well, I wouldn't need to if he understood the English.'

Mr Haseem is now just blinking pleasantly at me with no comprehension of the problem.

I sigh. 'So how long will it take you to write it out in Urdu?'

'I will take it home and do it there.'

Aaaarggh.

'But Mr Khan needs to sign it so we need it tonight. That's why you're here.'

'Ah... in that case, I will do it tonight. The translation takes about two or three hours.'

I think tears might actually be rolling down my face. 'OK, let's just get on with it.'

By the time the statement is finished, it's transpired that Mr Khan is not actually sure if he saw a gun at all. There's a stone chip to his car, but we all kind of agree that - would you credit it - it was probably caused by a stone. It's 2.30am. I decide to send Mr Haseem home and have Mr Khan come back in the next day to sign the final Urdu version of his statement.

'I can't believe it took this long,' he informs me, through the interpreter.

'Neither can I,' I say.

It's late and I should be at home now. But I still have to type up my statement for the detective dealing with the GBH at Green Path. As I switch my computer on, I notice that I have a new email waiting. I am almost overcome with excitement: surely it's too much to hope that someone has come into work after midnight to send me congratulations for the good work I have done that day?

The email is from an inspector I have never heard of in a department called Auditors.

'PC Bloggs,' he writes. 'Petra James has now called five times awaiting police attendance. I notice you are the officer responsible for her investigation and I must remind you of the Victim's Charter which states we are to keep our victims updated. The computer system shows that you have been doing nothing for the last four hours. This just isn't good enough. Please ensure officers from Overshire are asked to attend her address and inform her when you have done so.'

Petra James. The name's in the back of my mind somewhere. It takes me ten minutes to recall that she is the owner of the white

Range Rover I recovered from Wigmore Road a few hours earlier. It feels like three days ago now.

I wend my way home and find that my ex-boyfriend appears to have sent me some leaflets advertising pizzas. I look at my watch. Sadly, the pizza place closed hours ago.

And that is Tuesday.

4

Sex, Lies and CCTV

I'M SITTING IN THE briefing room later the same week.

It's nearly a quarter past four, and I'm patiently listening to the lads have the customary conversation - about engine parts and wind-breaking, that sort of thing - with which they fill the first fifteen minutes of each shift. I generally entertain myself during these conversations by rolling my eyes at Will. In fact, I realise, I've recently been entertaining myself by looking at Will quite a lot, lately. It used to be that we'd exchange comical glances, but lately I've taken just to staring. I blame his sun tan, because he certainly isn't the 'hottie' of our team (that would be Lloyd), but then again I'm not really a hottie kind of girl. Anyway, Will is far too studious to talk about engine parts or wind-breaking, and spends most of the daily briefing worrying about how he will manage to satisfy all the victims he has recently promised to satisfy. Right now, his eyes are half-closed in a sort of frown, as though he's ticking points off on a huge To-Do list in the air before him.

It is at this point that the Friendly Neighbourhood Officer, Phil Cox, enters. Phil has slightly more service than me, but he left Shift in the 2005 exodus and is now soaking up the good life in the land of milk and honey.

'Sergeant?' he begins, slightly hesitantly.

'YES?' Lloyd bellows, rising to his feet. Our actual sergeant, Chris, just sits there in a daydream, relishing the last few moments of sanity before he opens his email inbox.

'Er... there's a woman at the front counter,' Phil says. 'She's saying... she's saying...'

Something awful hangs in the air and we all gaze at him. It must be one of the three Rs: Robbery, Rape or Romanian Refugee.

Phil's voice drops to a whisper. 'She's saying she's been raped.'

Lloyd immediately regrets pretending to be in charge and sits down. His eyebrows turn towards Chris, and the bearer of tidings follows them. Chris nods slowly. 'Good, good,' he says. 'Get some details.'

This is not what Phil is hoping to hear. He stutters and burbles for a moment, and then spits it out. 'Er... it's a while since I've dealt with a rape.'

It takes me some time, but I suddenly realise that six pairs of eyes have swivelled in my direction. Becks is off sick, and I own the sole pair of boobs in the room (unless you count Rich's).

'Bloggsy, perhaps you could... er...'

Halfway through the order, Chris has a panic attack and stops talking.

I feign surprise. 'Me?'

Chris clears his throat. Lloyd is staring at the ceiling with an expression of someone trying desperately to think of something nice to say about car engines.

'It's not because I'm a WOMAN, is it?' I say. Sergeants and control rooms are always itching to send female officers to deal with rapes. That's all well and good, except that there aren't many women in the police, rapes take a long time to deal with and we still have the same non-rape stuff as everyone else to work on, too. Plus not all rape victims *want* a woman officer - most don't care and some even want a man.

Chris looks at me, and Phil shuffles out. We all sit, rigid-backed, for a second or two. Everyone's waiting to see what my next move will be. I contemplate the statement I'd been planning to take from the victim of a beer-throwing, and then let out a deep sigh.

'Hang on, Phil.' I get up and chase him down the corridor.

Our shift of eight officers deals with a full-blown rape about once a month. By full-blown, I mean one that has happened in the last day or so and which therefore involves CID, a doctor, and at least seven emails. In the 21st Century, there are now more ways than ever to commit sexual acts on people, including the use of objects, cameras, the Internet and, in some cases, cups of water. So, to clarify and simplify matters, by the word 'rape' I am referring to cases involving a penis. It is a little-known fact that if a male police officer actually hears or uses the word 'vagina', he will collapse. Fortunately, my shift is blessed with two females, which means the blokes can sometimes go for months without suffering in this way. For this they are eternally grateful and sometimes reward us when we take on their rapes by leaving choccies in our in-trays. Seriously.

This also means that my female colleague and I receive regular training in the womanly attributes of gathering evidence at the scene of a serious crime and taking important victim statements - things, I think you will agree, which are hardly in the remit of men.

When I reach the front office, Coxy shows me into the side room and I am greeted by a mini-skirt and bra containing some rather pink and fleshy skin. The face is plastered in cheap mascara and lippy; from the lippied mouth emanates a low crying that does not stop throughout the subsequent interview. The crying I can excuse, but the mascara is unacceptable.

Coxy does a vanishing act at the last moment and I sit down and introduce myself. The girl in front of me is Mandy Richardson.

'I've... been... RAPED!' she bawls, shuddering, and shedding another pound of foundation into her cleavage as she does so.

'Why don't you tell me what happened?'

Mandy proceeds to describe her ordeal. 'I was in the bedroom,' she starts. 'He was all over me… then he pulled me into a cupboard and raped me.'

After half an hour of digging, I piece together the story. Mandy met a guy at Fleas Nightclub in Blandmore. She texted him a few times in the ensuing week, and then decided to go to a party at his mate's house. She does not know the mate's name, nor his address, nor any directions as to how to get there, nor what the house looks like. Whilst at this undefined address, Mandy went into an upstairs bedroom with the guy. He kissed her but when he tried to take off her top she said no, at which he pulled her into a walk-in wardrobe and had sex with her against her will. She did not struggle as she feared he would murder her, and she did not scream as she was embarrassed in case someone heard. Oh, and it transpires it's the second time she's been raped - the first was two years ago, but she didn't report that one.

I carry out my police officerly duties by writing out notes of the account and taking as much detail as possible. I then relay this information to the Detective Sergeant on duty. Detective Sergeants are paid about £5,000 a year more than me to sit by a telephone and tell people how to do things which they've already done. Sometimes you really get your moneys-worth, and they tell you that what you've already done is wrong and that there is no way to change it.

Afterwards, I drive Mandy to the Rape Suite. This is a small house on a residential street with some horrific floral sofas and pastel lampshades that are designed to blot out the trauma of recently-committed crimes. They work: very often on seeing the Suite, the victims decide that they cannot remember the crime at all.

Rape complainants have to be forensically examined by a doctor and samples, like traces of semen or hair, taken; it's not a particularly pleasant experience, for anyone, but it's obviously vital.

A trained Detective Constable is supposed to attend at this point. Their role is to stand in the corner of the medical room with their hand out, catching medical exhibits thrown out by the doctor whilst making every effort not to catch an unfortunate glimpse of the examination itself. Each exhibit - they usually number over 20 - has to be sealed up forensically, labelled, re-labelled, re-sealed and signed by everyone who handles it.

While waiting for the DC to arrive, I try to speed up the process by getting out the list of police doctors and summoning one to the suite.

I phone the first doctor on our list to ask her to come down. She's away.

I phone the second. He is available, but says, somewhat apologetically, that he isn't trained to carry out rape examinations. Which begs the question, why's he on our list?

The third is on holiday, and the fourth is roaring drunk in a golf club bar somewhere in Scotland, and isn't actually on call.

Finally, the fifth name on our list confirms that, yes, she is trained, and she is also available. In three hours' time.

I arrange for her to come as soon as she's free, and we settle down to wait, Mandy sniffling quietly, me remembering the last time I was here. A young student was claiming she'd been attacked, and she was on the examination couch when it became apparent that it had not been cleaned since its last use. This threw up all sorts of questions, not the least of them relating to hygiene and forensics, but we had to press ahead anyway. I get up and check the cleaners have done their job this time.

After about an hour, a detective - DC Barnes - turns up. At this point I would normally leave, but Mandy finds the idea of this grizzled bloke watching things being inserted into her daunting, and says that she would really rather I stayed until after the medical.

DC Barnes has just managed to make himself and me some cups of tea (Mandy can't drink until after her mouth has been examined and must simply watch us having our fun), when we are all amazed to see the doctor's car pulling into the driveway.

The doctor gets out, but it isn't Dr Jenkins - the lady I spoke to on the phone, who said she'd be here in three hours. Instead it's Dr Green, the first one I tried, who said she was away but has now decided she was actually just up the road.

What follows is probably what you expect. Some searching, embarrassing questions, and then a searching, embarrassing examination.

Mandy cries throughout all of this, in spite of the doctor's gentle reassurances that she has seen far worse. I catch the exhibit bags without looking at them - call me squeamish but I just don't need to know that I am holding somebody's vaginal fluids - and toss them on to DC Barnes who begins the painstaking task of sealing them all up.

At last Dr Green leaves, Mandy is installed on the downstairs sofa with a mug of squash, and I settle down in the background listening to DC Barnes dismantling the story she told me.

'So you met this guy at a nightclub?' he starts.

'Um, yes.'

'How exactly did you start talking?'

'Er... I don't remember.'

'What were the first words said between you?'

Mandy blushes. She takes out a pocket mirror to examine her face. Unbelievably, she appears satisfied by what she sees and tucks it back into her handbag.

'Mandy?'

'Erm... I think I said, 'You got any coke?''

'I see.' DC Barnes makes some notes. I imagine that he has recorded the word 'Drugs', and probably underlined it.

'And when you went to this party last night, how much had you drunk?'

'About seven beers.'

'Is that a lot for you?'

She snorts. 'Are you joking?'

'Is it not a lot?'

'No. I usually have ten or twelve. I had those seven at home, before I got there.'

'This was *before* you went out?'

'Yeh.'

More scribbling. This is no doubt recorded as 'Drink'.

He confirms that Mandy had been flirting with her attacker by text message for several days previously, and had gone upstairs to the bedroom with him willingly. He said, 'Let's find somewhere private,' she says.

The detective nods, thoughtfully. 'Do you take any medication, Mandy?'

'Yeah, Prozac,' she says. 'I've been depressed.'

'Why's that?'

She shrugs and her tear-streaked face wrinkles in thought for a moment. 'Dunno.' Then she holds out her arms, displaying parallel cuts on the insides of both elbows. 'The kids have been getting me down,' she says.

'How many children have you got?'

'Three.'

'And the father?'

'Jodie's dad is dead, that's my eldest. Ryan's is a deadbeat, he's a violent pig. We broke up when Charlene was born. Charlie's old man is just drunk all the time. I don't see him much any more.'

'And was it one of these guys who raped you two years ago?'

She smiles, a timid, nervous smile. 'No, that was Matt. He got me onto crack when I was pregnant with Ryan.'

'Right.'

DC Barnes is making frantic notes, most likely including the words 'Mental', 'Promiscuous' and 'Serial complainant'. I suspect that Mandy is not scoring too highly on the checklist of credibility; suffice it to say, the DC doesn't look amused to have been called out to hear her story. He leaves the room, and I hear him phoning up his DS to arrange the arrest of the offender; the words 'pile of crap' may or may not have been used.

As I sit there, I wonder whether he is right, or whether his mistake is in applying the standards of ordinary, sensible men to this confused and chaotic woman.

I remember a moment of madness from my own life. When I was twenty, which is not all that long ago, thank you, I got drunk at a party and agreed to go home with a man I'd never met before. Once at his house, he started to undress me. His intentions eventually filtered through to my slightly addled brain, along with a few other things: that I did not fancy this guy, that I did not know him, and that I had no idea where I was or what I was doing there.

I told him to stop, he called me a taxi and I went home.

I would say almost all of my female friends have done this at one time or another. I don't think any have been raped, but then that's the sort of thing only your closest friends might tell you. Some have been very frightened. Some have gone through with the sex out of sheer embarrassment at having changed their minds. Some, like me, have been very lucky that the bloke who took them home had just got his wires crossed, and got all embarrassed and apologetic when he was put straight.

We all agree we were utterly stupid and that we were an unlucky roll of the dice away from being raped and, who knows, buried in a suitcase.

* * * * *

When DC Barnes finishes with Mandy, I'm released to go back to something far more important than holding a crying woman's hand: Crime Management.

This is the process of making sure that Blandshire Constabulary, and in particular, Blandmore's Area Commander, get the credit for the work PC Bloggs has done. As a 21st Century police officer, attending the incident and catching the baddie is not nearly as important as making sure you claim the DETECTION. I get a detection whenever I charge, report or give out a ticket to an offender - they don't have to be convicted. However, I can't claim it unless I also perform several other tasks, and these are known as Crime Management. (This should not be confused with Crime Management, Investigation and Detection Supervising, which is Charles Hammond's job and involves making sure that I have done my Crime Managing properly).

And so, my sergeant thinking I am busy looking at a vagina, I locate one of our more useable chairs and sit down at one of our working computers. The chair slowly slides down until my chin is level with the keyboard and it will not go back up again, no matter how many little levers I press. Reaching up for the mouse, I open my virtual 'docket' and view the jobs in it.

A job 'in your docket' is an open investigation which needs concluding.

The 21st Century police officer has two 'dockets'.

One is virtual, and consists of crime reports in your name which are stored on the computer (in the Crime Management System). This is because investigating is now 'paper-free'.

The second is a metal box which sits in a stack in the report room. It contains the paper belonging to the paper-free investigations and, for practicality's sake, usually a printout of the virtual docket.

I find myself staring at three open crime reports. One of them is entitled 'Exposure', which confuses me as I have only dealt with one Exposure in the last year and I charged a kid with it two months ago. I go into the report and find that it is indeed the one I charged a kid with two months ago. There is no information as to why the investigation has been reopened, nor why the 'Undetected' flag has been ticked. I send off an email requesting an explanation. I deal with the others as best I can and then switch the computer off.

My virtual housekeeping done for an hour at least, I scan the room for my metal docket. I left it on the window sill, where, incidentally, a member of the public need only reach in from the High Street and remove it. It has vanished from there, perhaps for good. What joy! I'm about to radio up to ask for some work to do when I spot the offending article in the stack for Team 2, the shift of Sergeant Rory 'Buns-of-steel' Williams (five teams of officers cover the 24 hours of each day on a revolving shift pattern; each team has its own sergeant of varying ability/cuteness, and Rory is at the upper end of the scale, cuteness-wise). Before retrieving it, I check the label on the front - there's always a chance I have been transferred to Team 2 without being told... but no, it appears to have been an error. I sigh: I can always hope.

Will enters the report room as I stand staring at Rory's name. He reaches up to the top of our team's stack and feels around inside his own docket. It probably isn't professional, but as he stands there on tiptoe I idly consider his buns: whilst more of a tin/zinc alloy than steel, they do the job.

He turns round, and I think I might be blushing. Looking hurriedly away, I take hold of my docket and hoist it out onto the desk. It seems unusually heavy today and as soon as I pull it out I find out why: a surprise parcel fills it up entirely. It's a huge manila envelope, bound up with lots of brown elastic bands. I drop it on the desk and it splits open, scattering video tapes across the floor. They are labelled as exhibits: 'EEB-1', 'EEB-2'… all the way up to 'EEB-10'. The only clue as to what they might show is the helpful words 'Copy of CCTV tape' written neatly on each one, which clarifies things immensely. I'm baffled: not only would I be likely to remember the unusual event of CCTV footage forming part of an investigation - it's almost always fuzzy and useless - but I'm sure I'd recall TEN pieces of footage. I shake out the envelope in the hope that they are accompanied by some information and a 'Video request' form drops out with my name written at the top. The rest is blank.

Will has completed his search and he withdraws a great curved Samurai sword which had fallen down behind the stack of dockets. It has been wrapped in brown parcel tape from end to end and sports a police exhibit label on the hilt. Will drops it on the desk in order to help me clear up the pool of tapes.

He sees me looking and shakes his head. 'Don't ask.'

'I won't.'

He gives me a dashing wink and trots out, swishing his sword.

As I sit contemplating my pile of tapes, I'm astonished to hear on my radio that CID have arrested Mandy's rapist. This is very concerning: DC Barnes could have been hurt badly trying to accomplish a basic police task like arresting someone now that he is a detective. Then I hear Lloyd asking for space to be found in custody, and I realise that it is in fact he who has arrested the guy.

I throw the CCTV tapes back into my docket. It will no longer fit in the stack, so I shove it back onto the window sill. I toy with the urge to tootle down to custody and peer at the woman-hater; eventually, I resist. Instead, miraculously, I locate some car-keys and go out to do some work.

I have two statements to take from witnesses for my ongoing investigations. One of them is the neighbour of a woman whose lawn was sprayed with weed killer. The neighbour saw the offender creeping in through the gate at night - she just happened to be awake at 4am looking out of her back window. That investigation is due to take a few weeks: we think the chemical was applied in the shape of some unflattering and possibly threatening four letter words, but until the grass finally dies back completely we can't be sure which ones.

The other statement is from a man who is being victimised by the Council. It seems the Council are planting listening devices in his loft to spy on his conversations, and when they came round to replace his smoke detector they put another gizmo in which now stares unblinkingly down at him, night and day. Unfortunately, my update on the incident log did not aptly reflect the situation and it has been designated rather haphazardly as criminal damage. Once I have the man's conspiracy theory down on paper, I'm hoping to persuade the Auditors to bin it on the grounds of mental health.

Whilst en route to see Mr Bugs I am rudely interrupted by the radio controller. 'Any unit to attend a report of a sexual assault by a taxi driver.'

Apparently Blandmore has thrown an impromptu Rape Day today. My finger is automatically on the transmit button. I know I'm going to end up attending the incident, so I decide to bypass the politics and just volunteer. In any event, the only other available unit is Rich and he will be sitting somewhere in the nick with his heart pumping faster and faster as he tries to think of an excuse not to go. Rich is not lazy - indeed, he is one of the most diligent, hard-working officers on the team and by far the best at saying 'Yes, sarge' and meaning it. Unfortunately, he is also absolutely terrified of anything more complicated than the sound of breaking glass and a hooded figure running away.

The controller elaborates on the incident at hand. 'Anne-Marie Culhart was taking a taxi back from Elsmith when the driver pulled over and tried to force her to give him oral sex. She's currently at home with her mother.'

The voice is that of the radio controller who does not mind using the word 'sex' over the air. Some of them like to phone you directly if the incident involves faeces, genitals or urination, out of embarrassment at too many people hearing them use naughty words.

'How old is she?' I query.

'Nineteen.'

The victim's name is familiar. I play with it in my mind, and then it comes to me. Culhart is Lisa Perril's maiden-name. 'Is Anne-Marie something to do with the Perrils?'

There is a pause which Lloyd fills - he's a walking family tree of Blandmore. 'Yes, yes. Lisa's sister.'

Lisa's family live in Carlton Way. I drift along the road, scanning for house numbers, and am amazed to find that the relevant one has a kindly-looking woman in the doorway, peering anxiously up and down the street. She sees me and beckons.

I park up and trot over. 'Hello. Mrs Culhart?'

'Yes, dear, thank you for getting here so fast.' How on earth did she produce Lisa Perril? This lady is absolutely charming. She is wearing a clean jumper and jeans, with large red fluffy house-slippers. She puts the kettle on without my even having to ask and I am ushered through to the back room, where a teenager sits on a sofa with her legs slung over the arm.

'Anne-Marie?'

'Yes.'

She is skinny, with dark hair stretched back in a ponytail and a pale face blotchy with tears. Whilst her pose hints at Chav, there is a subtle straightness of her back and an alert look in her eyes which suggests she might actually have done A-levels.

Before I've done more than deposit my backside in an armchair and order the beverage of my choice, my mobile phone rings.

'Bloggs? Any good?'

'Sarge...?'

'The assault. Is it genuine?'

'Er... Sarge, I've only just arrived.'

'You do know she's basically a Perril?'

Unfortunately, people from 'bad' families, and even ones who are simply related by marriage, or other, less stable relationships, can get tarred with the same brush.

'Yes, Sarge,' I say.

'Well, keep me updated.'

I then speak to Anne-Marie to establish how 'good' her assault is.

The initial information pretty much sums it up. The driver got into the back of the cab, gripped her round the back of the neck, unzipped his trousers and said, 'Suck it, and I'll halve the fare.' Anne-Marie started screaming, a Mini pulled up behind them and the driver put away his family fortune and dropped her off where she had asked.

'Did he charge the full amount?' (What on earth made me ask that?)

'Yes, and it was a rip-off, too.' She smiles a little.

I find myself analysing her facial expression. Is she just a little too happy? Is that, in fact, the face of a girl who *willingly* gives taxi drivers blow-jobs in exchange for rides? Gah! Now look what Sergeant Woodcock has done to me.

Anyway, my views are pretty irrelevant. Being a shift officer, I'm only trained to take basic statements about junk mail and weed killer, so an expert will have to take over before much more is said or done. I therefore carry out the urgent actions required and inform CID that they will have to spare someone from the in-depth discussion of Mandy's sexual habits to deal with this.

As I leave the Culharts' house, my mobile phone rings again.

'Bloggs here.'

'PC Bloggs, it's Dr Jenkins. I'm at the Rape Suite… are we ready to go ahead with this examination?'

I am baffled, until I recall arranging for her to come and examine Mandy, and forgetting to cancel her when Dr Green arrived. I apologise profusely - something at which I excel - and get back in my car. Dr Jenkins may or may not be willing to attend the next time she is called to the Rape Suite.

On arriving back at Blandmore, Chris accosts me.

'Well?'

'I've seized her clothing and taken swabs for DNA from her neck. There might be CCTV of the taxi rank and there's a black London cab to look out for.'

'Is she telling the truth?'

'Er... she was crying when I got there.'

Tears are always good. The courts like tears. If you ever get raped, make sure you cry a lot.

The sergeant is pacified; it sounds like a good job. He wanders up to pass this to CID. Before I can wander after him, I am dispatched to two burglaries. I attend these on auto-pilot, my mind dissecting the jobs I have dealt with so far that day. It's easy to misunderstand the role of the police at incidents like those involving Mandy and Anne-Marie. Rather than concentrating on securing perishable evidence, and taking an unprompted 'free recall' account from the victim, I should have been looking for those tell-tale signs that this was a 'bad job'. A 'Blandmore job'. A lack of witnesses, CCTV or cooperation from the victim, plus any lies told for whatever reasons, are all indicators. Moreover, a police officer should dig deeply into the complainant's possible motivations for making the allegation. In this case, the taxi driver had 'ripped her off', which may have prompted her to 'get him back' by giving up a year of her life to drag him through court proceedings. Few can grasp the sheer scale of a teenager's malevolence when it comes to men. For any budding 21st Century police officers out there, always remember this: on attending a report like this, your job is to be judge, jury and executioner, NOT merely to investigate.

Once finished with the burglaries, I return to the nick and discover that Mandy's rapist has been charged and remanded. Standing in the doorway to CID, I absorb the withering glances of people wearing plainclothes and say, 'I thought it was 'a load of rubbish'?'

'It won't go anywhere at court,' DC Barnes says. 'But it's a detection.'

Sometimes I yearn to be in CID so badly I can hardly contain myself. There the offences are so serious that you charge people with barely any evidence at all. It is the same in the Domestic Violence Unit. If one party says the other one did it, that is pretty much all you need to go ahead. If the courts later throw it out... well, we've done our job.

I descend to the report writing room for a well-earned cup of tea. Well, a cup of tea.

I need to update the investigation status of the crimes I have attended today, and input the actions I have carried out at each incident, so it takes two cups in the end. The joy of having two dockets is that you have to write everything down manually when you attend the scene and then transfer it all onto the paper-free system at the nick. This helps speed up your investigation and, in particular, it vitally assists your sergeant; he can now view the information in your virtual docket and transfer it into an email, which can be printed out and sent to the filing department.

Speaking of my sergeant, Chris comes into the room and groans when he sees me mid-Crime-Managing.

He looks at me, suspiciously. 'Bloggs,' he says. 'I've warned you about attending too many crimes.'

As my sergeant, he has to 'Review' all my investigations on a regular basis. Part of the purpose of a Review is for the sergeant to sit down with me and discuss the investigation, and give me ideas on how to solve unsolvable crimes. But more importantly still, the sergeant must then update the computer database (Crime Management System) to say that the Review has taken place.

If the sergeant fails to carry out these Reviews at set intervals, he will receive automatic emails reminding him to do so.

After eighty days and five Reviews, both of us will be hauled in front of the inspector for failing to solve the crime.

It's either a tremendously constructive use of the time and money spent on creating and employing a highly experienced police sergeant, or a soul-destroying, life-wasting avalanche of admin. I couldn't possibly comment. What I do know is that any crime I attend will add another quarter-inch of paper to the pile in his in-tray.

'It's OK, sarge,' I say. 'Two of them are burglaries.' Burglaries are OK because they tend to disappear off to the specialist Burglary Team - there's little follow-up work for the attending PC and, therefore, for her sergeant.

'Yes,' he says. 'But before the Burglary Team will take them I have to Review them. Are they ready to be filed?'

'Well, one of the victims' phones was used by the offender to call a landline number during the burglary.'

Technically, this is good news; we may be able to identify whoever it was the offender spoke to and get them, in turn, to ID the offender. However, in order to do that we need to trace the number called. Chris groans again, only louder.

'Oh God!' he says. 'You know that means more forms for the number trace.'

With the face of a true computer-hater, Chris trudges out.

I continue Crime Managing. As I tap away, I see that my earlier email - the one about the kid and the exposure - has been replied to. If there is a department whose diligence I cannot criticise at all, it is the department responsible for replying to negatively-toned emails. Whilst your unimportant annual leave and new uniform requests can go unanswered for weeks, as soon as you raise your electronic voice in complaint you can guarantee a same-day response.

This email is from Enid Pimento, the 'Scrutineer'. She is the link between a number of different departments, some of which try to generate detections for Blandshire Constabulary, others whose job it is to take them away again.

Enid's role is to balance the importance of the weekly performance figures against the insidious lies told by police officers. The relationship of a PC with her Scrutineer is akin to that of the unpopular newly-wed with the mother-in-law who lives next door: occasionally, she startles you by paying a bill on your behalf, but more often you arrive home and find her poisoning your soup.

'PC Bloggs,' reads her email, '*your detection for Exposure has been removed as you have not entered the suspect's custody number. The custody number is BX/2342P.*'

My fingers hover over the keys. I want to type, '*Can't you just enter that yourself if you know it?*' but Chris is getting sick of pretending to tell me off, so I restrain myself.

I go instead to the Arrest page and attempt to enter the reference number. Up pops a helpful message: '*Access denied.*'

It's getting close to 1am, and therefore going home time, so I send off an email to IT Support asking them assist me, and shut down the system. At least it isn't Detection Night; the Exposure can wait another day.

* * * * *

I see Mandy leaving the nick as I pass the front office. It has taken eight hours, but someone has finally found a Polaroid camera and photographs have now been taken of a minuscule scratch on the inside of her forearm. She seems to have washed and changed. At least, she has replaced the thick layer of makeup with another thick layer of makeup and her breasts are now hanging out of a new top.

'Hi there,' I say. 'Did it go all right?'

She shrugs.

'You know he's been charged?'

'Yes.'

I nod vaguely, not sure of the right tack to take.

'I know no one believes me,' she blurts out.

'Of course they do,' I say.

'I shouldn't have gone upstairs with him.'

She shakes her head.

No kidding.

Mandy wanders out into the street and off into the night. I watch her go, wondering what possessed her to go to a party in a strange house with a man she hardly knew, and then agree to go upstairs with him?

Then I turn and walk to the locker room. Do I believe her? I think I do. Does it matter? Not really. I've done my bit, insignificant though it was, and it's for others to take forward now.

Every now and again, a nice girl from a good family is snatched off the street and attacked by some bastard in a balaclava. Quite rightly, the police will pour huge resources into finding her attacker. She will be believed and supported and when, as is likely, her rapist is found he will be brought to justice (or sent to jail for a couple of years, anyway).

But your usual rape victim is a girl like Mandy, vulnerable, inarticulate and lacking the skills to explain herself properly - or act in a sensible manner on a night out. Their rapist is almost always someone they know, often an ex. When the rape occurs, they don't struggle or cry out like they do in movies. They have no injuries. No one witnesses it, or records it on CCTV. They have been raped before and they don't report this one for days or even weeks afterwards.

Does all of this mean it hasn't happened? It quite likely has nothing to do with it either way.

Does all of this mean the chances of proving the offence in court are zero? Probably.

Yet women like Mandy keep coming forward, ever-hopeful that a mystery witness will be discovered in the corner of the crime scene, or the prosecution barrister will pop up at court and perform a Columbo-type reconstruction of the event that will vindicate them in front of everyone.

He won't.

I squeeze my stab vest and belt into my locker.

A lot of police officers believe that most rape allegations are simply made up. I'm sure some are.

The sad truth, I realise, is that I am a serving policewoman of good character, who does not drink, much, or take drugs; yet if I were raped, other than by a total stranger, I am not sure I would bother to report it.

5

Tea and Testimony

EVERY TIME A police officer attends a Mop's house to take a statement, fill out a form or merely to bleat platitudes at someone who has been severely let down, he or she faces the age-old question: Tea or no Tea?

I have devised a simple test to resolve this dilemma: if I will need to wipe my feet on the way out, I do not take tea.

A much trickier scenario is when all the positive criteria are met - a half-clean kitchen, signs that someone in the premises knows what a bin is for, lack of dog mess on the floor - and yet no-one actually offers to stick the kettle on.

At times like these, I love being crewed with Lloyd. He has a number of strategies for eliciting tea from reticent Mops and absolutely no compunction about using them. Being six-foot-four, built like a tennis pro and with a mop of curly brown hair, he rarely has to try hard.

This evening, however, his skills are put to the test. We have arrived at a five-bedroom detached country 'cottage' to speak to two small boys who have been approached by a stranger in the park. A family gathering is in full swing, with children racing around the driveway and across the lawn, and the front door is standing wide open.

Lloyd enters first and rests his giant shoulders in the kitchen doorway.

'Evening all,' he says. He loves saying things like that, and always uses his deepest voice for the job. 'Mrs Brayburn?'

'Oh, hello!' A flushed woman pops her head round from the open fridge door. She's stacking Tupperware boxes, or rearranging them. 'Sorry,' she says. 'Do sit down. And it's Minnie, please.'

She clears us a space at the kitchen table, blowing frizzy blonde hair out of her eyes and sweeping aside a couple of plates of half eaten pizza slices and a bowl containing five or six home-made chocolate cookies. The kitchen is full of the smells of baking and cooking; it's 8pm and I've not eaten since 3am. This is because today is 'Quick Changeover Shift', a fiendish ornament to our working arrangements designed to 'normalise' our sleeping patterns. I've just finished a row of nights (ending at 7am) but we're required to come straight back in for a 5pm to midnight shift the next evening. The result of this is that between sleeping and dressing for work again you almost never get round to eating. Right now, I am suffering from an abnormal hunger that is almost tangible. The aroma of the pizza and those cookies is unbearable.

'Right,' says Lloyd. 'OK.' He rests the side of his folder on the table and glances around. 'Gosh, that smells good.'

Mrs Brayburn smiles. 'I usually bake on a Thursday,' she says. 'The children love my cookies.'

Surely we will be offered one any minute?

Am I stretching the bounds of credibility if I tell you that Minnie Brayburn sits down and starts to tell us her tale without any such offer?

'Adam and Robbie were playing in the park,' she says, putting her hair behind her ears. 'They came in about half an hour ago and said some guy had come up to them and tried to put Adam in his car. We didn't really twig at first, then it hit us and we all went racing out looking for him, but he was gone.'

Lloyd clears his throat. 'Are the boys around?'

'Yes, I'll get them.' She leans out of the kitchen window and shouts to another woman standing on the lawn. 'Sarah? Are the boys there?'

The woman shouts something back and I can see her chivvying some small children towards the house.

She turns back to us. 'We've tried not to upset them by making a big deal out of it, but they were in quite a state when they came back.'

'Mmm,' we both say.

There is a short pause as we wait for the kids to materialise. But still no sniff of an offer of tea and/or cookie.

Lloyd tries again. 'I hope we're not interrupting your coffee or anything... feel free to make yourself one.'

'No thanks,' she says. 'I had one earlier. With a cookie.'

I can almost hear Lloyd's teeth grinding.

There's some noise in the hallway and Minnie gets up, looking towards the door. By chance, the kettle is vaguely in her line of sight. 'Here they are,' she says.

'I'd love one!' says Lloyd.

'Sorry?'

'Oh, sorry,' he says. 'Er... I thought you asked if I wanted a tea. The old hearing going again, don't worry about it.'

Minnie laughs with this dear, sweet, mildly eccentric copper, and brings the children over with the other woman.

'This is Adam, my son,' she says, pointing at a skinny, freckled boy who looks about five or six. 'This is Sarah, my sister. And Robbie, my nephew. He's her boy.'

Robbie is a little older than Adam, with black spiked hair; he's wearing an England shirt with ROONEY on the back.

'Boys,' says Minnie. 'These are the police officers who are going to ask you about the man in the park.'

The boys huddle together and gaze up at Lloyd, who towers over them even sitting down. They look very apprehensive. 'All right, lads?' he says. 'Nothing to worry about.'

At that, Adam starts crying. He points at me. 'I want her, Mummy.'

Lloyd shrugs with no trace of personal affront whatsoever. 'No worries,' he says. 'I'll stay and have a cup of tea while you pop into the next room and have a chat to PC Bloggs.'

My jaw drops at his cheekiness, but I take Adam and Minnie into the study. Over my shoulder, I see Lloyd making himself at home with the kettle and chatting amiably with Robbie and Sarah. The boy has climbed up onto the kitchen table, and my last view is of Lloyd getting his big mitt on one of the cookies. Without me.

I sit Adam down and do my usual preamble, about telling the truth and just saying if he doesn't remember something, and not to worry about getting in trouble. Kids as young as five can be hard to interview, especially if they are from nice families who have brought them up to respect the police. They tend to nod and agree with everything you ask and are so desperate to please you that they will sometimes make the answers up.

'So, Adam,' I say. 'Just tell me about what happened.'

He winds his chocolatey fingers together and stands up. 'Well, we were playing over by the swings and he came up and said you look cold and I said I wasn't and he said did I want to go for a nice holiday and I said no then he grabbed me' - Adam grips his own arm at this point - 'and he pulled me to his car and I shouted no and then Robbie shouted no as well and we ran away.'

My tummy rumbles audibly as I make notes. 'Can you describe this person?' I ask.

'I writed it down.'

I glance at Minnie, who produces a scrap of paper. 'He wrote down what he could remember when he came in,' she says.

I look at the torn page of a notebook and twist my head to make out words. '*It was a he?*' I say.

'Yes,' says Adam. He giggles nervously.

'Can you remember any more about him, Adam?'

'He was really really tall and had a pink head.'

'Right. Tell me about his car.'

'Er… I think it was white.'

'OK. Is there anything else you can tell me about the man?'

'Well…' Adam looks with some embarrassment at his mother. 'I think he was a Stranger but I'm not sure.'

I finish my notes and wrap up the interview. CID will be pleased to know they are looking for a tall he-stranger with a pink head.

By the time I return to the kitchen, Lloyd has the satisfied expression of someone who has eaten a cookie, possibly two, and drunk a cup of tea. As he has now struck up a rapport with Robbie, and they are discussing whether Wayne Rooney should play in a forward role or in the hole behind an out-and-out frontman, I decide that he can interview the second child to give me the chance to have a cuppa myself.

Robbie's mother is summoned and Lloyd slopes off with them. Minnie is back in the kitchen. I can hardly just help myself to tea right in front of her, so I sit on the edge of a wooden stool with my hands tucked under my thighs and I rock there for a good five minutes while she goes about her business. Finally, I clear my throat, just a touch, and say, 'Er, I couldn't have a cup of tea, could I? It's just I haven't slept in twenty-four hours.'

'Oh, you poor dear!' she says, a look of horror on her face. 'Of course!'

Minnie bustles into action and presents me with an entire teapot and - to my delight - a neat row of cucumber sandwiches with the crusts cut off. Sometimes the direct approach is best.

I sit there for another 15 minutes, getting pleasantly full and listening to Minnie Brayburn talk about this and that, until Lloyd wanders back in and it's time to leave.

Chances of catching the pervert? Almost nil.

A complete waste of time? Certainly not. Robbie and Adam now think that the police are the most patient and compassionate adults in the world, their mothers know we care (which we do), and I've eaten the best sarnies I've had in ages, albeit with an awfully long wait. I never got a cookie, though.

* * * * *

There's something about the Quick Changeover shift that sends Blandmore into a frenzy. For instance, we usually get endless, back-to-back 'blue light' jobs; it's almost as if the local scrotes know that every officer on duty has been up the whole of the previous night and really wants to get home on time. Lloyd offers to write up the report for CID on the attempted kidnapping and I snatch some precious moments to put my docket in order before our three days off. I always attempt some email pre-emption on Quick Changeover. This consists of opening up each virtual crime report in my name and writing something into the update field explaining why I have made no progress on it whatsoever.

My online docket has grown to about seven outstanding jobs, with the Grahams harassment and now three burglaries added to it. I notice the Exposure staring at me with the cold eyes of the undetected, and I open my inbox to find a response from IT Support about it. Apparently, I am not authorised to enter custody numbers into our crime system - this can only be done by a trained civilian on the Crime Desk. This is because civilians have no vested interest in entering false custody references, whereas presumably PC Bloggs could make good money out of the scam.

As a side-note, you may be wondering whether the Crime Desk is the same thing as the Crime Centre, or whether I am being deliberately confusing. I would like to assure you that all of these departments exist. I have actually simplified the structure of my force considerably for fear of being written off as far-fetched.

I consider picking up the phone to the Crime Desk and then burst out laughing at my own naïvety. It is almost 10pm - why would they be on duty at this hour? So, email it is. My next obstacle is that there is no email address for 'Crime Desk'. I try several permutations and finally I just email the request to every member of the entire department, asking them to put the requisite custody number into the requisite crime report and allocate me the requisite detection. And could they please do it by Wednesday night as Charles Hammond might then bring me a doughnut.

A further email draws my attention to an update in one of my crime reports. With the skill of a master novelist, the Crime Centre employee who has sent the email has kept me in suspense as to the nature of the update. I have to log into the Crime Management System again to locate it.

It appears that the lawn-spraying incident I am investigating has now escalated to a mean letter being left on the doormat. The update goes onto inform me that the letter has been seized by another officer *and* a statement taken, but only because that officer was unaware that I was already the victim's personal bobby. The officer has also been kind enough to inform me that the offender has been identified and lives in Nutcorn - a small town in the far north of Blandshire. Apparently, the suspect grew up in the house next door to the lawn-owner and he has, for some reason, always blamed her for the debilitating cancer that killed his mother. This will mean a fax (the horror, the horror) to Nutcorn police station for an arrest. Sighing, I add it to the list of things I'll do when I get time.

I check in with Lloyd: he is happily typing away and there's little I can do to help, short of standing over his shoulder telling him what to write. For some reason, I get called bossy when I do that.

Will is not in the office for me to stare at, so I find myself at something of a loose end. My mind turns to my 10 CCTV tapes. It's now five days since they materialised *en masse* in my tray, and I have made no attempt whatsoever to view them. I grab them and set off to locate a video recorder. I try custody first, but the moment I walk in the door with the stack of tapes under my chin I am yelled at by Sergeant Hayes to get out of her custody suite with my crap.

Most sergeants have to do a stint in custody during their career, where their astute legal knowledge and people management skills are put to good use instructing officers to ask someone else their questions, deciding how many sugars to put in the prisoners' coffee and how long to make the next officer wait to talk to them. Even so, it can be quite dull, so Sergeant Hayes keeps herself entertained by sticking rigidly to force and government policy no matter how ridiculous it may be; the current custody policy is that no one is allowed in there for anything other than matters relating to prisoners or to bring her a cup of tea, so I reluctantly depart.

I mooch upstairs to the Burglary and Robbery Team offices. Being as it's after 10pm, I can cruise most of the police station without interference from non-uniformed employees, but none of the departments appear to have VCRs. I locate one in CID itself, but there is no television with it. I tentatively sit down before it, wondering where I can get a telly from. Then the duty Detective Sergeant enters and screams at me to get out of his office with my crap.

I check all other unlocked offices and come up with nothing. In desperation, I toy with the idea of trying to sneak past the eagle eyes of Sgt Hayes back down in custody. I stash my tapes in the front office and return, incognito, without them. The first two interview rooms have no video players. The third is in the throes of a huge CID interview and they are putting the VCR to vital use as a tray for their teacups. The fourth and fifth interview rooms not only don't have video players, they don't even have tape recorders. One of them also has no chairs. I admit defeat, and leave. On the stairwell I run into Lloyd and find out that we have been given another job by the skipper.

'But it's after ten,' I say. 'The night shift are on.'

'Apparently they're already all busy,' he says. 'It's just a quick enquiry.'

'Oh, no… not a quick enquiry.'

Those are usually the most complex kind.

'It's for Guy, it'll be fine.'

'Guy' is PC Guy Mitchum from our shift; he's been in Lanzarote for three days trying to forget the tower of paperwork he'll return to. Apparently, he needs somebody to pop round to Wayne and Lisa Perrils' place and take down Wayne's mobile telephone number. I grudgingly agree that that does indeed sound like a very quick enquiry.

Tea and Testimony

We've handed our marked car over to the night shift - in fact, Joanna from Team 1 almost pick pocketed the car-keys from my belt as I walked in the door, though this was almost certainly more to do with wanting to bask in a seat warmed by Lloyd's behind than with wanting to do some work.

Lloyd and I go out covertly in a plain car instead. I once did a three-day attachment to CID, so I know where they hide the keys to their vehicles and have a high success rate in sneaking them away. To be fair, they don't really mind operational officers using them, as long as it's for less than half an hour and we return them at the precise moment they think they might be about to use them. I think this is because they know that if they don't leave the station within thirty seconds of the thought occurring to them, the feeling will pass and they won't leave at all.

We wend our way up to the Perrils' flat. I raise a hand to knock. Just as my fist hits the wood, I hear the sound of screeching coming from within. I freeze. I hear the unmistakable tones of Wayne. 'You bitch!' he shouts.

'Get off me!' wails Lisa.

I can scarcely believe it, but it seems we have accidentally arrived in the middle of a domestic. I knock again and the door is jerked open, forcefully; in front of me is the semi-clad form of my old friend Wayne.

'What?' he says.

'Good evening,' I say. My eyes take in the tramlines of blood across his chest. 'Is everything all right?'

'That cow from downstairs didn't call you again, did she?' he says.

Lloyd raises both hands. 'Hey, steady on,' he says. 'We just came by to get your mobile number for PC Mitchum.'

'Oh yeah.' Wayne calms down, somewhat. He's drunk and doesn't appear to have changed his trousers since I last saw him.

'Are you hurt?' I ask, gesturing at the blood on his chest.

'Nah, that's not mine,' he says, wiping it off with the back of his hand.

Lloyd and I look at each other, and then at him. Eventually, he realises what he's said.

'Oh, er, she just, er, cut herself doing the vegetables,' he says.

That's a fatal mistake; neither he nor Lisa have prepared or eaten a vegetable in the last five years.

'I think we'd better come in,' I say.

'Nah, it's fine,' he replies. 'No one called you, so it ain't your business.'

Fortunately my fifteen weeks of legal training enables me to ignore this. I put a hand heavily on the door, and it slams open.

'Lisa, are you all right?' I say.

She staggers into view. I wonder whether she has started lap dancing. There can't be many other explanations for the classy little black skirt she is sporting around her waist, and the teeny thong that is now being displayed to all and sundry.

'Yeah, I'm all right,' she says.

I tilt my head. 'You're bleeding.'

Blood is seeping down the inside of one thigh and into the crease at the back of her knee. Lloyd takes Wayne's arm and leads him outside, and I squeeze through. I quickly establish that Lisa has a four-inch slash mark horizontally across her leg. Over her shoulder into the bathroom I see a bloodied knife on the floor.

'How did you do that?' I say.

'How d'you think?' she snaps. 'He did it, didn't he?'

'Well, did he?'

'Yeah.'

I catch Lloyd's eye in the hallway. He's holding Wayne against the wall, fingers spread against his bare chest. I perform the international sign for handcuffs - touching the insides of both wrists together - and he nods. Lisa cottons onto what is happening as Lloyd is halfway through the caution.

'Why are you arresting him?' she shouts.

'Because he's stabbed you, Lisa.'

'Why you doing this to me?' She steps back into the bathroom and abruptly begins to fumble on the floor. I realise she's trying to find the knife.

I grip her wrist and jerk her back into the lounge.

'Don't be an idiot,' I say, breathing hard. 'You can't put up with this, Lisa.'

'But I dunno what to do,' she says. 'He don't mean it. I love him.'

For some reason, victims of domestic violence always talk about 'love', as though that had anything to do with anything. Briefly, I think about pointing out the inconsistencies between 'love' and knife', but then I drop it.

'Are you going to give us a statement this time?' I ask, surreptitiously folding the bloodied blade into a latex glove in my pocket.

'No,' she says. 'In fact, get out.' She wrenches herself away from me and falls back onto the sofa, screaming her despair into the cushions.

'Can I at least call you an ambulance for the cut?'

'No.' She turns her thigh out. 'It's nothing. Look.'

I look closer at the injury; it actually isn't deep, and has almost stopped bleeding. Wayne is starting to get anxious in the hallway, so I say, 'Someone will be back to see you later, Lisa,' and assist Lloyd in carting him outside.

You may be wondering why I persist in persecuting this innocent couple when they have absolutely no desire to see or deal with the police. The answer, of course, is that I have to. It used to be the case that police officers were let loose on the streets and allowed to make decisions about whether or not to arrest people on whatever whim they chose. This was a terrible state of affairs, obviously, as it meant that the investigation of crime was allowed to rest on the judgment of dumb white males with thick necks, whose only expertise lay in having attended hundreds of similar incidents. Here in the 21st Century, senior managers in the police and their political masters have realised that police officers *cannot and should not be trusted*. This is the key component in Blandshire Constabulary becoming a guiding light to other forces. They have simply decreed that police officers *must* arrest people whenever they physically can. (Technically, that's not an absolute; we *can* decide not to arrest, but we will be questioned by senior officers later to determine why we didn't. At these meetings, it will become clear that we have not considered the 'bigger picture'. Low-ranking police officers foolishly sometimes try to attend incidents without downloading a single policy, or looking up a single statistic. Once this important lapse has been pointed out to us by a senior officer, it very often appears that our original decision not to arrest was wrong after all.)

Of course, if you replace police with automatons in uniform, you don't have to worry as much about the integrity of your employees, and in time that will negate the requirement for trusted and responsible supervisors. This can only be a good thing. Think of the budgetary savings!

In the case of the Perrils, no doubt most police officers would be inclined to leave them there to stab each other to death all night. But we have our policies and statistics to keep us from our murderous desires.

It's 2am before Lloyd and I sign off-duty, but not before he has spent the customary ten minutes fending off Jo's coquettish advances. In the end, he gets away from her by informing her that she will have to interview Wayne for us. I take out my work mobile to turn it off, and discover that a voicemail has been waiting for me since 4pm. I throw my kit into my locker, listening as I do so: it turns out I am due in court on Monday morning at 9am. It is now Monday morning at 2am.

Bollocks.

Mind you, it's not as if I have a personal life or anything.

I retrieve my mangled tie from the back of the locker and remove the epaulettes from my stab vest. I had a spare set of epaulettes once, but I left them in a panda car one day and somebody filched them. Given that they were adorned with my badge number, I cannot imagine what use they would be to anyone else, unless I have a stalker who collects memorabilia of me and sticks it up in a shrine in his or her bedroom. I can only hope.

I have absolutely no idea which case I am giving evidence in, so I wearily log back onto the system; there's a chance I'm the Officer in Charge of it and might therefore be expected to bring the exhibits with me. (Exhibits are items recovered from the scene and relevant to a crime. In movies, they usually consist of clumps of the attacker's hair or blood-covered murder weapons. In real life, the hair turns out to be from the dog and the knife has ketchup on it.)

The system confirms that I am due in court on Monday morning but the space where the case reference should be is blank. I replay my voicemail, and this time I pay attention.

R v Leeman.

Which means that I, *Regina*, arrested someone called Leeman at some point and am now going up *v* him in court.

I can't for the life of me recall who Leeman is and what I might have arrested him for.

I could surf three other systems to try and locate the original case, but the time till the court opens its doors is rapidly diminishing. More importantly, surfing the computer systems is not something for which I can claim overtime. I call it a night and set off home.

In the past, I've expressed sarcastic thoughts about the Courts in my blog (http://pcbloggs.blogspot.com/, in case you're interested). This was very wrong of me. In fact, I love and cherish my court appearances. Particularly when they drop on me a couple of days beforehand and are scheduled for my rest day, as the Working Time Directive means if you have to work on a rest day with less than five days' notice you get paid double time. (If I do accidentally happen to see a notification more than five days before the court date, I quickly make a call to IT services claiming that my email has gone down, I have forgotten my password, or that my eyes were blown out in a bomb and I need to have all my court notifications sent to me on tape.)

Court appearances follow a predictable path. I roll out of bed at 8 or 9 and have a leisurely breakfast. Sometimes I even get to iron a shirt. Then comes the first voicemail check. If that is clear, I begin to stroll towards the court. Very often, the phone-call telling me that the case has been cancelled will arrive just as I enter the court building. If not, I order a few cups of tea from the Witness Service and watch the lawyers running about for an hour or so. I might read a gossip magazine, and find that the woman who wouldn't give me a statement last year has sold her story of domestic violence to *Talk!* At about 11am, the CPS will visit me in the witness waiting room. Their file will be incomplete and they will have several additional questions such as, 'Is the victim coming?', 'Where's the transcript of the interview?' and 'Was there CCTV or not?' I'll have no idea, being just the dogsbody who arrested the guy and handed over a pile of paper to someone else. The officer who actually knows these details will not have been asked to show up and will be sunning him/herself in the Caribbean with his/her phone switched off. After another hour, the Magistrate or District Judge will get fed up and bin the job, and I'll be sent home with the feeling that it is somehow, once again, the police's fault.

Of course, once in a blue moon, all the witnesses have turned up and the CPS hasn't lost part of the file; on those occasions, the 11am visit will instead follow the lines of, 'He *might* be about to change his plea.' This is because the defence barrister has realised that time has run out and his client is about to be found guilty on the irrefutable evidence that they have known about for six months. A plea bargain is agreed by 12pm and once again I can go home.

About once a year, I end up sitting at court all day only to be told at about 4pm that there is no time to hold the trial. Or that the guy pled guilty at 10am and no one bothered to tell me. Even so, it is still six hours work for eight hours' double time, so who's complaining?

On this particular Monday morning, after about four hours' sleep, everything goes according to the above plan until I arrive at Blandmore Magistrates' Court. I take off my coat to discover that I'm only wearing one epaulette and I haven't brought my tie.

Sighing, I introduce myself to the usher, and tell her I'm here to send Mr Leeman to prison.

She glances up and down her sheet and shrugs. 'There's no R v Leeman on the list,' she says.

I blink at her. 'Well, I got the message last night.'

She checks again. 'No. Was it definitely Blandmore?'

My blood runs cold. I fumble for my phone and listen to the message again.

'Yes, it definitely says Blandmore.'

'You'll have to call the Witness Service, I can't help you.'

I spot a passing Witness Service employee and hurry over. He listens patiently for a moment or two, head on one side. Eventually, he says, 'Yes…I'd call the Witness Service if I were you.'

'Is that not you?' I ask.

'You need to call the office,' he says.

I call the office.

The person I speak to is extremely helpful.

'Let me see,' he says. 'PC Bloggs… Leeman… Ah! Here we are. Yes, you're definitely due in Blandmore Crown Court this morning.'

I go hot and cold. '*Crown* Court?' I say.

'Yes.'

'But my message said Blandmore *Mags*.'

'Oh. Is that not in the same place?'

No, it's not. Crown Court is across town and has no free parking. I nip into the nick, borrowing some epaulettes and a tie from an unlocked panda, and set off at a trot. I'm now sweating with stress. As soon as I get there, I hear myself being paged over the echoey public address system to attend the CPS office urgently. I hasten to the stairs and climb four flights, two steps at a time (I never take the lift in case I find myself sharing it with the defendant), and arrive gasping for breath at the door to the CPS.

'R v Leeman?' responds the office clerk. 'Oh that's Charlie's case.' Charlotte Grant is the prosecutor in my case. 'She's in court already.'

'But I was only just paged. Just now? PC Bloggs?'

'Yes, but she had to go to Court 3.'

I jog back downstairs and hover outside Court 3 for ten minutes. I'm about to wander back down to the police waiting room when Charlotte Grant emerges.

'Ah! PC Bloggs.'

'Yes, you called?'

'We have a slight problem with the file.' She takes out a bright purple folder and struggles through it for a scrap of paper. 'It says... *here*... that a scientist has confirmed that the drugs are cocaine. But he hasn't done a statement.'

I stare at her blankly. 'I'm afraid I don't know what case this is.'

'Leeman? Chap with a stash of cocaine?'

I dredge the depths of my memory; somewhere, I recall dealing with someone else's arrest one morning, and charging a man with possession of half a kilo of crack. 'Ah, yes,' I say. 'The scientist definitely did a statement, I remember because I sent it on.'

'We don't have it. Could you possibly get another copy? The judge has given us half an hour.' She looks at her watch. 'And that was two minutes ago.'

I race down to the police room and make five phone-calls. Having obtained the number for the file unit, I dial through to them. The phone rings for what seems like an age. Now I look at *my* watch. This is going to get binned. 'Come on,' I say, under my breath. 'Come *on*.'

The phone answers. The civilian on the other end is quick and efficient, and to my amazement the statement whirs through on the fax with only three lines blurred to the point of illegibility and a minute and a half in hand. I grab it and rush back up to Court 3.

It's empty.

I wait for a few minutes, wondering what to do. Then the CPS page me on the public address system again. I race up to the CPS office again. The sweat situation is now such that I'm not sure I can return my borrowed epaulettes without washing them. When I get there, they tell me Charlotte has gone, but I might find her somewhere around Court 5.

I finally catch up with her, feeling like I've run several more metres than a police officer rightly should.

'Here it is!' I gasp, passing the statement over.

She takes it with a smile. 'Don't worry,' she says. 'He pleaded guilty. You can go. But thanks, anyway.'

I'm almost disappointed as I float home.

That little jaunt cost our little local budget about £160 in my overtime and petrol, not to mention the £100 to pay someone else to cover my shift for me.

I go through the same experience 10 to 15 times a year, as does every one of my colleagues.

6

Let Sleeping Sergeants Lie

I HATE THE FIRST in a run of night shifts. I feel too inert if I spend the day lying in bed, but if I don't then 10pm dawns and I face the prospect of a nine-hour shift without sleep.

This is a far-reaching dilemma. As a reasonably young, single white female, with a job that entails dressing up in uniform and kneeling on people until they come quietly, you might think I have men flocking around me. In reality, I have a choice: I can spend my free evenings fluttering my eyes at hopeful candidates, or I can turn up for work vaguely bright-eyed and with a hope of staying awake until the end of the shift.

There is a third alternative, the preferred choice of most single police officers: date other police officers. Even though you'll no doubt be working opposite shift patterns and therefore only see each other briefly as you pass in the dark, at least when you do see each other you'll understand why you're both in such a bad mood.

And so I approach my night shifts with mixed feelings, and it's worse when they start early in the week. Thursday through Saturday, I charge about most of the night with my blue lights on, remembering why I joined the police and complaining about how busy I am. But early in the week I drift around at about five miles per hour through fog-strewn streets, wondering whether I might not be better off doing something else after all and praying that someone, somewhere is about to have the worst night of their life so that my adrenaline can kick in.

Tonight it is both a first night shift and a Wednesday. I trudge to work five minutes late without any great remorse. Entering the briefing room with my stab vest open, my shoelaces undone and one epaulette in my hand (mine, this time), I'm dismayed to see that the inspector has decided to grace us with his presence. Suddenly, five minutes is five minutes.

'Er, sorry, Guv,' I say, and sit down quickly.

'No problem, Bloggs,' he says. 'Just bring me a doughnut later.'

I have fallen prey to the doughnut rule. There have been a few of them knocking around, lately, which is disastrous for me. Being a woman, I'm always on a diet and can't afford the present rate of two or three a week. I wonder if the inspector will settle for chocolate éclairs?

Inspector Bainbridge has twenty-six years' service and walks around with the air of a man who has managed to be promoted to a decent salary in enough time to claim a reasonable pension when he retires. He is one of the few inspectors who tries to attend incidents, and there's an ancient myth that he once dealt with a car accident on his way to the nick.

The reason for the Guvnor's visit soon becomes apparent. He is here to read us an informative email from the Detective Chief Inspector Responsible for Informative Emails.

'DCI Pauling has sent this out to you all,' he says. 'You should be getting it in letter form too.'

Becks is handing out the post, and, sure enough, there's a brown envelope for each of us; you can tell it's from the DCI because it looks like junk mail.

'I'll read it,' says Insp Bainbridge, 'so there can be no doubts as to whether you've all been informed.'

He clears his throat.

To all Operational Response Officers,' he reads.

This is a letter to remind you that Domestic Violence is our Number One Priority.

Victims of Domestic Violence are not getting the service they deserve. From now on, on attending all domestic incidents, you must carry out the following tasks:

1. Take a statement from the victim, even if drunk or refusing to give a statement.

2. Take a statement from any witnesses, even if drunk or unwilling.

3. Knock on doors even if it is 4am - people who have witnessed the incident will not mind being woken.

4. Consider forensic evidence.

5. Take photographs of any injuries.

6. Write up your own statement describing what you saw.

It goes without saying that you will be making an arrest wherever possible, in line with the force's Positive Intervention policy.

Any officer who does not carry out these actions at EVERY domestic incident, will be hearing from me and will be expected to explain why not.

Thank you.

DCI Ben Pauling, Senior Management Team.'

There is a short silence after he finishes.

Lloyd breaks it. 'I just can't believe that,' he says.

'I know…he said *Thank you*,' says the sarge.

Lloyd just shakes his head. 'Doesn't he think we try to do all that anyway?'

'Well, you need to try harder,' says the inspector. 'Look, all I do is read it out. Just listen or not as you choose, file it away in your heads or forget about it instantly, and we'll leave it at that.'

The shift subsides. I can't believe Lloyd's shoddy attitude. Personally, I think it's marvellous how the DCI took the time out to write each of us a personally-typed letter reminding us how to investigate crime. I'll take it with me and show it to Wayne and Lisa Perril's neighbours the next time I call round. It'll only be the third time that week they've been woken at 4am to ask if they saw or heard anything.

Once I am clear on what my Number One Priority is to be tonight, I'm summoned by Control: 'PC Bloggs, can you attend the High Street. Ambulance asking for assistance with a violent male.'

I don't know about other areas, but I imagine that the police in most places generally try to provide speedy attendance for other emergency services, especially if they are in trouble. We certainly do. It's partly camaraderie and partly a hope that the same will be returned to us (particularly when it comes to waiting in A&E). So I drop any plans to start my shift with a coffee from the doughnut shop and look around for a crew-mate. I'm supposed to be crewed with the sergeant tonight, but he has a good hour of reviewing and emailing to do before he'll be able to go out to play, so I nab Becks and we shoot out of the nick with blue lights blazing.

We arrive at the High Street within about a minute. It might have been quicker to walk, but if we end up grappling with a violent male it is always good to have a vehicle to grapple him into.

I see two paramedics, my friends Andy and Bill. They tower over a familiar figure who is sitting on a bench with his head in his hands. It is TD, the Town Drunk. Bill is leaning over him, peering at a minuscule cut on his temple.

We approach and I say, 'You called?'

Andy points. 'TD's fallen down again.'

'Is he OK?'

'He's fine, just a bump. We're not taking him in.'

'Good.' Wondering if I imagined the word 'violent', I repeat, 'So… you called?'

'Well, we took him home last night.'

I'm suitably impressed. 'Good show,' I say. 'Well done.'

'He can't walk.'

Andy seems to be trying to invoke a particular response from me and I have a feeling I know what it is. I'm not going to make it easy for him.

'Terrible, terrible,' I say. 'The demon drink, eh?'

Bill helps him out. 'He'll fall again.'

'Yes, I imagine that's a strong possibility.'

We stand in a small square, the space between us filled with portent.

Andy breaks the moment. 'Well… we'll leave you to it.'

They shuffle off with - to be fair - a certain amount of embarrassment.

I approach TD and establish his state. He is, officially, sozzled: he thinks I'm his brother and can't see Becks at all. Mind you, she is standing a good twenty yards away chatting to a rather dashing passer-by in a suit.

'Not *again*, TD,' I say, despairingly.

'Sorry, broth.' He is swaying where he sits.

'What happened to your new duffel coat?' It's not new, and it may not even be a duffel coat, but it is splattered with vomit.

'Is it time for tea? I wanna go home, broth.'

'Shall I call you a cab?'

'I got no money, broth.'

'I am female, by the way.'

'Take us home, broth.'

'No.'

'Please.'

'No.'

'I'm about to be sick.'

'You're not selling it to me.'

Over my shoulder I see Bill and Andy lurking. They raise their eyebrows, as if to say, 'You aren't going to leave the poor man there, are you?'

'I'm not a taxi,' I call over.

'Nor are we,' they call back.

I take a step towards them. 'Why did you call us again? Something about violence?'

Andy's tone becomes plaintive. 'It's your turn,' he says.

Then, before I can respond, they pile into their van and drive off.

'Cheeky sods,' I say, to no-one in particular.

Becks has managed to wrench herself away from Mr Dashing. 'Look at the state of him,' she says, staring at the wretch on the pavement.

'I have been doing,' I say. 'Come on, let's leave him be.'

I lead the way to the panda, but I can't help looking back. TD is wobbling back and forth like a Subbuteo footballer. I have this vision of him falling, hitting his head and dying. I wince. I'd be suspended and have all my clothing seized. I waver. Then I turn back.

'Oh sod it,' I say, with a deep sigh. 'Let's take him home.'

There's always the chance that an incapable drunk inserted forcibly into his own home will die later that night, and if that happens I will still be suspended, but at least it will have happened out of public view which means I'm less likely to be fed to the media and will be able to be slowly reintroduced to society after a suitable period in purdah.

Becks and I undertake the awful task of arranging TD between us. Becks is not a reedy little girl. She is several inches taller than me, and I would describe her as 'solid'. She is also ridiculously fit, lifts weights and even 'runs' on her days off. Yes, when she could be having her nails done. I mean, honestly, is she a woman or what?

Nonetheless, TD is even more solid, and it takes some serious effort to drag him over to our panda. He is guided in head first and promptly falls asleep across both back seats. I'm probably breaking the seatbelt laws, but I drive him home anyway - it's a good job I know where 'home' is, as he certainly doesn't. My plan is just to dump him outside his address, but on arrival he is virtually catatonic. So we have to half-carry him up the stairs to his flat. As I hoist his stinking form onto my shoulders, I remember why I try to avoid going out drinking with blokes. From Becks' expression, and the way she's twisting her neck to keep her pony-tail from falling onto TD's sweaty neck, she shares my feelings.

He falls asleep happily on his sofa - it crosses my mind to wonder how much underwear a man can own that he can afford to leave so much of it lying unwashed around a house - and we exit with a feeling of a pointless job not in the slightest bit well done. I wipe my feet on the doormat before I dirty the outside street.

The car now reeks of stale beer and old urine, and I check with a flash of my torch for bodily fluids which will allow me to submit it for cleaning and get a new one. Unfortunately, it is just the air in the space recently occupied by TD. The windows go down; I'd rather freeze than inhale that for the next hour.

I wonder whether I've done the right thing. It's certainly not our job to take drunks home, but very often we can't afford not to. There are other circumstances in which we can't risk abandoning a Mop at the side of the road. If you're not paralytically drunk but would like a free ride home in a panda, try getting kicked out by your girlfriend and threatening to go back in and smack her if you're left there. Or say you've been abducted and dumped in a country lane which happens to be near a pub. You could say you've been followed down a dark alleyway and you think the bloke is somewhere nearby. If all else fails, wearing a mini-skirt and expressing admiration for the shiny red, yellow and white car containing an oh-so-handsome policeman may do the trick. Just hope you don't get Becks and I, who are neither of us amused by mini-skirts.

As I have not yet been summoned to crew up with the sergeant, it appears we have some breathing space to circle Blandmore aimlessly. This exercise is known as PATROLLING, and apparently reduces crime.

'That was foul,' says Becks. She wipes her palms on her trousers and then pulls out her hair and re-does her pony-tail. The fashion at Blandmore nick at the moment is for female officers to have long, luscious hair. The fashion is also for them to be far younger than me and far more brunette than me, but I try not to hold these traits against them. It may be possible for a girl to be young, pretty and have long hair and still be a good police officer, for all I know.

'How's Luke?' Becks continues as we drive once again into my favourite haunt, the Porle.

'Oh,' I say. 'We broke up a couple of weeks ago. He just couldn't put up with the Job any more. And I couldn't put up with him not putting up with it any more.'

Becks is nodding, but she's looking over her shoulder and suddenly interrupts, 'That's the car suspected of all those burglaries.'

I see the rear bumper of a gold Mondeo just leaving the drive-through McDonalds and floor the accelerator to reach the next gap in the central reservation before it disappears from view. I achieve an acceptable amount of wheel-spin during my U-turn and we drop in behind the Mondeo with an efficiency that surprises both of us.

The driver does not accelerate away when our blue lights go on, which is a pretty good sign that he is not doing anything illegal, and we stop him in the chevrons at the next roundabout. The car boasts three baseball-capped, hoodied young men, all of whom I have arrested in the last six months for varying degrees of theft.

Naturally, Becks and I are both terrified to be in the presence of three blokes and are on the verge of total collapse. Fortunately, I've brought along my smelling salts.

Although the three delightful youths will almost certainly be found burgling later tonight, we don't find anything illegal on them now. This means they are free to go, once we have filled out both sides of a four-page form containing their names, dates of birth, hair colour and Zodiac signs.

We resume our journey into the Porle. It's midnight, now, a time when two respectable young women really ought to be home in bed. But the remorseless fight against crime goes on.

'I must say,' Becks says, 'it's a relief to work with you for a change. I'm lucky if I even get to draw my cuffs when I'm out with the blokes. It's as if they think I'm worried I might break a fingernail. They mean well, and everything, but Bongo almost threw me out of the way the other night arresting a drunk.'

I raise an eyebrow; perhaps I ought to steal a few arrests from Becks myself.

'You're OK working with Will, though?' I say.

'What could be bad about working with Will?' she says. 'He's so keen he takes on all the investigations and he'd take half my own work out of my docket if I let him.'

'You looked like you were having fun the other day.'

Becks narrows her eyes. 'It's OK, Bloggsy; we all know he's hands-off except for you.'

I don't know how I look, but I feel bright red on the inside. 'He is *not*! Why would you say that?'

Just then, my radio crackles. It's the sergeant, summoning me back to the police station to crew up with him. He naturally anticipates his orders taking at least half an hour to be actioned, so Becks and I nip to Tesco for some coffee and to pick up some doughnuts for the Guvnor before heading back to Blandmore nick.

As I sit down, a disorder sparks off on the other side of town. I have an important alcohol-related-incident email to send, and some other emails to delete, so Becks reluctantly goes out to the fight with Guy, leaving me alone to manage my emails and wait for the sergeant. I'm still fighting the flush that Becks' remarks brought on, and am even a bit annoyed with her for saying it. I mean, can't a girl and guy be friends these days? Can't they chat and flirt harmlessly, or even kiss occasionally, and can't she stare longingly at him for a good part of most days, without everyone assuming something's 'going on'?

Turning my attention back to the computer, I'm ecstatic to find that the Crime Desk has replied to my message about the Exposure job.

'We have updated the crime report with the custody reference as requested,' it says.

No mention of the detection.

I used to groan when this kind of thing happened, but now I just quietly exhale another smidgen of hope and enthusiasm and take it on the chin. I reply with a less-than-polite request for them to update the crime report since - as I'd said in my last email - the custody reference is now in and I would dearly like to be permitted to claim at least one detection towards my monthly target.

I then re-read their email and find that they have already informed me they cannot create a detection - this has to be done by the Scrutineer. In anticipation of a supervisory 'chat' over my sent email, I forward their reply to Enid Pimento and lie my head down on the keyboard for a short, self-flagellating nap.

* * * * *

Let Sleeping Sergeants Lie

At last, Chris Woodcock finishes his paperwork and we go out on patrol. There are pluses and minuses of being crewed with one's supervisor: on the minus side, he tends to fall asleep in the passenger seat therefore cannot entertain me with thrilling conversation all night. On the plus side, any wrong decisions we make together are on his head.

By 1am, the steady flow of non-existent fights and smashed car windows has died down and, as predicted, we are left drifting aimlessly through town and country to reassure the public and prevent crime. With the diesel engine thrumming, we're probably doing a better job of waking the public up and providing a cover for crime, but it's the thought that counts.

At a quarter-to-two, proceedings get underway with a burglary in progress. A rather nice-sounding couple have just disturbed a male in their living room and he has fled over the garden fence.

A burglary in progress is the sign for every available officer to splurge onto the streets and race to the scene. This is mostly because it involves a blue light drive, a fleeing villain and the chance of a fight. It's what we call a Gucci arrest, with - best of all - very little paperwork. It will be investigated by the Burglary Team, so once you've pretended to carry out house-to-house enquiries and summoned the Scenes of Crime people to the address, your job is done.

Here's how I normally deal with a burglary.

Step One: Attend, look at broken window/door, nod and make encouragingly expert noises.

Step Two: Record details of what has been stolen.

Step Three: Explain to the victim that we will be doing house-to-house enquiries, local intelligence checks, CCTV, and identifying people from line-ups.

Step Four: Do no further work, but hand over the whole investigation to Scenes of Crime.

That generally does the trick. Mind you, I occasionally torture myself by imagining the horror of turning up to discover that your nice-sounding victims are in fact the Beckhams, or Jeremy Beadle. A Celebrity Burglary would immediately trigger a requirement for a higher level of service, including all the above actions and more, as there is also a high chance that the burglary was done by a Stalker. This combines a crime which is impossible to solve with intense press coverage and a crazed lunatic (in the case of Beadle, at least).

I should add that I have nothing against trying to catch burglars. Indeed, in terms of pleasure, I'd say that catching an actual burglar is the equivalent of filling out fifty stop-check forms, easily, and that's quite some achievement. But I just have this ingrained stubbornness that says, if a department is there to investigate a certain type of crime, is it really necessary for me to do the entire investigation for them? I mean, the Burglary Team don't get out of bed on Friday nights and assist us in dealing with drunken yobbery, do they?

On this particular night, we pull out all the stops and I am surprised to hear that a dog is on its way to aid us.

The dog-handlers are all officially based at Tapping, where the kennels are, but they post themselves out to an area for their shift and our local handler is usually Saira Freeman. Five foot three, Indian, with short, peroxide hair, Saira is diamond-edged. In fact, there is only one person I would less like to meet alone in a dark alley, and she travels around in the boot of Saira's car.

Tonight, Saira is only minutes from the burglary, so we all plot up at strategic locations to form a loose containment of the area where the villain was last seen. As I explained before, this is standard practice when the dog is on scene - there's little point the dog searching an area exhaustively, only to find that the bad guy fled over the back wall two hours before. Saira goes in to see the nice-sounding couple and to warn them to stay indoors, and then deploys Clarice, her German Shepherd bitch. Forty-five kilogrammes of hackles, saliva and glinting eyes lock onto the trail of the rascal - and the dog is following the scent, too. Saira updates us by commentary on the radio, and before long we realise that she and Clarice are heading in our direction. I begin to pay slightly more attention than I was.

Suddenly the sergeant nudges me, and I see a lad mooching across the square in front of the shops with his hands in his pockets. He matches the description perfectly, in that he is wearing a hoodie.

Chris and I hop out and tell the boy to stand still.

'Who the fookin hell are you?' he says, with a scowl.

The sergeant doesn't often raise his voice, but now it goes up a notch. 'You're nice, aren't you? Just stand still, or the dog will have you.'

'What fookin dog?' he says, and starts to slouch off. Over his shoulder, he sees Saira and Clarice heading his way, and he hesitates. They grow nearer and he shrugs. 'Nah, that's just a puppy, man.'

But he stands still and I can see past the bravado.

Clarice reaches us, and erupts, barking and snapping; she starts at thigh-height and rapidly rises to the youth's throat. Saira's arm is almost yanked out of its socket by the baying dog.

The youth starts to slide away and Saira screams, 'Stand still! Stand still or she'll have you!'

Clarice is now slavering at the jaw, flecks of foam hitting the asphalt and glinting in the orange street light. She does not like this boy one bit. He starts sniffing, and his eyes redden, and he stands stock still, hands gripping the sides of his trousers.

'Now, speak to these officers.'

Chris and I establish the boy's name and address. It turns out he's been grounded, which was why he was anxious not to be found outdoors. While he talks, he cannot help but eye up Clarice. Suddenly, she breaks into more barking, standing up on her hind legs and leaning all her weight against her handler to try and take a piece out of the lad.

'Stop it!' he cries. 'I ain't done nothing.'

'Stop staring at her,' says Saira. 'You don't like people staring at you, do you?'

His eyes drop to the pavement. We hear from officers at the scene that the burglar was actually an Asian lad wearing all white, so after a stern gypsy's warning regarding night-time wanderings and gobbiness in the presence of ladies, our man is sent on his way.

Saira ruffles her dog's head. 'Not bad for a pup, is she?' she says.

Chris and I both nod, approvingly. I love dogs, but Clarice strikes the fear of God into me and I admire anyone who dares touch her head, even to pat it.

Further information comes to pass that the offender climbed into a vehicle outside the address, and was not on foot at all.

'Oh well,' says Saira. 'Call it a night?'

We wait for her to walk ahead and put Clarice back in her cage before following. She wraps her dog-lead around her body, a la Indiana Jones, and we chat for a moment or two, we girls; it's remarkable, we agree, how Clarice doesn't seem to think she's weaker than male dogs, or a slower runner. No-one's told her she can't do the same jobs. You might even think Clarice is oblivious to her gender, and just gets on with it.

Mid-sentence, Saira is summoned via radio to Brickville to track down a fugitive gunman. Chris and I have more mundane pressures at hand, so he dispatches a non-sergeant-containing unit to do the paperwork for the burglary, while we wend our way through the dark streets to locate the neon lights of the nearest petrol station. Coffee is needed.

Ten minutes later, as we sit sipping our double latte chocamochatinos in the car, the controller radios the sergeant and says she needs him to pop up and view an incident on the computer.

'I'm not at the nick,' says Chris. 'I'm out and about. Can you just tell me about it?'

'No, it's Restricted,' she says. Which means us lowly PCs are not allowed to know about the job.

I ferry Chris to the police station so he can log in and view the excitingly secret item. A moment later, as I am battling with a statement I have not yet done for an interview I did two weeks ago, he pipes up on the radio. 'Uh, that Restricted log you wanted me to view...?'

'Yes?'

'It's Restricted. I can't view it.'

'Oh, right. We'll try to get you access. Wait one...'

About three minutes later the controller calls up again, 'Sergeant Woodcock, unfortunately we require a Control Room supervisor to give you access to that log.'

'Fine.'

'We have no supervisor on at the moment. We'll sort it and get back to you.'

'Fine.'

Chris doesn't sound too bothered; I'm not sure he really wanted to view the log in the first place. At least if he's locked out he can't be blamed for doing nothing about it.

Twenty minutes later, I'm disturbed from my statement-writing again by the sounds of frivolity echoing in the corridor. I poke my head out and see Guy and Becks standing at the entrance to the sergeant's office, doubled over in stitches. Will is watching with his head leaning on the door-frame and a wry smile on his lips. I toddle along and try to judge the right distance to stand from Will so that I don't look like I'm shagging him, without it looking as though we've had a fight. I now see what they are all watching: Lloyd is placing cones around the sergeant's seat and tying Police tape between them to cordon off Sergeant Woodcock, who is snoring gently. The scene is completed by a large POLICE SLOW sign and then captured on the Domestic Violence Polaroid camera. For some reason, the camera can never be found when there is actually a battered woman there to photograph, but if there's a police officer in a personally humiliating situation it arrives in moments. Lloyd sticks the Polaroid to Chris's stab vest and we stand in a huddle to wait for him to notice.

Not a word has been spoken on the radio for over half an hour now, so it is a shock for us all to hear the controller's voice. 'Sergeant Woodcock?'

He jerks awake, and notices half his shift giggling at him from the corridor.

'Don't you have any work to do?'

It's one of the quirks of our job that we all have dozens of things to do, but we can only do them by the light of day when the office-dwellers and Mops we need to speak to are awake. I mean, you can make phone-calls to your victims at 4am informing them that you've made no progress on their three-month-old investigation, but I personally only do that when they've made at least one complaint about my lack of regular contact.

'Sergeant Woodcock?' repeats the controller.

'Er, yes, go ahead.'

'That log is now ready to view.'

Chris brushes drool off his chin and disentangles his chair from the Police tape. He logs in and spends a minute scanning the screen. Then he calls up on the radio. 'Control, I've read that log. Was there anything you wanted me to do?'

'Um, no not really. Just for your information.'

'Yes, copied.'

I shake my head. 'They made you come in and wait nearly an hour for that? Was it anything good?'

'Nope. Neighbouring force doing an arrest warrant for a murderer on our border. They just wanted to let us know.'

'So why did you need to see it?'

'Control room staff are civilians and are therefore not qualified to Risk Assess to the high level that we are. They tell me about the job and that way if I fail to do anything and it all goes wrong, it's on my head.'

'Sarge, you only needed to say 'Arse-Covering'.'

He gives a short laugh and yawns for about thirty seconds.

'How come you're so tired?'

'Kids and postmen.'

We are interrupted by the disturbing sound of my being addressed by name over the air. 'PC Bloggs, can you attend 14 Bishop Drive for a Fear for Welfare.'

The sergeant groans. 'I really need to catch up on my Reviews,' he says. 'Take Rich with you, he loves suicidal birds.'

Fear For Welfares come in at a rate of between one and five a day, and they range from elderly neighbours who haven't been seen for a few days, to lost children and suicidal relatives. Our job in such matters is to locate the relevant party and solve whatever crisis led to the concern for their welfare in the first place. This is usually fairly simple and can be achieved by a quick snap of the fingers and muttering of some magic words.

The incident at 14 Bishop Drive is the sort of thing which will be attended daily in each police area across the nation.

The controller elaborates. 'Caller is from the Mental Health Team. They've received a call from a patient saying she is going to kill herself. Could you attend to check on her welfare?'

The Mental Health Team is part of the local authority's Social Services Department. They have a Crisis Team on duty 24/7. Despite that, it naturally makes sense to send us: after all, police officers have the psychotherapeutic training to counsel a suicidal woman and the necessary legal powers to deal with her. Don't we? The answers are, 'No' and 'Sometimes'. Section 136 of the Mental Health Act allows us to detain a person who might pose a danger to themselves or others if they are in a public place. In the privacy of your own home, however, you are free to be as mad as you please. People *can* be sectioned from their own homes and locked up against their will, but this is done by doctors and social workers (such as members of the Mental Health Team). But they have far more training in Arse-Covering than we do so, as here, their back-up plan is to make sure it is the police's fault (see *Victoria Climbie*).

Let Sleeping Sergeants Lie

Being a cold-hearted public servant, I'm generally not too fazed by these calls. You turn up, find the crying person, comfort them for a short while and then phone the Mental Health Team back and say, 'Are you on your way?'

The answer is invariably 'No', which leads to the customary batting of responsibility between us and them. This can take up to an hour. Sometimes the problem can be solved by phoning the person's estranged mother who now lives abroad, waking her up and blaming her for her daughter's imminent suicide if she does not immediately get on a plane and come to her side.

Failing that, the Ambulance service is always there to take final responsibility should we leave and the person tops herself later. 'Well, she was checked out by paramedics,' we say, with a regretful shake of the head. 'They refused to take her to hospital so don't blame me.'

It turns out we have been called to Colleen Moore, a manic depressive anorexic in her late twenties.

When we arrive she answers the door in her underwear, which is one of the signs I look for to identify a 'maddie'. Rich doesn't do skinny women in grubby underwear, so I have to ensure Colleen is wrapped in a curtain before he can enter. Once inside, she moves out of the curtain and into the lounge virtually naked, which means that Rich says very little for the rest of our stay. I think I can safely say that Colleen is the saddest woman I have ever seen. The sadness just pours out of her; it is suffocating. She is clearly starving herself, her bones sticking out under grey skin, her lank hair just hanging off her head. The whole impression is of a kind of deflating soufflé. Within three minutes, I almost want to kill *myself*.

Usually, a suicidal person will happily tell you all their woes - about how their sister just killed herself, their brother is in jail for rape, their parents abused each other and her... in a way, it's actually quite reassuring. You think, *You don't end up like this unless you are extraordinarily unlucky in life, so maybe I'll be OK.*

Colleen, however, says not a word. She just sits in the corner, with her back against the wall, thin knees pulled up to her chest, and sunken, red-rimmed eyes staring into space. She's immune to my questions about medication, alcohol, illnesses and the like. Rich and I stand off a little and go through the various parties we could pass responsibility to, discounting ambulance, mental health, social services and family. Finally the time comes when we have to leave, the prospect of her suicide looming. A quick phone-call to the sergeant ensures that this, if it occurs, will be his fault.

I try a last-ditch effort. 'Colleen, is there anything you want from us... even something you might not think the police can do?'

Tears rolling down her face, she looks up at me and whispers her first words. 'Just a hug.'

I don't hug people much, and certainly not members of public. This isn't because I don't care, nor that I don't sometimes want to. I just don't. So I take her hand and pat it, feebly.

'There, there,' I say.

She looks up at me and nods; I think she understands my inability to do the one thing she needs.

'Thank you,' she murmurs. 'God bless.'

And we leave.

We wander in for some tea and sandwiches and the rest of the night passes at a crawl. It gets to 07.00hrs and I'm ashamed to say that I have not affected Positive Intervention once in all of the nine hours I had in which to do so. I've returned a drunk home, reinforced street discipline in a wayward teen and spent fifteen minutes holding a lonely woman's hand.

I haven't met a single target, or filled out one form. As far as the Senior Management Team is concerned, I may as well have stayed at home.

Maybe tomorrow night I will.

God bless the police.

7

How A Bus-Stop Ends Up
In A Police Car

I AM DRIVING.

I've been driving for twelve hours, yet still I drive.

There have been breaks, of course, moments when I have run from the car towards someone for some reason, but largely it's been driving.

The reason for the twelve hours is TERRORISM, which is also the reason for a lot of my overtime this year. Terror-related overtime is paid for by the Home Office, as opposed to Blandshire Constabulary, so it's eagerly snapped up.

The reason for the driving is that I am working alone and have therefore been tasked with the vital role of ferrying articles from one police station to another.

Earlier, I ferried some paperwork to Charl nick, where there are two overflow Blandmore prisoners, and then I ferried some different paperwork back again relating to two overflow Charl prisoners being held at Blandmore. After that, my radio broke, so I ferried it to Liveron where the spare radios are kept. Then it was decided to swap the Charl prisoners for the Blandmore prisoners, so I went back to Charl. When I got there, the custody sergeant had changed, and the new one thought the swap idea was ridiculous and cancelled it.

I am presently doing about 50mph in the middle lane of the motorway, hoping that the next exit will be Blandmore but suspecting that it was actually the last.

My milometer is reading over two hundred miles for the day so far.

Even after years of it, I still love driving marked police cars. You can throw them around like toys, because you're not responsible for the maintenance. You can pull out directly into whichever lane you want and someone will give way to you. You can drive down footpaths, into playing fields and you can park on double yellow lines. You can even try out handbrake turns and other manoeuvres on the Porle estate in the dead of night. If you set a police car in first gear and let it drift along Cossum Hill, the driver and passenger can actually run round and change seats before the car hits anything.

Or so I have heard.

Being a woman, I am a very poor driver. I haven't even managed to crash a panda yet, which is something I am working on.

The blokes on my shift, on the other hand, are Good Drivers. Lloyd is good at everything, Nick is ex-army and Will owns a motorbike, so therefore he must be good. Guy is good because he drives very, very fast. He's had three accidents this year, *that's* how good he is. (Believe it or not, police officers have a large number of minor crashes. Given that it is frequent for one officer drive over 700 'work' miles in a week, on top of whatever he drives at home, I would like to see more praise heaped on us for the number of times we *don't* crash.)

I lurch back into Blandmore in time to see Guy setting off to a criminal damage in progress. He passes me on two wheels at the roundabout. I admire his dedication. No amount of road deaths is too many to catch a miscreant youth smashing a car windscreen.

I'm too tired to stop at the next red light and I feel a detached air of surprise as the round red circle floats behind me out of view. I *think* I looked both ways before I did it.

I get to the nick and lock up the panda; Chris sees me leaning on it for a moment with both elbows.

'You look mullered,' he says.

'Uh huh.'

'You shouldn't really drive if you're that tired.'

This piques my interest, and I squint over my shoulder at the sergeant. 'What would happen if I said I was too tired to drive one day?'

'Er... well, you would be sent home, I guess.'

'Sounds like a plan.'

'Of course,' he says, 'if you *kept* on getting too tired, someone would probably question whether you were fit for active duty.'

'Isn't there some kind of suggested concentration span for

drivers?' I say. 'Like one hour, or something?'

Chris stares at me for a moment. 'Bloggs, you aren't a 'driver', you're a police officer.'

'That's what I thought.' I blink redness out of my eyes and trudge into the report room where I can relax in the pleasant fluorescent flicker. I try to remember the last time I was not tired. Whenever it was, it was before I ever got my hands on a warrant card.

I decide to book myself off-duty and, as I log in, an irresistible force draws me towards the Crime Management system. The screen flashes up and a surge of adrenaline washes the fatigue from my body. I sit bolt upright and exalt in the goodness of mankind.

The detection has been put on for the Exposure job!

I am now a third of the way to my monthly target, and it has only taken three weeks to do it.

(I might or might not be driving home at this point. Either way, I end up in my bed with the endless whir of a diesel engine chugging in my ears.)

* * * * *

Minutes later, it seems, I am back at work.

We are working twelve hour shifts every day this week - 7am to 7pm - due to the entire late shift being sent to sit on their arses in a wood.

I am crewed with Guy today and, as usual, he has arrived an hour early for work to nab the first available set of car-keys. Guy is the newest member of our team. He was tutored on the Neighbourhood Team, which is an unfair start for the best of us, and since then he has been struggling to master the job. There is talk that he only joined up to manhandle people and drive fast cars, but then again there is talk that I am a kind-hearted soul who enjoys doing other people's work for them. Gossip can be cruel.

Anyway, we are designated the lead Response vehicle for the day, which is more exciting than words can express and will enable me to spend over three minutes filling out vital paperwork that arrived in my tray last week with a deadline of last month on it. On the other hand, I will get to collect five more investigations to provide me with paperwork for next month's deadlines.

Being a Saturday, it is never too early for a drink and a fist fight, so at 7.30am we are dispatched to an alcohol-fuelled domestic at 42 Ratchet Path. I check my palms to ensure that the pores are prepped for sweating and I brace myself for a Guy-drive.

Our blue and screaming panda is soon hurtling down the dual carriageway to Blandmore's northernmost parish. A car has broken down on the roundabout, causing a small queue of early weekend drivers to build up, and they part for us like the sea before Moses. Which is just as well, as I see no sign of Guy slowing down if they don't. One taxi driver is delighted to see that the entire road of vehicles is giving way to him for no reason and he pulls out into our path in the compulsory manner.

Guy flicks the wheel right and left and utilises the Laws of Relativity to squeeze us through a gap that a cyclist would probably shy away from. We erupt from the roundabout like a blue-horned bull and charge our way out of town with no further obstacles to slow our progress.

Parking takes too long, so Guy just flings the car onto the kerb in the vicinity of number 41 and we jump out. I watch my crew-mate racing into the cul-de-sac and decide that I will first establish whether we are anywhere near the right address before I perspire any more. As I suspected, No41 backs onto No51 and the house on the other side of the road is No82. I follow the path round and finally locate the right one, by which time Guy is back in the car and roaring up behind me.

We can see the rear garden to 42, which prompts Guy to begin a scramble over the wall. I watch him for a moment and plod round to the front door where a brass dog stands guard over a fetching wood-and-stained-glass porch.

A bustling woman in a business suit opens the door. 'Oh, hello officer!' she says.

It takes me all of three seconds to establish that this woman has probably only ever called 999 once in her life and that was when she saw a mugging in London.

'We had a call that there was a domestic going on here?'

The woman is joined by her husband. He puts a hand on her side in a wholesome manner.

'Here?' they say, in unison, looking at each other and then at me. Consternation is written all over their faces.

'Yes, here,' I say. 'Someone called us to say they heard a domestic row? Has there been any problem at all here?'

'I suppose they might have heard me shouting at the dog,' chuckles the lady.

'Or me cursing the news,' says the man, and they both titter.

'It might well be that,' I agree.

Flushed with the joy of being called 'officer' and the greater joy of finding no evidence of a domestic, I update the Control room and tootle back to the car.

As I am starting the engine (the keys having remained in the ignition), I feel like something's missing. Something large and fairly boisterous. At that moment, my radio bleeps to indicate a person-to-person call.

Ah, yes! Guy.

'Yes, go ahead?'

'Um... Bloggs, could you give me a hand?'

'Where are you?' I crane my neck but can't see him anywhere.

'I'm... er... I'm in the back garden.'

'Can't you get out?'

'Well, I can, but...' His voice lowers. 'I ripped my trousers climbing over and if I turn around to come out they might see my...'

I make my way towards the back wall, against which I lean, giggling uncontrollably. 'You'll have to come out somehow.'

'It's not funny,' he says, looking hurt.

'I beg to differ.'

In the end, I distract the occupants by ringing their doorbell once more on the pretext of thanking them and letting them know we're leaving, while Guy shuffles back over the wall and into the car.

It takes me some time to catch enough breath to make sense of what the radio controller is telling me, but finally it becomes clear that she is talking about a crime reference number for the domestic we have just attended.

'Um, control, there *is* no domestic.'

'Yes, but I'm trying to tell you that a crime report has already been started.'

'But... for what?'

'Assault.'

'Assault? All the caller heard was shouting.'

'Unfortunately, the civilian operator has started the report and now it can't be deleted.'

The law of deep police magicks again.

'Well can you just update it that there was no domestic?'

'I'm afraid you'll have to do that.'

I was very much afraid of that, too. 'Yes, copied.'

'I can't believe they've started a crime report already,' says Guy.

I shake my head in agreement. 'The barefaced cheek of it.'

We return to the nick at a far more sedate pace, and in far more merriment than we left it.

As we walk into the main corridor, the front office clerk catches me. 'PC Bloggs, there's a man out here to see you.'

I poke my head out into the public waiting area. I instantly recognise the forty-year-old white guy with Rasta plaits, but can't remember why.

He follows me into the corridor. 'WPC Bloggs, how happy to see you again. How was your holiday?'

I frown. 'I haven't been on holiday.'

'Yes you have.'

'My last holiday was twelve months ago,' I say, perplexed.

'Yes, WPC Bloggs, when you sent me to court for abusing my ex-missus.'

'Ah...' I rummage in the attic of my memory and produce a name. 'Mr Carson.'

I charged Mr Carson with harassment sixteen months ago. He'd been sending blood-stained letters to his then girlfriend.

'Yes, indeed, WPC Bloggs.'

'It's just PC Bloggs. How are you, Mr Carson?'

'I am very well, thank you, WPC Bloggs. I have been exonerated of guilt.'

'You were acquitted?' I usually discover the results of my court cases from the suspect, as it's almost impossible to find out any other way if I'm not called to give evidence.

'I have been cleared. My name is unbesmirched; I have no stain on my character.'

Which means someone botched the prosecution and he managed to get off.

'That's nice.'

'I have come to ask for my writings back.'

'Your writings?'

'You took writings from my house, WPC Bloggs.'

It is a severe test of my mind, but I somehow remember that we wanted to analyse his handwriting and did therefore take some paperwork from his office to compare with the offending letters.

'It was a diary, wasn't it?' I say.

'Yes, WPC Bloggs,' he says. 'For the year 2003.'

'And you want that back?'

'Yes, WPC Bloggs, I do.'

'OK... wait right here.'

There's a well-worn saying that only three things can get a police officer fired: Paperwork, Property and Policewomen. I don't sleep with Policewomen and I just about cope with the Paperwork, but Property is the bane of my life.

When someone is arrested for anything involving an object with a corporeal presence, that corporeal presence will, likely as not, end up in the Property Store. This is either a dark dungeon located in the basement, or a Portakabin, with aisles, shelves, racks and drawers stuffed full of drugs, weapons, clothing, mobile phones and random articles seized by Scenes of Crime examiners.

With all this vital evidence stashed in one place, the opportunities for loss and destruction are numerous.

In Blandshire Constabulary, a foolproof system has been developed to tackle this potential disaster. Every item that goes into the store is labelled with a unique title and reference number and the label is signed by the officer who has seized it. The same title is then transferred onto another label with another completely unique reference number. The item and both labels are put into a bag and sealed by a seal marked with yet another totally and utterly unique and individual reference number. A carbon copy of one of the labels is kept by the officer so they can locate the item again and another copy is kept by the Property Manager so that he can locate it again, too.

The sealed, bagged, triply-tagged exhibit is then duly chucked in a small cupboard, where it sits in a pile of other similarly bagged items until the Property Manager stows it away in the dungeon. The smaller pieces are quite happy to drop down behind the shelving unit and store themselves forever in the temporary cupboard. The rest will stay in the dungeon until the case is over, by which time the officer who put it there will have left the force or forgotten of its existence.

Believe it or not, in spite of this remarkable system, property can and does wander off. More often than not, the stray items can be found in someone's docket, or kit bag, or locker. Occasionally, the exhibit will turn up in a panda car boot, or travel home in someone's stab vest by accident. If not found in any of these places, there is a high chance that the officer seized it immediately before rushing to another incident and the exhibit got out there. If the item is located in the store, it will probably have been stashed underneath something a lot heavier, or will have been chemically treated, left in a damp spot or dropped by the expert examining it, and will have been damaged beyond repair.

Either way, if anything you own ever falls into the hands of the police through your fault or another's, do not expect to see it again. It is for this reason that I advise people who are being harassed to just change their number and forget about it, because if you hand us your mobile phone for analysis you may as well just buy a new one.

Oddly, there are Mops who will not accept this fact and actually expect their personal items to be returned to them when the police no longer need them. Mr Carson is one of those people.

With fingers crossed, I summon up the relevant file on a computer and locate the property reference for the diary.

To my astonishment, it takes the Property Manager about five minutes to bring me the diary and I run it along to the front office with a kind of stunned elation and the pleasurable anticipation of someone who is about to satisfy a Mop.

But Mr Carson has gone. I look out into the public foyer, I ask the front office clerk, but there is no sign of the man who has waited sixteen months to reclaim his personal belongings: the extra ten minutes were just too much. I return the diary to the store and sign it up to say that if the owner returns, he can have it. With the story of Guy's trousers still to tell to the shift, I put Mr Carson from my mind.

* * * * *

Before I can even mention the word 'breakfast', Guy races past me towards the car park. He is wearing a new pair of trousers.

'Some kids are smashing up McDonalds,' he says, breathlessly.

'Food critics, perhaps?' I say.

Ideal: a foot-chase, *then* breakfast. Our tyre-burning exit from the nick scares an old man off entering and we are halfway to McDonalds when my mobile rings.

'PC Bloggs?' It's Sergeant Hayes. 'Can you attend custody please and deal with your bail prisoner?'

'My bail prisoner?'

'Mr Neville.' In the background I hear a voice raised in agitation. 'Sorry, Mr Neville Saunderson.'

I point out a left turn that Guy is hooning past and we just make it by forcing a Mini into the bus-stop. 'Mr Neville... I don't know who that is.'

'Bailed from Nutcorn Police Station on 3rd March to you, here, today.'

Nutcorn... it sounds familiar. 'What's the offence, please?'

'Criminal Damage and Harassment. Something to do with a lawn.'

'But...'

I faxed Nutcorn four weeks ago asking to have Mr Saunderson arrested for spraying the F-word on Shelley Grimmick's grass, but I don't recall any response, and certainly nothing about bailing the prisoner to me.

A prisoner is bailed when there are more enquiries to do before making a decision as to whether to charge them or not. Not being ready for a bail date is a serious matter. It can indicate an Abuse of Process, which can mean the case being thrown out and/or disciplinary action. Officers who continually fail to handle their bails properly will be called into the sergeant's office and, if no improvement is made, maybe even the inspector's!

For this reason I think before answering, then say, 'But no-one told me.'

My words must have been drowned out by the siren as all I hear in response is Sergeant Hayes shouting my name. Unfortunately, at that moment we draw into the car park of McDonalds in time to see three scruffy kids drop their spray-cans and stones and leg it into the park.

We try, but have no hope of catching the little scrotes along the getaway paths put in by the Council. On returning to McDonalds, we discover that the staff have managed to detain one of the window-smashers and he is duly arrested.

When I arrive in custody, I approach the desk to explain my shoddy behaviour to Sergeant Hayes. I open my mouth to begin, but she cuts me off, holding up her palm and reaching under the desk to produce a cheese and salad sandwich. 'Lunch,' she says, by way of an explanation. I wait, gobsmacked, as she sits back down in the same place and begins taking small bites from the sandwich.

After a moment of two, I try to speak, but the palm is raised higher and the chewing intensifies.

After 10 minutes of watching Sergeant Hayes eat, both the sandwich and the palm are gone and she is ready for me. She informs me that Mr Saunderson has been re-bailed to the following week, and that I had better come up with a good reason for making the poor man travel 80 miles for nothing. I'm still in shock over the sandwich business and can do no better than stammer at her, before she produces a sheaf of papers and says that she already called Nutcorn and has discovered that I was not informed of the arrest or bail.

'Don't worry, they sent these in on the fax.'

The papers appear to relate to a can of weed killer and some handwritten technical reports which are now residing in Nutcorn Property Store awaiting my disposal. I shovel them into my stabbie pocket and agree that it just is not good enough; if you're going to send faxes in this day and age you really should follow them up with two or three emails.

The week drags on. If possible, the days get longer and longer. I haven't left my house except to go to work and work's been so busy I haven't even had time to ignore Will in front of the rest of the team. By Thursday, I'm to be found strewn on a swivel chair that is in the inexorable process of folding in half. I spend a few moments rattling at the jammed levers, for no real purpose, and then slump forwards and give up. I am drafting an email to the Scenes of Crime officers in Nutcorn to request that they send the weed killer and reports over in their next dispatch to Blandmore, and no matter how many 'pleases' I type, it still reads 'pissed off'.

Most of the shift has gone home now, and it's just Guy, Bongo and me trying madly to effect email limitation before our long weekend off. As we hand the panda keys over to the next shift, the radio bursts to life with reports of a car driving dangerously round the Ring Road. The night shift gushes onto the streets, their faces full of grins and chatter that put the three of us to shame.

Logging off the four systems that I have running, I throw my tie into my docket and trudge home. My bed must be missing me.

* * * * *

Monday afternoon begins with much excitement. The Superintendent is in briefing, and he is bearing an email.

'On Thursday night,' he says, 'PC Macrieff was involved in a pursuit with a black Volkswagen Golf. The vehicle crashed on Ropel Road and PC Macrieff got involved in a fight with the driver. He was single-crewed and had no backup nearby. At this point PC Guy Mitchum, who was on his way home from a twelve-hour shift, happened to pass. He stopped and assisted PC Macrieff in handcuffing the offender, thereby saving a colleague from possible serious injury. This is an example of what our work is all about and PC Mitchum deserves the highest praise for his actions. I would hope that any of us would do the same, no matter how tired and stressed we all may be.'

Only a Superintendent is in possession of enough shoulder-metal to deliver a message of this import, and I can see he's delighted to be doing so.

'I just came to thank Guy personally, and to let you all know what happened.'

We stare across at Guy, who shrugs modestly. Lloyd punches him lightly. 'Nice one,' he says.

'Yes, well done,' says the Super. I wonder how many Leadership courses you have to go on before you can nod with such gravity.

'No problem, guv,' says our young hero, having the grace to blush slightly.

'Right, sarge, I'll let you get on with it,' says the Superintendent. 'Don't forget, people, only two days to get another thirty detections this week... keep at it!'

Briefing unfolds and we troop into the report room, Guy staying behind for a few moments to bask in his glory with Sergeant Woodcock.

Lloyd looks at me. 'You were here Thursday late, what happened?'

I shrug. 'Don't ask me. When it's time to go home I take off my battery and chuck the radio in my locker.'

'Guy doesn't,' says Will. 'He'll have been listening to the pursuit on his way home.'

There is a short silence.

'You think he drove that way deliberately to try and join the pursuit?' says Becks.

There is a mass of throat-clearing among the guys and more than a few timid glances into the corridor.

'Wouldn't be the first time,' mutters Lloyd.

Guy saunters in at this juncture. From his unaccustomed bashfulness at recounting the tale, I surmise that the shift has guessed correctly. Still, no one can knock the outcome, so it's best just to smile and congratulate him. As I am six years older than Guy, and not remotely attracted to him, I am able to get up and ruffle his hair in a motherly fashion, while the rest of the team shakes his hand and Becks just nods.

Guy is what I affectionately refer to as an 'ARV-wannabe'. There are men who join the police because, in the depths of their testosterone-fuelled brains, they want to be presented with thirty inches of polished metal and be told to point it at people. They never put much effort into learning the niceties of life: where they're going, such trivia will merely hold them back. Instead they hone the gruffness of their voices, their sandpaper jaws, and the use of their steel-encased bodies to squash random strangers. The Armed Response Vehicle officers have the thickest necks in the force. They can carry three loaded firearms at any one time. They drive vehicles that have over two-litre engines. If you are out clubbing on a Friday night and you see, standing between two fluorescent-jacketed stick figures, a burly male clad all in black, arms folded and gaze burning bright and fixedly at a quivering drunk teenager, you will have seen one of these Titans. Do not attempt to engage him in ordinary conversation or you risk upsetting the simplistic wiring of his brain. But if you are assaulted, threatened or raped, this coiled man-beast should be your first port of call to sic onto the offender.

Guy is not one of these men and he will never get further than submitting the form which would allow him to become one. Yes, he has mastered the tactlessness and the poor paperwork skills, but his voice is more of a shrill whistle, his jaw a little too smooth, his body a pliable beanbag. I think, somewhere inside, Guy knows that he will never be an ARV, and that thought drives him to more and more desperate acts to prove himself.

In this case, his desperation has resulted in a fine act. It only goes to show that the rest of us should not be so quick to book off-duty at the end of the day. By merely keeping the radio on for ten more minutes, we could find ourselves in a position to arrest shoplifters, record domestics and fight with passing crooks. The good news is that anything that did not result in a detection could go unrecorded as no one would even know we had been there.

(In case you're wondering, women do become ARVs. As a female, it's actually hard not to become one, as every week we are urged to attend Firearms Awareness Days to ease our passage into this most male-dominated of departments. It's yet another indictment on our foolish nature that very few women take up this opportunity to force people to the floor at gunpoint and then hand them to someone else to deal with.)

A great deal of Monday is spent encouraging Guy to recount the details of his heroism, interspersed with moments when people actually drive out of the police station to attend jobs. I have been allocated an inactive radio call-sign today in order to put my docket 'in order', which means I make no attempt to retrieve car-keys and am to be found at all times sat on my backside in the report writing room. Nick can't find any keys so he sits beside me for a moment, then stuns the team by announcing his intention to take a bus into the Porle. Nick has been in the police since before I was born and is a good sort, if a bit old-fashioned. Not only does he bus himself around Blandmore *in lieu* of sitting in front of the car-key board for hours, he also walks and cycles around the place, too. Plus he has side-burns, and wears his hat on attending crime scenes.

By 7pm, I have put my paperwork in order of importance, with the oldest jobs stuffed back in the bottom of the tray. There is now no hope of achieving victim satisfaction with those, so I may as well concentrate on the ones that have yet to result in complaints. Among my old jobs is the paperwork for Neville Saunderson and the weed killer, as well as a burglary I don't remotely remember attending.

As I sort through the newer investigations, I'm shunted to one side by Guy as he pulls out his own docket. He's holding a sheaf of papers in his other hand which he inserts onto the top of his paperwork and then presses the contents of the tray down hard in order to slide it back in.

'Look at the state of your work,' says Will. 'You need to sort that out, mate.'

Guy shrugs. 'I've been sent to a fight.'

'If you just put the papers for each case together, it will be a lot easier and it doesn't take a minute,' says Will. He pulls out his own tray to reveal an immaculate array of brown envelopes labelled with names and timescales. 'I'll help you later if you like.'

'Yeah, cheers, mate.' Guy departs with his fighting gloves on.

I stare down into my own docket, with its odd pages of somebody's statement floating in the bottom alongside a Scenes of Crime report from an investigation that I filed two months ago. There was a time when my docket looked the way Will's does, but a year is a long time in the police and at some point during my service I just stopped caring about paper.

As Will and I discuss the pros and cons of filing, we hear that Nick has arrested a robber on the bus - which is exactly why I don't take them. Will departs to assist, carrying a map of the local bus stops.

A few minutes later, Guy's voice flares up on the radio. 'Vehicle making off!'

Those three words are the reason a lot of people joined the police. Within moments, every useable vehicle, whether marked or plain, is being driven out of the nick. I leap into the back of a CID car and we are halfway up the road when the driver asks me where we're going.

Guy is still on the radio, describing the car chase he has just begun. 'Vehicle is two up, driving at five-oh miles per hour, turning left left left into Markus Way... right right right onto the Ring... no deviation... now recip... back onto the Ring...'

I won't bore you with the meaning of all this jargon, but suffice it to say if it is not used you can expect the control room sergeant to abort the chase before you have had a chance to wipe out a single parked car or pedestrian.

Three minutes later, Guy is still going, which is fairly impressive for a little old Response driver. The detective I am with has circled the town centre in an attempt to keep abreast of the chase, but has now pulled up on a bridge where we sit listening to the commentary and trying to work out where the offender might be going.

It's important to remember during police chases that it doesn't matter so much what the driver has done wrong or why he is fleeing, but more how fast his car is and whether or not we can catch him. Most pursuits are over within three or four minutes, if not seconds. If they last any longer there is a good chance that we will win.

As I sit on the bridge listening to Guy's frantic messages, I remember my first pursuit. I'd been an operational police officer for two days when my tutor constable whisked me off to a fight outside a pub involving eighteen men with sticks. The fight turned out to be a loud conversation, the eighteen men were three women and the sticks were merely hands, so we ended up chatting with the licensee while someone else took down people's names.

As we stood in the low sunlight, having a thoroughly calm and pleasant evening, there was a roar of exhaust and a car bombed past us so fast that the old lady on the corner didn't even have time to open her mouth in disgust. My tutor yelled at me to leap in the panda and the chase was on. We caught up enough to see the registration, which revealed that it was a stolen car from North Wales and had just left a local petrol station without paying. All good news, insofar as justifying what followed.

After four minutes of weaving around traffic and using gentle inclines to assist our 1.5l diesel in the task of acceleration, our target shrank to a dot and then vanished the other side of a roundabout. My tutor kept his foot flat to the floor for another minute and we were just about to give up when we rounded a corner and found a scene of carnage before us.

The stolen car was half way across the kerb. One wheel was rolling down the opposite side of the road, and a plume of smoke was hanging in the air. One hoodied figure was staggering from the passenger seat, and the driver was rattling his door handle and letting out screams of despair. By the time he thought to climb over the handbrake and flee out of the other door, my tutor and two other officers had collared him.

I ended up waiting on scene for the recovery truck and talking with the small crowd of onlookers who had appeared from nowhere to marvel at the crash site.

'Did you see what happened?' I asked a lanky man in hiking boots holding a carrier bag.

'I was waiting for the number 32,' he nodded. 'It just came round there and hit the post box.'

I looked up and down the road, aware that I would probably have to draw a diagram of what he was telling me. 'So you were waiting where?'

'For the number 32 bus. At the bus stop.' He held up the carrier bag.

Assuming he was pointing, I scanned the road. 'Exactly where?' I said.

'Here,' he said. 'Right here.'

I suddenly realised he meant he'd been waiting where we were standing.

'But where's the bus stop, then?' I asked.

'Here,' he said, holding up the bag again.

I took the carrier bag and opened it gingerly. Sure enough, there was the bus stop, compressed from nine foot seven to about six inches square.

'I wasn't sure if you'd want it for evidence,' he said.

'To be honest, it's my second day on the job,' I said, 'so I'm not exactly sure either.' Thinking it was better to be safe than sorry, I tied the carrier bag back up and placed it in the boot of our panda.

About half an hour later, we waved off the recovery truck and headed back into the nick. After only a short diversion, when we saw a number 32 bus wandering plaintively up and down the road and thought we'd better fill the driver in, we filed a surprisingly concise report on the incident and I went home thinking that being a police officer was exactly like being on *The Bill*. I think the bus stop stayed in the boot of that panda for about six months.

By the sixth minute of today's chase, all other work has ground to a halt and every police officer in the town is holed up in strategic positions on the off-chance that the ultimate crash will occur near them.

A Traffic car now emerges from the ether in which they reside and Guy is ordered to concede the pursuit. Traffic Officers are highly trained Advanced Response and Pursuit Drivers, which means they get to crash at much higher speeds than us. To the amazement of everyone listening, the chase goes on and on, and now four Traffic cars are involved. The offending vehicle has reached Charl and notched up two wing mirrors and a pheasant.

Finally, they all hit the motorway. The force helicopter is unable to assist, due to a couple of clouds being in the sky, but other than that the radio tells us there is a good complement of officers engaged in the affair and the outcome seems promising. The pursuit heads down the motorway for at least ten miles, during which time the control room sergeant has some serious thinking to do about the health and safety ramifications of putting an end to the nonsense by squashing the fugitive in a box of three Traffic cars (the notorious T-PAC). It takes a good ten minutes to consider this problem before the manoeuvre is authorised, at which point the vehicle leaves the motorway and the option is discounted.

With great excitement, we now hear that the offender has done a full circuit of the roundabout and is coming back down the motorway. My detective driver parks us up on another bridge and we peer over the gantry like schoolchildren.

It's getting dark and it's easy to pick out the first blue light that cracks the horizon. One by one, more lights join it until my eyes contract slightly. Now I can see the subject car - a Rover 214 - blazing down the centre lane with sparks flying from its rims. It roars beneath us and I stare in awed silence at the array of police cars that froths in its wake. One, two, three... I count eight Traffic cars by the time they reach us.

The light-show passes by into another force area and I return to my grey little police station. I have seen a glimpse of another life, a bright world where police officers chase criminals with a fanfare and a crunch of metal.

Sadly, some of us have real police work to do, and glumly I break out my pen.

8

PC Bloggs Investigates

WHENEVER I zoom to an address for the third time in the same night, it occurs to me that I am the privileged observer of the mysterious Chav tradition known as 'Call-the-police' Day.

Most normal Brits may dial 999 for the police just two or three times in their lives - when they are attacked by muggers, say, or find themselves in a bad car accident. They may dial a few more times on witnessing other people in trouble but, for themselves, it tends to be during those mercifully few moments of extreme terror.

Not so the Chavs.

For the average Chav, calling the police forms an essential part of his or her everyday life. It's most usually done during a long, bored evening, following the consumption of much cheap lager, and is a way for one family of Chavs to assert its superiority over another. Frequently, both sides in an argument will call us; Chavs compete for the title of 'victim' by trying to beat each other to the phone.

This daily ritual climaxes on 'Call-the-police' Day. This falls on a different day for each individual Chav.

He or she will commence proceedings with a quick call in the morning along the lines of, 'My ex-partner stared at me when I dropped the kids off at school.'

They'll follow this up at lunch-time with, 'I've received three text messages from my ex-partner saying sorry for staring at me and I feel she/he is harassing me.'

If time allows, a third call will come in at tea-time to say that the ex-partner has driven past the house, an event usually accompanied by a coded gesture (raised and extended middle finger or shaken fist) at the victim to let them know that the proceedings are due to kick off that night.

After tea, 'Call-the-police' Day is launched.

The festivities begin with a ceremonial 'banging on of doors', performed by one party on the front door of the other, with the accompaniment of obscene, guttural roars.

The other party will dial 999, which is the signal for their friends and family to join the celebrations by attacking the Door-banger. The police will attend and usually arrest the Door-banger, sometimes taking a few of the family away, too.

The next phase comes about two hours later. This time, the original caller will have gone round to the other party's house to return the Door-banging, whilst simultaneously phoning 999 to tell the police what they are doing. The trick is to have left the scene before the other family comes out or the police attend.

This will trigger the final phase in the ritual, when both families meet in the park and have an all-out rumble.

At least three parties to the fight should then call the police and - if the whole rite has been properly observed - this is the point at which random members of public and neighbours begin to dial 999, demonstrating a ripple effect that unites the whole community.

For beginners, one way spot that a 'Call-the-police' Day has occurred is that every custody suite in the police force area will be full and the shift that comes on duty in the morning will be handed at least five hundred sheets of paper relating to the job.

The first of our next run of early shifts begins exactly like this. The sergeant presents us with a pile of paper relating to various offences that the O'Milligan family have been arrested for overnight.

I read out the offences. 'Drink-drive, common assault, disqualified driving, harassment, nuisance messages, possession of an offensive weapon, criminal damage and attempted murder.'

There is a short pause. Then Lloyd says, 'I imagine CID will be dealing with this one then.'

'Well, it isn't much of an attempted murder,' says Chris. 'Basically, Lee O'Milligan tried to run over PC Barnaby at 60mph. Fortunately for PC Barnaby, O'Milligan didn't see the bollard that was standing between them.'

'I still imagine CID are dealing,' says Lloyd.

Chris shrugs. 'If the prisoner-handling team won't take it, then it's us.'

'For attempted murder?'

'The feeling upstairs is that it will most likely be charged as a traffic offence,' says Chris. 'You can't expect CID to deal with a job that won't result in any detections.' (As traffic offences are non-recordable under Home Office rules, charging people for them does not count.)

Lloyd snorts. 'I suppose the fact that they would have to deal with the old man for all the other offences might be something to do with it.'

Privately, I think that Lloyd has the wrong attitude. As we have only limited resources to choose from, the experienced detectives must save themselves for those incidents involving people who have murdered their family and already admitted it. Prolific offenders like the O'Milligans will never successfully be sent to prison, so they are best palmed off on officers without any kind of special training, who have nothing to lose.

In the end, Will and I are dispatched to custody to deal with the three O'Milligans in the traps. It takes two cups of tea to read through all the statements, whereupon we announce our presence to Sergeant Hayes. Another cup of tea later, the first solicitor arrives. He is well over six feet tall and, I cannot help noticing, devilishly attractive.

Will has taken control of the Lee O'Milligan offences and I am to handle his wife Katye (yes, that is the correct spelling) and daughter Shimona.

The solicitor introduces himself. 'Hello. I'm Kevin Dapper.'

You certainly *are*. I find Will looking at me sideways as I shake Mr Dapper's hand, in what I hope is a coquettish, but professional, manner. I notice that Will is watching with a slight frown on his face.

Solicitors - even the ugly ones - are a vital part of the criminal justice system. Thanks to the Police and Criminal Evidence Act 1984 (PACE), suspects have an inalienable right to legal representation as soon as the magic words, 'You do not have to say anything...' are said aloud.

The fact is, most police officers have a cruel and oppressive streak in them that drives them to beat confessions from the most innocent of men. All we desire is to convict, convict, convict, and damned be the truth. We are professional at faking CCTV and tape-recordings, we are expert computer hackers and, let's face it, we just love locking people in cells and starving them for no good reason. I don't know about anyone else, but that's certainly why I joined up.

Without solicitors, the poor criminals would be prey to our depravity. Some of them might even tell us the truth, and that would never do.

Will begins to describe the saga. 'Basically, your client's wife had an argument with their daughter which resulted in their daughter hitting their son, whereupon he got into his car and tried to run over a police officer, while drunk.'

It takes another few attempts to explain this, whereupon the solicitor makes a few notes.

'And Katye O'Milligan, why is she here?'

'You mean you are the solicitor for all three of them?'

'Yes.'

'You can't be. Two of them are making allegations against each other.'

Dapper sighs. 'I didn't know that. If you tell me about the case, I can decide if there's a conflict of interest.'

A conflict of interest is when the two prisoners in question give their lawyer different stories, thus confusing his poor brain and running the risk of him doing something illegal. The custody sergeant is consulted and decides that Dapper himself is the only person who can really decide if there is a conflict of interest. This is because he is the only one who stands to lose out by not representing all three clients - in the form of a lesser paycheque. We therefore disclose the details of Katye and Shimona's evening spat.

In the end, Dapper decides that he can represent Lee and Katye O'Milligan, but Shimona will have to find someone else. Shimona is also only sixteen, which means that she will also require an appropriate adult to assist her in concocting a defence and to tell the bad police lady to go away.

While Will discusses the finer points with Dapper, I go to see Shimona. Peering in through the hatch of her cell door, I see a podgy kid sitting on the bed, her knees drawn up as close as they can get to her chin. She has twisted her hair back in a ponytail, the tip of which she has inserted into the corner of her mouth. She is sucking on it furiously.

'Shimona.'

'Yeah, what.'

'You need an appropriate adult.'

'Whatever.'

'Is there anyone you'd like us to call?'

'I'm seventeen.'

'No, you're sixteen.'

'I was born in 1991.'

'Yes, that makes you sixteen. It's 2007.'

'Oh.'

'Shall I just call Social Services?'

'Whatever.'

'Fine. They'll take about four hours.'

'What!' At this Shimona leaps from the bed and races for the hatch. 'You bitch!'

Once again my touchy female nature defeats me, and I snap the hatch back into place. 'See you in four hours, Shimona.'

'You bitch-fookin whore!' She begins to kick and punch the door behind me and I saunter back to the custody desk with the corridor shuddering. The solicitor is standing by the desk waiting to speak to Lee. He looks a little perturbed at the noise I have created, so I explain. 'That's the client you turned down.'

He is too professional to smile, but the quick opening of his book gives him away.

Lee is brought out - a great, sweating hulk with fire-blond hair and a deep hatred of police officers. He shuffles past us like Frankenstein's creation and into consultation with Mr Dapper. I watch the pair sit down in the solicitor's room and see Dapper's broad grin as he shakes his client's hand. I am awed at the man's professionalism, as he manages not to wipe the hand on his trousers afterwards. Why, he doesn't even wrinkle his nose.

Consultations are usually about fifteen to twenty minutes long and are the only time the solicitor has to brief his client on the best story to tell in interview. If the client is too dumb, confused or guilty to tell a convincing tale, the outcome will be a 'No Comment' interview. Perhaps unsurprisingly, this is when the customer answers every question with the words 'No Comment'. Modern police training encourages us to ask all the questions anyway, just in case the prisoner decides suddenly to answer one or two - which actually happens fairly often.

I don't mind 'No Comment' interviews. Sometimes, I rather enjoy them... the lengthy drawing out of questions, and the palpable air of boredom that fills the room. You get so little time to yourself just to sit and think these days.

An hour later, I have sat on and slipped off the custody counter twice by accident, once as the inspector walked in. I have been hugged by a custody assistant who said I looked 'sad' and been bustled out of the way by another who described me as 'moody, more like'. I've told Will to go and start preparing the file for the Crown Prosecution Service and three times taken calls from him to tell him to carry on. All this while, Lee O'Milligan is in deep consultation about the whys and wherefores of the universe with the ever-patient Mr Dapper.

While I sit there waiting, I see a familiar face walking into custody. It's my old friend, Wayne Perril.

'I don't believe it, Wayne,' I say. 'You're answering your bail on time. Well, *almost* on time.'

'I'm only a day late,' he says, with a defensive shrug. 'I don't wanna be remanded again.'

'Hang about, though,' I say. 'I thought we'd charged you? It's that criminal damage, right? The one from 11th February?'

'He's here for a stabbing on 25th February,' says PC Hurley.

'Oh, right.' I separate the two incidents in my mind and recall the one that I had happened upon with Lloyd. 'What's happening?'

'Charge, on CPS advice.'

'Did Lisa give a statement then?'

'No. It'll be dropped at court, but the CPS are doing their usual Arse-Covering exercise.' He shrugs. 'What do I care? In the end, I get a detection, the police are seen to be doing something positive, and Wayne gets a day out in court at the tax-payer's expense where he learns that it really is OK to stab and beat his wife as long as she doesn't really mind too much.'

I nod gravely and watch proceedings. Wayne is informed that for stabbing his wife in the thigh he will be charged with Common Assault and be bailed with strict conditions not to contact Lisa until after the court case. If he breaches these conditions, he will be arrested within a week or two and put before the court who will reiterate that he really, really must try not to contact Lisa. Alternatively, if he appears incapable of keeping to the conditions, the courts could take the draconian step of taking them away altogether.

Wayne mumbles something about razors, booze and love, and then allows PC Hurley to let him out of the nick. No doubt the experience has left him a chastened, changed man.

I wait fifteen minutes more before rapping on the door to the consultation room under the pretext of offering Dapper and his client a cup of tea. It is my way of asking how much longer they are going to be, and ogling Dapper, without being oppressive. Dapper says they're both fine, thanks, and will just be a few more minutes.

I've almost lost the will to charge O'Milligan when he finally surfaces from consultation with the sigh of a man who by all rights is really too fat to commit crime. Will is astonished when I ring him up with the news and he dashes to custody in glee.

O'Milligan answers 'No Comment' to all questions. I can only imagine that it took the lawyer the hour and a half we've been waiting to explain how to pronounce the words.

Finally, we move onto Katye. To my amazement, she admits slapping her daughter around the face, and is dispatched swiftly with a police caution. She goes to sit in the public foyer to share a cab home with her husband. In the meantime, a social worker has arrived to see Shimona and then left after being told to eff off.

Sergeant Hayes is now on the phone to Social Services: it's their job to be told to eff off, after all. Unfortunately, it appears they disagree. While the debate rages, Will and I go to prepare an epic package to fax to CPS Direct regarding Lee O'Milligan.

Since not much crime happens on Saturdays, what with very few people going out on the town and getting mullered, much of the Criminal Justice System has shut down for the weekend. One such part is the in-house Crown Prosecution Service lawyer. During the working week, he's installed in an office within Blandmore Police Station. At weekends he's installed at home in leafy Barton-on-the-Wold.

So we telephone the wonderful call centre that is CPS Direct.

James McBrant, one of their duty lawyers, picks up with the dreary lack of enthusiasm we have come to expect of public sector workers. 'You've reached CPS Direct.'

Will has put it on speaker-phone and I listen as I quickly type up a summary of the interview. 'Hello, we're in Blandmore and we would like to charge someone, please.'

'Has it passed the Threshold Test?'

The Threshold Test means that the custody sergeant has reviewed the evidence and has decided to charge the person regardless of what CPS think. CPS lawyers will not review your case unless this test has been passed, as it saves them the bother of reviewing the evidence themselves.

'Yes, indeedio.'

McBrant doesn't join in with Will's waggish happiness. 'Email me your advice request.'

'Already done.'

There is a pause while McBrant logs into the CPS Direct inbox and locates the email. Then comes the dreaded request to fax through the evidence, in this case consisting of four police statements and a rather mangled car. My allotted task is to stand over the fax machine feeding the pages through one at a time; otherwise the machine will take them all at once and get jammed. The trick is to wait long enough that the rollers do not just grab the next sheet and take it through with the one before, but not so long that the machine thinks the fax has ended. I decide not to fax the car itself.

'Are you getting it?' Will asks.

'Yes. There's rather a lot. Hold on.' McBrant goes silent for several minutes and I suspect he is phoning up the Samaritans on the other line.

While we wait, I watch Will tapping his biro frenziedly on the desk. At last he looks up at me. 'So... bit of flirting going on there, with the solicitor.'

My jaw drops and I am about to fire back a retort denying all allegations, when James McBrant re-emerges onto the speaker-phone.

He has obviously had a pep-talk. 'I can't possibly review this by phone. I would need to see pictures of the car and medical evidence from the officer. It's hardly an attempted murder.'

Will and I exchange glances. Once lawyers start talking about 'evidence', you know that your prisoner will not be charged. Will wavers for a moment and then plants his finger firmly on the Release button, cutting off James McBrant in mid-criticism. One of the wonders of modern technology is that there is now no way to call McBrant back, as a call to the national number will select the next prosecutor on the list. A nightmare should it happen when you have a gung-ho, charge-em-and-to-hell-with-it cowboy on the other end, a blessing in this case.

We now have no choice but to start again.

The next prosecutor to pick up is Julie Parsons. Her first request is drowned out by the loud gargle of a baby and she apologises profusely: if she doesn't burp him now he'll throw up on her later.

Julie is horrified to hear about the nasty man who tried to run down a nice police officer, and is determined to send him to prison immediately. It takes all of eighteen minutes and just four attempts to use the fax machine before the decision is announced to charge O'Milligan and keep him in custody overnight.

Then, just as her advice is chugging out of the fax, there is a power cut and the page stops printing at the words, 'I propose to deal with O'Milligan in the following way:'

When the generator kicks in and the fax continues, the rest of the sheet is blank.

With ludicrous complacency, Will has already hung up. We spend the next ten minutes frantically faxing the number Julie gave us with requests for her to send it again, before Will's inbox surges to life and produces an email version of her fax.

At this juncture, I am gripped by a sudden chill: I've done no Crime Managing all day! The System will not have logged Katye O'Milligan's caution, and if I don't input it within the next three minutes, quite possibly I will be fired.

Will returns to read out the good news to Lee and I settle down at my computer for a Crime Management fest. Half an hour later, I've updated all of my ongoing investigations, which now number nine. It's a little-known fact that if left to their own devices, investigations can actually multiply. If I am doing my job properly, nine should continue to rise until it becomes fifteen or Sergeant Woodcock receives three complaints about me, whichever is the sooner. At this point, I can expect to be given three days to 'sort it out', which may include coming into work on a rest day without pay. Hence, I log in regularly in an attempt to whittle the figures down as quickly as they rise.

On this occasion, I don't succeed in getting rid of any work, but I do at least update each investigation to say that the reason I have not got rid of any work is because I am in custody dealing with three prisoners.

I dimly notice that a burglary I filed last week has reopened itself and the non-existent domestic that Guy and I attended the same week - the one where he tore the seat out of his trousers - is still 'awaiting action'. On the plus side, the Scrutineer has filed Mr Grahams' harassment, stating that 'the officer in charge of the case has now waited too long for an arrest to be justified'. A victory of sorts, and the last we'll hear of Mr Grahams.

My final act before returning to custody is to open my email, something I'm driven to do daily by a perverse self-hatred. I nearly always regret it.

I have an email from Scenes of Crime in Nutcorn stating that they cannot possibly go all the way to the property store to retrieve my weed killer and send it to me. Helpfully, they say that among the long list of things Scenes of Crime Officers are not, they are not 'couriers'.

I decide to be proactive and telephone the Nutcorn duty sergeant. You might think that it would be simple to find out the telephone number for another officer in my own force. I said, you might think that. After 10 minutes, I'm in possession of the number of someone who might know the relevant number. I dial it and lo, I find myself speaking to an officer in the same room as the Nutcorn skipper. She passes me over.

'Sarge,' I say. 'PC Bloggs here in Blandmore.'

'Hello, PC Bloggs of Blandmore, and welcome to the show,' he says. This only confirms what I have always thought about officers in rural stations.

'Some officers from your nick arrested a guy for me last week and bailed him back to Blandmore,' I say. 'There were some exhibits relating to the case and I need them sent over to me.'

A short silence indicates that my request falls in the category of Never-been-done-before. I hear the long intake of breath known as the Plumber's Sniff. 'Can you come and get them?' he says.

'Well, I would,' I say, 'but we're on minimum staffing levels all week and it's a two-hour round trip.'

'I see... why do you need them again?'

'I want to send them away for fingerprinting and handwriting analysis.'

'Fingerprinting, I see...'

'I'd be really grateful if someone would just put them in the internal dispatch.' I am batting my eyes and pouting furiously down the phone.

It works. Still got the old magic, Bloggs. 'Tell you what,' he says, 'as I'm sooo nice, I'll help you out.'

'Thank you, sarge, you've no idea what a lot of hassle it will save me.'

'Here's how I'll help you out: email Scenes of Crime and they can pop the exhibits in the dispatch for you next time they're over here.'

I rub my eyebrows vigorously. I can feel a headache coming on. 'Um, right, thank you. Is there no way that you could...'

'No point a police officer wasting his time digging through the old property store when those guys are in it every day. Glad to have been of service. Good day!' And he hangs up.

I stare in mounting rage at the dead receiver in my hand and take my revenge by updating the Crime Management System with the contents of the conversation. A bit of an overreaction, but a woman scorned and all that.

It occurs to me, as I sit there, that the report room has emptied out in a manner that suggests a police-related activity somewhere: either someone has brought cakes in, or there is a fight going on. I lurch into the corridor in time to see five black-clad hulks tramp through the door to custody with their thumbs tucked into the sides of their stab vests. Aaaargh! A group of ARVs is in the station and I am missing it!

I race to custody and discover that the party is in aid of Lee O'Milligan, who is about to be told he is not getting bail. For some reason, people can react badly to being told they'll stay in custody overnight and when those people weigh twenty-five stone - even if twelve of them are made of blubber - some back-up is in order.

O'Milligan doesn't seem to have noticed that twelve officers now surround him while he's offered his charge forms to sign. He signs and then slowly twigs. 'Where's the bail form?'

Sergeant Hayes twitches the signed papers back over to his side of the raised desk and puts them safely out of sight before replying, 'I am remanding you for the safety of the public.'

O'Milligan's right foot twitches slightly in a pawing motion. His fists clench. His skin turns white. I identify these as danger signs of aggression.

He circles his head from left to right, taking in the five arm-folded man-machines that surround him and the seven white-shirted weeds next to them. For a moment his face contorts with the expression of someone who is multiplying twelve stone by twelve to see if it is less than twenty-five. He then tosses his pen down and plods back into his cell without a word.

'Thank you, boys,' says Sergeant Hayes.

The ARVs slope off, muttering about how last time they had to hold a prisoner out like a stretcher and roll his fingers one by one onto the scanner to take prints. I consider attempting to flirt as they stampede past me but the sheer quantity of stubble on display overloads my circuits and I shy away. Once again, I find Will watching me with that same curious frown.

Hayes spots me. 'Bloggs, a long-lost cousin or auntie or someone has arrived for Shimona so she can now be interviewed.' The sergeant gestures to a skinny woman with glasses and streaked hair who is standing in the corner.

'Sister, actually,' she says.

Will cries off to go and begin the ginormous file which must now be submitted in time to travel to court with Lee O'Milligan in the morning, leaving me alone with Shimona and her beloved big sister. It takes several minutes to fulfil Shimona's pre-interview demands of a cigarette and one cup of water and another of coffee, and then we settle down in Interview Room 2, the bulk of which is taken up by an enormous television and video-player.

I balance Shimona's sister underneath the television and station myself opposite the girl to be interviewed. She is leaning on her elbows on the table and the ponytail is back in the corner of the mouth.

The interview starts well, in that I manage to unwrap the tapes and press 'record'. Then I am interrupted.

'I want a brief.'

I press 'stop' and stare at Shimona. 'You just signed to say you were happy to be interviewed without a solicitor.'

'Yeah, whatever, I've changed my mind.'

My teeth may or may not be gritted. 'No *problem*,' I say.

Shimona is hauled back to the custody desk where the sergeant listens to her change of heart and then says, 'Take her back to her cell.'

'Oh man...' Shimona glares at her sister. 'See what you done now!'

'I never told you to have no solicitor,' says the sister. 'Don't you look at me like that, you snotty little bitch.'

Things teeter on the brink of a sororal catfight, and then Shimona looks away. 'I don't want one no more,' she says.

Sergeant Hayes barely bats an eyelid. 'Fine, take her back to the cell while we call out the inspector.'

'What? Why!' screeches Shimona.

'Only an inspector can authorise an interview to go ahead without a solicitor when one has been requested,' says Sergeant Hayes.

'That's fookin stupid! Why?'

'In case PC Bloggs has oppressed you into not wanting one any more.'

Shimona looks me up and down with a sneer. 'Her?' she says.

'Can't you just phone him?' asks the sister.

Hayes sighs. 'It's a 'her', actually. But I suppose we can.'

The inspector feels it would be better if she attended, so Shimona is reinserted into the custody block and I find myself at a loose end yet again for another half hour. I consider going to help Will with his file, but given the last couple of looks he's given me, I doubt I'd be welcome. I take the opportunity of re-bailing Neville Saunderson (the weed killer attacker), as it appears I will no longer be ready to deal with him this week. A few minutes pass. I lean on the fingerprint scanner and half-close my eyes. Suddenly, I think about my short stint in interview with Shimona and a thought occurs to me. A minute later, I'm playing one of my ten CCTV tapes in the comfort of Interview Room 2. I watch with bated breath as a petrol station forecourt is displayed to me in jerky freeze-frame. A car draws in. A male gets out. He appears to fill up with petrol. He enters the shop. He returns. He drives away. End reel.

I remove the tape and sigh. The other tapes must be different camera views, one of which will no doubt enlighten me as to why the mountain of videos was placed in my docket on that cold, midwinter morning six weeks ago.

The inspector has been and gone, so I return tape 1 to my tray and collect Shimona from her cell again. We pause while I get Shimona yet another cup of coffee and, finally, we're underway.

You may be wondering why I pander to this child's every desire. The answer, once again, is PACE and its Codes of Practice. Not only am I complying with an historic piece of legislation designed to assist the guiltiest of offenders in their endeavours for freedom, but I am Covering my Arse against allegations of oppression at the same time. Plus with a few cups of sugary caffeine down her gob, Shimona will be more likely to give me some straight answers.

The tapes are on, the interview begins. I perform the introductions, explain the Caution and ask my standard opening question: 'Do you understand why you have been arrested?'

Believe it or not, sometimes these words alone can prompt a confused confession.

'I haven't been arrested,' says Shimona.

Not exactly a confession.

'Well, you have, because you're here.'

'I was never arrested, though. No-one never put handcuffs on me.'

I put down my pen. Somehow, I don't think this is going to be the level of interview for which I need to make notes. 'You actually don't need to be handcuffed to be under arrest,' I say.

'Yeah, I do. Right, Sonia?'

Sonia nods emphatically. 'You do need it, me Ma said so.'

In an attempt to steer the interview back on track, I look down at PC Cansat's statement. 'Look, it says here, "I then said to Shimona O'Milligan, '*I am arresting you on suspicion of assault and criminal damage*.' I cautioned her to which she replied, '*Whatever*'." Does that ring any bells?'

Shimona titters. Then she gets serious again. 'Does he say he handcuffed me, though? Cos he's a liar.'

'No, he says he arrested you.'

'Well, I wasn't listening.'

'This may surprise you,' I say, 'but you can be arrested even if you aren't listening.'

'No, you can't. Not if you're inside a house. I know the law.'

If there is one thing I like more than a gobby teenager, it is a gobby teenager who knows the law.

'Shimona, you are going to have to take my word for the fact that you were brought here under arrest and you are still under arrest now. Let's move on.'

'Whatever.'

'Just tell me what happened.'

Shimona describes how the argument broke out because she had been ejected from Waitrose earlier that day. 'The store guys in there just follow you round,' she says. 'This one guy was in my face, following me up and down the aisles, watching me going in and out of the shop for ten minutes. It was well rude, I'm like, fuck right off, will you, it does my head in.'

'Why do you think he was following you?'

'Cos he's a cock. Store detectives always fookin harass me when I go shopping. I done nothing to them, I was just hanging around looking at DVDs.'

'Fine. What happened next?'

'I asked him what his problem was.'

'And then?'

'He said I was out of order, and the two of them gripped me up and chucked me out the shop. I was bawling in the street and smashing Dad's car up when Mum came down and slapped me round the face.'

I ignore the enormous and seemingly illogical leap between being ejected from a shop and destroying your father's car, and ask, 'Do you think that maybe you were just a tad out of order?'

'No way! Those guys are out of order - they just follow you for no reason, yeah.'

At this, Sonia pipes up. 'That is well true, issit. The store detectives in there always follow you up and down, man. They does it to everyone, yeah.'

I privately think that I have never once been followed around by store detectives in any shop, let alone Waitrose. We continue with the interview, but essentially Shimona admits both offences despite claiming that a reasonable response to being hit by her mother was to turn and hit her brother.

Finally, she is charged and released, whereupon her mother begins to scream at her in the front foyer and they are both ejected into an unsuspecting taxi.

I go to find Will, who is sitting in the report writing room generating detections on the Crime Management System. We have run into overtime and Team 3 have started work, which means a queue of two or three officers standing over our shoulders waiting to use a computer.

Will and I tot up our detection figures for the day: Lee charged with three offences, Katye cautioned, Shimona charged with two. The fact that five of the six charges relate to offences within the family, that no one wants anyone prosecuted for, or that not one victim or offender will ever turn up in court or go to prison for them, does little to deflate the enthusiasm I feel at meeting my detection target for the month all in one day!

The one offence with a truly aggrieved party is the near-running-down of PC Barnaby, for which Lee has been charged with Dangerous Driving. Since that is a traffic offence, and not included in our performance figures for the detection of violent crime, no one really cares about that.

All in all, a good nine hours' work.

I pause outside the locker room and decant my stabbie and kit belt onto the floor. As I chuck my tie and epaulettes into my kit bag, I see Will exiting the guys' locker room, car key in hand (the motorbike's only for sunny days).

'Hey, Bloggsy,' he says. 'I'm knackered.'

I undo the top couple of buttons of my shirt and lean against the wall for a moment. 'Yeah I know what you mean.'

'Well, I'll see you tomorrow.' He walks past me to the top of the stairs, then looks back. 'Fancy a couple of beers?'

I waver.

'I'll drive.' He dangles his keys temptingly before my face.

'Um...'

I may be a 21st Century Police Officer, fearless and relentless, and all that, but I do drink beer. Sometimes.

I pick up my bag and follow him out.

9

The Unfair Sex

BOOKING LEAVE is one of my favourite activities. If you're one of those people who never bet on horse-racing except on Grand National day, booking leave is a little like that. Except I get to do it twenty times a year.

First, you fill out the form. The most vital section is the part where you describe exactly how many hours you plan to book. Accuracy is the key. For example, if you're working day shifts the week you want to go on holiday, and you accidentally claim just 7am-4pm off (omitting the hour between 4pm and 5pm), you will find yourself rostered to work one-hour days that week and will have to fill out another form to resolve the problem. This is because the Duties department runs an automated system, whereby humans read the form and take it completely literally, offering no advice nor remedy for errors. The onus, quite rightly, is on officers to ensure that they are aware of their working hours eighteen months in advance, despite having no clue what team or station they will be working from the week after next.

The form thus filled, it goes by email to Duties, who are 'Out of Office' until after the time you had hoped to take as leave. So you re-draft the form and email it to the person who is responsible for your leave in Duties' absence.

Now comes the exciting part. You wait up to three days to hear back, hoping against hope that maybe, just maybe, you have won your holiday.

Then the emails arrive. *'Unfortunately your team are on minimum manning that day. Sorry.'*

'Minimum manning' is the number of officers below which it is considered that the public, and we, are at risk of harm.

Taking it on the chin, you change the dates and re-submit the form.

The Unfair Sex

Once again, it is rejected. You ask your inspector, who phones Duties directly and asks whether, given that the relevant date is eight months in the future, another officer or Special Constable might be imposed upon to change their shift to cover for PC Bloggs' absence.

Of course, this is *completely* impossible.

Finally, you accept that you are going to have to be ill later in the year and forget about the idea of time off.

Today, the 10th April, is one such day. Back in November, I tried to book today off to go and stay with friends and was told that I was a heartless animal for wishing to endanger Blandmore in this way. I cancelled the engagement and moved on, in the magnanimous way we women can.

A few days before the date in question, I receive an email informing me that I am in court on 11th April and will therefore be unable to work a night shift the night before. I will work from 2pm-10pm instead. This will render me worse than useless to my team, who begin the shift at 10pm. Out of nowhere, a Special Constable is produced to work until 3am instead of me.

I come in at 2pm, and am met with a blank stare by the duty sergeant for Team 1. He knows nothing about my court dates, nor my change of duties, and cares less. He tells me to get on with my own work, which is code for 'sit and have a cup of tea'.

As I get tea-d up, I catch a glimpse of a figure vanishing into the Neighbourhood office, and follow it at a half-jog.

'Frances?'

The girl stops and swings back to greet me. I have not seen Frances for well over two years, since she left our team to have a baby. Charlie must be well over a year old now, but she's still off frontline work.

'Hey, Bloggsy, how's it going?' She shows me into the Neighbourhood office, a place of awe-inspiring calm and relaxation, where the two sergeants are practising rounders with a cardboard bat and rolled-up paper ball.

'You're working here now?'

She nods. 'I take statements for them.'

'You take statements for Neighbourhood officers? Is there such a job?'

'I'm getting back into response, but it works out better here as I can choose my own hours. I have the baby every morning and work evenings.'

'And you're quite happy?'

'Oh yes.'

I recall the day that Frances came into work and told me she was pregnant. We were making a tray of tea for our shift, and she waited until the noise of the boiling kettle obscured greedy ears from picking up the gossip. I was barred from telling a soul for at least a month while she determined what was to be done, and then one day she 'came out' and I never saw her again.

Rumour has it that she spent four months making spreadsheets for CID and was then promoted to scanning photographs of wanted criminals to create the posters that go on the briefing room walls. Every now and again we would hear whispers that she had asked the Superintendent whether she might not do something more worthwhile and interesting, but eventually she went on maternity leave and the outrageous whispers died down.

A year on from the birth, Frances explains to me that she has forgotten how to use the radio or make arrests, and there are a dozen new criminal offences she has never heard of. This is par for the course for any police officer off the front-line for two years.

'But the Job's been brilliant,' she says. 'They let me work whatever I want and now they've put me here where it fits in perfectly with my life.'

'But what about the sergeant's exam, or your CID attachment?' She had been on the brink of both before foolishly allowing her husband to knock her up.

She shrugs. 'I can't think about either until I've gotten back into things. It's two years since I even drew my handcuffs, Bloggsy.' She sounds somewhat wistful.

I glance at her belt; she's not wearing any of her kit, anyway.

We sit and chat for five more minutes and then I tune into some action on the airwaves. I find her frowning at me quizzically and explain. 'There's a robbery just happened, Palm Drive.'

She nods. 'Phew, I don't miss all that! Have I shown you a picture of Charlie yet?'

I coo over the baby headshot for a moment, and we are then interrupted by Sally Marshall, who had her boy at the same time as

The Unfair Sex

Frances. She appears to have just wandered in from the Domestic Violence Unit for the purposes of filling in some time; at any rate, she perches on the desk-edge without apparent urgency.

A discussion strikes up about local nurseries, and whether men are bastards or just incompetent. Palm Drive becomes more appealing, and I disengage myself from the chitchat of these consummate professionals to drive at a perfectly reasonable speed through Blandmore's pedestrian zone.

As I drive, I decide that I, too, am going to have a baby.

I long for the day when I can swan up at nine o'clock, having called to say that my poor little tot has a temperature, dash off home at twelve to sort out a car-seat-emergency, come back in for a few hours and then knock off feeling 'tired'. When I start to build up my hours (if I can be bothered to do so at all), I won't really feel like working lates, so I'll find a nursery that closes at four. Then I'll ask to work solely early shifts with the exception of bank holidays, when I would like whichever shift will mean running into overtime, and when I am fully fit and ready to milk them for all they are worth, I will claim that I can't afford to do the job any more unless they let me work extra hours here, there and everywhere.

I support the police in their discriminatory tactics, but I do think they run the risk of encouraging non-baby-producing officers, like myself or even males, into thinking that we, too, should be allowed to work flexible hours. Of course, it's ridiculous to suppose that any right-thinking man would want to work different hours simply in order to see his spouse, child or golfing partner. Just because the more pathetic of us can't handle spending days apart from our loved ones, living in perpetual exhaustion and being spammed with overtime on the one night per month we actually have planned something sociable, doesn't mean the management should give in to our moaning.

Obviously, once pregnant, I will become a negative figure insofar as resourcing goes. Whereas now the management see my name among those on the duty list and feel smug in the knowledge that they have five healthy officers on duty, they will be forced to remember that officially, I no longer count. You see, being pregnant is a very delicate condition. At any moment, I might be subjected to an extreme pile of paperwork and the baby could just fall out of my pants. This would cause a mess in the briefing room, and negative headlines.

The management must find somewhere safe to put me until I am out of danger. Thus, the invention of restricted duties. No fighting, no driving, no danger. No night shifts, no early shifts, no extremely late shifts and no tiredness. No confrontation, no responsibility, no stress. No crime, no crime prevention and no investigating.

The only solution is spreadsheets and statements (it was most unfair of them to inflict on Frances the stress associated with scanning). Safely ensconced in my office-paradise, I will have no need to concern my pretty head with thoughts of career progression and exams.

The above approach is known as RISK ASSESSMENT and it is FOR OUR OWN GOOD.

* * * * *

I circle the area of Palm Drive until I am satisfied that a Team 1 unit has located the victim and begun a paper trail leading to another officer. I then close in and inform the control room that I am present.

Before long, a description of the mugger is passed: drunk white male, aged mid-twenties, tattoo of an England flag on his neck. Should be in possession of an iPod, a pair of Oakley shades and a mobile phone.

I transmit on the radio. 'That sounds to me very much like Wayne Perril. I'll head for Corinthian Way in case he goes home.'

Twenty yards into Corinthian Way I spot Mr Perril; he's half-jogging and is uncharacteristically alert. He halts when I pull up beside him and grins lopsidedly. He smells of beer.

'Good afternoon, Wayne,' I say, taking his arm and glancing quickly up and down him for signs of an incriminating mp3 player or trendy sunnies. 'I'm arresting you on suspicion of robbery.'

'No, you fookin ain't.' His arms tense as he prepares for the familiar routine of snaking both wrists up and down in circles to prevent me handcuffing him.

I sigh. 'Oh, come on Wayne. We've always gotten along, haven't we?'

'You *ain't* arresting me.'

I side-sweep his legs in an attempt to surprise him to the floor. Instead I find myself clinging to his elbow as he swings me round in a circle. In fairness to Wayne, he makes no attempt to hit or kick me, or even to escape. It seems more a matter of pride that a woman half his size shouldn't be able to arrest him easily.

Unfortunately, he is proved right and despite a number of heel-jabs to the back of his calf, I only succeed in descending to the pavement with him where we wriggle, unprofessionally, in slow motion. By now, I have pressed my orange emergency button, which sends out a warbled beep to all officers and gives you priority to speak on the airwaves. I ignore the controller's request for an update, and allow Wayne's shouts of 'Fookin pig' to speak for themselves. Very soon, I hear the troops flocking to my aid.

It is an odd feeling, grappling with a male in a public street. Before joining the police it was not something I would have undertaken lightly. Or at all, actually. And yet I'm not particularly afraid for myself, despite the writhings of the much-stronger person I'm trying to control. I'd have been more scared if I'd known this was going to happen beforehand, and I probably wouldn't have gone there alone to start with. But now the adrenaline is pumping, and I know help is on the way.

Eventually, we roll into the middle of the lane of traffic and a car brakes to avoid driving over us. The driver sits patiently at his wheel waiting for the fight to finish. Somehow, I've ended up on top, and I'm sitting on Wayne's calves and leaning on his back as he lies face-down on the Tarmac. He's not quite strong enough to fling me off, and I rack out my baton and use it as a bar across his shoulders. The sirens are just round the corner.

I hear the sound of Doc Martens on asphalt and breathe a sigh of relief. I turn my head in time to see John Ash from Team 1 colliding with Lisa Perril's raised Niked foot. It appears the foot was flying in the direction of my head when he intercepted it.

'Wayne!' she screeches. 'What are you doing to him?'

'Stand back!' Ash orders her.

'Get the fuck off him!'

'You swear again and you'll be nicked, too.'

'Fuck off, you pig!'

Ash grabs her.

Now two more pandas roll up and Wayne finds himself cuffed and restrained in an instant. Lisa Perril is causing more of a problem. She writhes, screams, punches, kicks and spits at everyone who comes near her. Various official techniques are discarded in favour of four men and me jumping on top of her and pinning every limb and her head down on the floor. You would think that might stop her, but even the tips of her elbows and her knees are still striking officers wherever they can.

By now Joanna from Team 1 has arrived and successfully quells the offender into submission by thrusting a manicured thumb into the recess behind Lisa's ear. Somehow Jo manages this without even smudging her mascara.

Lisa then decides to summon some assistance and starts screaming, 'Help! Help!' at the top of her lungs.

Two passers-by of an elderly persuasion hove into view, and I glance up at them as I roll up and down the road. The man bends down to catch Lisa's eyes. 'Are you all right, dear?' he says.

Her response is to flail a Nike towards Ash's head which he diverts with a booted heel to her thigh. The elderly couple pass by, shaking their heads. 'That's a bit harsh,' I hear one say.

I consider asking them to swap places with us.

Wayne is under control and thrust into the back of a panda, his exertions reduced to a few sweet nothings shouted in our direction. Jo's nail still inserted into Lisa's mandibular angle, it takes five more minutes to truss her up, and we then have to hold her motionless for the fifteen minutes it takes the Transit van to arrive. In that time she succeeds in biting Ed Garson's finger, provoking some four-letter utterances that are most certainly not Home-Office-approved.

As she is hoisted into the Transit, I spot an iPod on the floor where I first hit the deck with Wayne, and pounce on it triumphantly. A passer-by stops to inform me that it fell out of Wayne's shorts while I was trying to restrain him.

'You saw it all happen?' I say.

'Oh yes. I wanted to help you, but you know...'

I feel breathless and upset at this, the more so because I know I'm meant to tell him he did the right thing by not getting involved. At least he bothered to wait and give his name. Maybe he'll even show up in court.

One of the male PCs finds the Oakleys on Lisa a few moments later - Wayne must have passed them on - so it would appear we've done a reasonably good day's work.

The Unfair Sex

We arrive back at the nick, and I see that I've picked up a variety of scratches and bruises on my arms and face. I dive into the bathroom to examine the damage - I may even be breaking out in a tiny little black eye, which is simply thrilling for a tough street-fighter like me. While I'm here, I undo my top button and pull my collar down an inch, squinting into the mirror. No, I'm not sure that love bite will really pass as being inflicted by the Tarmac of Corinthian Way. Looks like I'm keeping my tie on all day after all.

The fact of my having arrested Wayne means that my attempt to avoid dealing with the robbery has gone awry. I collate the paperwork for it and, in the course of this, I speak with the victim. He is nineteen-year-old Sean Andrews. He has never spoken to a police officer before, and he will definitely not be showing up in court. His voice trembles as he speaks of his attacker. I leave him in the capable hands of the PC who has begun taking the statement, and find myself at a loose end waiting for the rest of the evidence to be brought to me. This must be how detectives feel.

A moment is spent wondering whether I should be shaky or worried following my tussle. Then my blacked eye falls on a spare computer and I realise that what I should really be thinking about is the fact that no one has yet created a crime report for the incident and a crisis is imminent if it's not done soon. I generate this via the Crime Centre and spend a precious 10 minutes updating it with the details of Wayne's arrest. While logged into the Crime Management system, I feel the old urge and I make the fatal mistake of checking the status of my virtual docket.

The Exposure is back.

I open it up and find that the detection has been removed. There is no explanation for this in the notes, nor in my email inbox. I feel shaky and worried, and even a little tearful. I send an email to the Scrutineer demanding she re-detect it.

The email inbox contains a further disaster. There's a message from the Property Manager to do with Mr Carson's 2003 diary. It has been sitting waiting for him since he came into the police station demanding it, and the Property Manager warns me that the diary will be destroyed if it isn't collected in another two weeks. He suggests that I ring Mr Carson to inform him of this fact and I email him back to say that if Mr Carson would like to leave me his telephone number I will happily make as many calls as is necessary to rid him from my life.

The last bit of paperwork for the Perrils is presented to me and I collate it in a pleasingly thick file, ready to thrust into the arms of a willing detective. There is a special team who deal with Robberies, as they are considered a particularly nasty sort of crime entailing the use of violence to steal, and therefore merit the attention of highly-trained officers. This means that PC Bloggs goes to the scene to gather all the evidence and, once all the work is done, a detective will interview the offender. If no suspect is identified or arrested, the detective will take on the taxing job of filing the crime report, although PC Bloggs will still be responsible for telling the victim it has been filed.

The only thing missing from the case is the mobile phone; sometimes, a robbery victim will introduce the existence of an imaginary mobile phone for insurance purposes, but in the case of trembling Sean Andrews the general consensus is that he is telling the truth.

I join Team 1 in gearing up for a house search. As I enter the store-room to locate the 'bust box' (a briefcase full of all kinds of goodies useful in seizing evidence), I find Jo already in there checking the contents of the box. She is with Ash and between them they have identified that the box consists of five small 'drugs bags' and about a hundred elastic bands, but no normal evidence bags, exhibits labels or search booklets. There are, however, two continuation booklets.

Jo runs down to Scenes of Crime on a shopping trip and I help Ash carry the bust box out into the report room.

Ash pauses on the stairs up from the basement to get a better grip on the box. 'Maybe you can shed some light on the rumours I've been hearing,' he says.

My hand flies instinctively to my throat and I find myself blushing uncontrollably. I knew I shouldn't have gone for those beers with Will. Someone was bound to see us leaving work in his car. Although surely no one could have seen us leaving the pub in that self-same car? And certainly not driving home in it together, and then coming back to work in it again the next day?

'Um, rumours?'

'About her and Guy,' he adds.

I get even hotter, this time in relief. It appears our secret is safe. 'Who and Guy?'

'Jo. They got together last week. I always thought it was Lloyd she was shagging.'

We enter the report room and are forced to curtail our conversation, but I am astounded not to have heard of this sooner. As in most workplaces, gossip in the police usually travels faster than the events themselves, and I'd have expected to hear this rumour at least three weeks before anything actually happened. For example, according to the rest of the shift, Will and I have been an item for at least two years. Tragically, it has merely been vicious rumour. Until the beers, that is.

Stories of sexual misdemeanour are always highly relished in the police service; I don't know if we have more sex than other people, but I'd like to think we do, and if you can get to my level of service without being forbidden to work with a good two or three of your colleagues, you just aren't doing your job properly. You need not *actually* have slept with any of them: what is important is that people think you have.

Before we can head out on our search, the Team 1 sergeant has the inspired idea of getting the stolen phone pinged. For my uninitiated readers, mobile phone companies can triangulate the rough location of a mobile phone by checking which transmission mast it's nearest to. This will establish at least whether it is still in Blandmore, or is in the process of being whisked away by an accomplice.

Because information relating to mobile phones is covered by the Data Protection Act, you have to have authority in order to get to it. This means someone who has passed two exams and made friends with the right people will decide yes or no. It can only be done in certain circumstances.

Sergeant Blacklock logs his request with the control room. It takes all of three minutes for the Tactical Inspector to reject the idea.

'It doesn't fit the criteria.'

The sergeant is most aggrieved. 'Why not?'

'Data protection - we can only ping phones when life is in danger.'

'But whose data are we protecting? The victim wants us to ping it so he can get it back.'

'Yes, but we are still invading his privacy.' He pauses. 'Or the privacy of the thief.'

'You're having a laugh.'

The inspector's silence says it all.

Here are some other circumstances in which the inspector will not authorise a 'ping'.

Someone's just burgled my house and stolen my mobile phone. The phone is still on, can we ping it to find out where the burglar is? No.

My brother just rang me to say he is in the woods with a shotgun and he is going to kill himself. Can we ping his phone to find him? No.

My 10 year old child has been missing all evening. Can we ping her mobile phone? No.

Someone I know just stabbed me, wounding me seriously, and ran away. He's hiding somewhere. Can we ping his phone? No.

While on the subject of 'authority', here are some other circumstances in which you can ask for privileged information (and the answers you will receive).

The guy who robbed me used my mobile phone to make some calls. Can we ask the mobile company who he called so that we can to track him down? We can indeed, but we have to submit three different forms and wait three months for the answer. The first of these forms is to confirm who is the subscriber of your phone. But it's me. Yes, but we have to confirm that by a month-long wait.

My ex-boyfriend has been harassing me. In interview he claimed that I phoned and texted him just as much as he did. This isn't true and I want you to take my mobile phone and look at it to prove it. OK, but we have to submit three different forms and wait three months for the information. *But I'm telling you it's OK to look at my phone.* Yes, but we have to fill in the forms anyway. *This is taking too long; I desperately need my phone for work. Can I have it back?* No, it has gone missing somewhere in the Crime Property Store and you will never see it again. You should have thought of that before you gave it to us.

Someone has been phoning me and threatening to kill me. I have no idea who this person is, but they seem to be watching me all the time and yesterday my brake pipes were cut. Can you find out who is the subscriber to that mobile phone number? Yes, but it will take three months. *I'll be dead by then.* Yes, but at least we won't have unlawfully invaded anyone's privacy.

As you can see, the Tactical Inspector does not have too many laughs.

In the end I am nominated to go and search Wayne's flat with Ash, on the basis that he was heading in that direction and might have sent the stolen mobile on ahead. Unsurprisingly I do not find it, although I do locate Lisa's crotchless-underwear collection and Wayne's used-stabbing-implement drawer. On the way back, I'm thinking gleefully of my one hour in court tomorrow when I am distracted by a small car. It's the sort of car that's only really safe with about two people in it, and this one has three or four times that many bobbing around inside. I check the time. I've got five minutes. I'll give the occupants a dressing down. I flick on the blue lights and start flashing my headlights in what I hope is an annoying fashion.

The driver indicates and pulls over. As I stop behind him, he pulls out again and continues. The second time I flash at him, he sticks his arm out of the window and waves me by. Normally, I give this a few more attempts but today I am tired. I pull up beside him and scream out of the window, 'Pull over!'

This time he gets the message.

I get out, and don my fluorescent jacket in an attempt to make him think I am a traffic officer who is proficient at giving out tickets.

As I draw level with the car and open the rear passenger door, my jaw falls open. He's clearly on a family outing - an outing, that is, for about three families. I count one, two, three, four, five, six kids seated in a neat row, and a seventh laid across their knees. Not one of them is over the age of eight. I now open the front passenger door, intending to unleash my full repertoire of sarcastic remarks, and discover a woman in the passenger seat with yet another child on her lap.

I am speechless for a good few seconds. Finally, I ask, 'Are these all your kids?'

'Yes,' says the driver, beaming proudly.

'Well... you can't just put them all in like that. They need seatbelts and booster seats.'

'Well, I'd need a bigger car for that,' he says.

'So buy a bigger car.'

'I can't afford one.'

My eye falls on the woman in the front. I goggle. 'Are you *breastfeeding*?'

'That's why I have him on my lap,' she says, defensively, and hastily concealing a gargantuan boob.

I have nothing against women showing off their impressive bosoms in public, whether breastfeeding or not, but an old-fashioned part of me does object to infants being held in the front seat of a moving vehicle without restraints.

'Well, I'm going to have to report you for this,' I say. 'You can expect to go to court.'

The man looks crestfallen. Devastated might not be too strong a word. 'Can't you just give me a lecture and shout at me a bit?' he says, hopefully.

It's the first time I have ever been petitioned for some shouting and I am tempted. 'Would that make you buy a bigger car?'

He is silent.

'I didn't think so.'

'Consider yourself reported for carrying eight children in a car designed for... oooh... none.'

I leave him standing at the side of the road and drive back to the police station in disbelief. The man will now wait approximately six months in anticipation of receiving a summons to court, when what will actually happen is that I will forget to submit the file. One of the downsides of the Crime Management System, if it can be said to have a downside, is that you get so accustomed to receiving emails prompting you to perform simple tasks that when you deal with a non-recordable offence like seatbelts, you find yourself incapable of remembering what to do.

I walk into the nick at the same time as Will, who is arriving for the night shift.

'You're early,' I say.

'Came to see you.'

It isn't the most gushing compliment I've ever heard, but then he is a man.

'You been fighting?' he adds, looking at my face.

'Oh, I'll tell you all about it later. First...'

At my behest, we duck quickly into the locker room for a few moments to check that he has been as discreet as I have about our beer-fuelled liaison. We both agree that discretion does not really enter the equation, as anyone we don't tell will just make up their own version of events anyway. I also take the opportunity to inform him that love bites are, and have always been, rather too teenage for my liking and that I would thank him if he refrained from inflicting them in future. Or positioned them further inside my uniform. A lot further.

Leaving Will to find his stab vest, I go back downstairs and heave out my docket to check that nothing vital has arrived in it in the last hour. In it I discover an exciting looking brown bag with a note stapled to it. It reads: 'Here are your exhibits.'

I tear it open and find that some saint from the early shift has driven to Nutcorn in response to a desperate email I sent out the week before, has collected my weed killer and reports and brought them all the way over for me. Their note says that it took three hours, allowing for traffic. This gives rise to the rarest of all occasions: the opportunity to send a grateful email to a colleague.

It also gives rise to the opportunity to fill in a ten-page document to accompany the weed killer to the fingerprint lab and a second ten-page document that will go with the reports to a handwriting expert. I would not normally complete this much paperwork right before bed for fear of nightmares, but the case of the sprayed lawn is getting so old that the lawn is probably a patio by now; I make an exception to save Sergeant Woodcock from the catastrophe of an 80-day review.

The rest of my own team have now started arriving, and I get to show off my war wounds. I also show off the thick handover package waiting in my docket. The team is suitably impressed, although naturally skittish in the presence of that amount of paper. With reassurances that the Robbery Team have already agreed to deal with the Perrils, I power up a computer for the final time tonight.

Once logged in, I type up a quick statement about the seatbelt incident, just in case. As I do so, Ash comes in and tells me that Lisa Perril has been released early from custody because the doctor said she is pregnant and it would not be good for the baby to spend the night in the traps. She has been bailed and will come back in a week on the off-chance that she is no longer pregnant by then.

I do wonder about babies. I wonder about policewomen who accept a blight on their career to start a family. I wonder about people who can afford eight children but not a car big enough to carry them all. I wonder about men who stab a girl one day and give them a baby the next, and I wonder about doctors who treat pregnancy as a kind of disease. I wonder if I will ever have a baby, and if I'll even tell my force if I do. Before it's really obvious, I mean.

Women. I guess we just wonder too much.

10

The Long Dark Tea-Time
of the Cells

I ARRIVE AT WORK this afternoon to be greeted with the dreaded words, 'There's a cell watch.'

This happens every few days or so, and means one lucky soul will be dispatched to custody to sit on a chair in the open doorway of a cell to keep a constant watch on its occupant. The watcher must be alert for the signs of suicide, catatonia, or vomit, plus escape. The occupant is alert for a chance to escape, by means of feigning suicide, catatonia or vomit.

A cell watch is triggered by the announcement that a prisoner has recently harmed themselves, has a medical condition which makes them prone to death, is awfully drunk or has declared themselves CLAUSTROPHOBIC. For my unscientific readers, claustrophobia is the fear of having no one to talk to all night.

In this age of technological genius, where cameras and microphones adorn custody suites and civilian gaolers service our customers' every need, you still can't beat good old-fashioned sitting as the best way to monitor our more vulnerable guests. Sergeant Woodcock is a sterling chap and always assures the Chosen One that he or she will be relieved after two or three hours, to spread the grief among us. In reality, after two or three hours Sergeant Woodcock will be endeavouring to guard two crime scenes and take three statements with his three remaining PCs, and will have forgotten all about the sitter.

It's Saturday night, and I am allotted a drunk, claustrophobic, suicidal and vomiting female to guard. If the subject is female, it will be Becks or I who is dispatched. With two out of eight on our team being female, and an estimated half of cell watches being females, this is only fair. You cannot really expect a male officer to sit alone with a woman in a cell block in case he gets scared.

Tonight it appears there is a high chance of this happening. I scan the supervision log to see what notes the previous watcher has made. Meryl Chance is MAD. She has been arrested on a court warrant for failing to answer bail last month which means there is no chance of her being released until the morning, and there is also no chance of her sitting quietly and falling asleep until that blessed time.

No sooner have I settled into the unmoving metal chair, than Meryl pipes up.

'Gaw, you're pretty, aren't you!'

She is lying on the mattress which has been moved off the bed into the middle of the floor. The bed boasts a row of goodies, including all the tissues from the tissue box laid out end to end, a puddle of a yellow liquid which I decide not to investigate, Chat magazine, two tampons and a pink jumper.

In an effort to look intellectual, I take out an educational book and open it at page one. I have learned through bitter experience that once you let on that you are able to converse in the English language, you will be forced to do so all night long.

At my silence, Meryl shuffles to her feet and makes a rush for the door.

'Whoa!' I leap up, dropping my *Guide to Crime Management* into the puddle of yellow liquid as I propel the prisoner back into her cage. 'Stay in there!' I say sternly.

Meryl thinks this is the funniest day of her life.

I pick up my sodden book and gingerly insert it into a paper bag which will be inserted into a bin later. I now take out my copy of *The Da Vinci Code* and move my chair forwards so that a toe rests on the ajar cell door, which I can now flick shut in case of another mad escape attempt.

Sergeant Hayes arrives at the end of the corridor and signs my clipboard to affirm my presence. She stands there staring at Meryl for a minute and then takes in my appearance. 'Inspector Bainbridge is in tonight,' she says.

I nod. 'Is he?'

'You might want to put your tie on.'

I glance down. My tie is hanging from my radio-clip. 'Really?'

The Long Dark Tea-Time of the Cells

'There's a bit of a clamp-down on cell watches at the minute. Professional image and all that. Plus, if you're reading… what is it? *The Da Vinci Code*, that's good, that is, I read it on holiday… if you're reading that, you're not really watching her, are you?'

'I'm here for nine hours, sarge.'

'So?' Hayes straightens her back in a manner which suggests that it is hardly her fault if I never joined the Army and am unable to sit motionless for days at a time.

'Er… right.' I put Dan Brown under my chair and my fingers start scrabbling at my top button.

Sergeant Hayes slopes off and I clip the tie back where it was. Aware of the camera just above my head, however, I leave Dan Brown where he is and fix my gaze on Meryl. My arms folded, my chin resting on my chest, I contemplate the five hundred and thirty-five minutes I have left. What was the average human's concentration span again? This question once again prompts me to consider: are police officers human? Meryl lies on her back before me, pushing herself across the cell with her bare feet so that the grime of the floor can stick to her clothes and skin. She is laughing to herself and counting the number of times the F-word has been graffiti'd into the ceiling. I suppose the general consensus would be that Meryl is human, which leads me to conclude that it is a fairly broad definition.

I can see my reflection in the metal sink further up the corridor. A better question might be, can we be human? *Should* we be human?

Like most humans, as soon as I am unable to move or call for assistance, I immediately need the toilet and develop hunger pangs. I get up and use Meryl's call-button to contact the custody desk.

After a bleep, a disembodied voice joins us in the cell. 'Yes?'

'Hi, it's Bloggs. Can someone relieve me for two minutes for a bathroom break?'

There is a world-weary sigh and Geoff the Gaoler plods down to the cells.

'You don't need to use that.' He gestures towards the button. 'Just ask us.'

'It's so far to the desk, though, you'd never hear me.'

He shrugs and takes up my seat without a word.

I consider doing an Atlas and leaving him there for an hour or so, but duty and Sergeant Hayes call and I return within my allotted two minutes and resign myself to a further five hundred and thirty without respite.

Meryl is now sitting in the entrance to the cell with the balls of her feet lying flat across their opposite thighs in a meditative pose. Her meerkat eyes are eyeing me brightly and she begins to chirrup away without regard for the silent staring competition I am playing.

'You are pretty. Do they let girls become police officers? The guy who was here before was sexy. So was the sergeant. Sergeant Sexy, I called him. But the new one's ugly. She's a bitch too. Are you a bitch? I don't like bitches much. Have you read *To Kill a Mockingbird*? I have, it's not very good.'

Removing my stab vest to hang it over the back of the chair passes another few seconds and then I sit back down. My back is already aching from the hard chair I have been given. I actually have to wipe away a few tears at my predicament and can only console myself at the thought of the email I will be sending to Occupational Health tomorrow night.

Occupational Health is the one department in Blandshire Constabulary which is fully devoted to the needs of police officers. If you are ill, it will provide a nurse to give you instructions about booking an appointment with your GP. If you are stressed, someone is there at the other end of the telephone to advise you to resign immediately. Best of all, if you are injured horribly on or off duty, Occ Health can email you the five-page form you need to fill in to be relieved of frontline duties.

Moreover, the department advertises itself as being primarily interested in our safety and our health, which sets it apart from every other department in the force, which are only concerned with Health and Safety. There is a difference. If you're being asked to attend unsafe incidents on your own, find that an item of uniform designed only for Kate Moss is doing your back in, or are forced to sit rigid in the corner of a freezing empty corridor for nine hours, you can leave as long an answer-phone message as you want about it and no one at Occ Health will mind in the least.

* * * * *

The Long Dark Tea-Time of the Cells

I have been in custody for an hour and Meryl has not stopped wittering, not even for a minute. Part of my duties involve reporting the activities of my subject in the cell watch log. I gave this up within five minutes, as I couldn't write fast enough, and am now just updating it every 10 minutes with the words, 'Still talking'.

I hear a bit of a commotion going on around the corner and take a quick peek from the end of the corridor. Bongo is dragging an unhappy customer up to Sergeant Hayes with Becks and Lloyd clinging to the man's thrashing legs. Some words are exchanged, and Hayes directs the group straight to the nearest cell - in my direction. I recognise the prisoner as Martin 'Big G' Bradshaw.

The other officers fall into Cell 1 with their charge and I hear a variety of shrieks, bumps and groans coming from within. Meryl has now joined me at the doorway, however, and I reluctantly escort her back in and sit back down in my chair. One of the many skills of the cell watcher is the ability to restrain yourself from joining in the action going on all around you and on the radio. I decide to turn my radio off.

'He's not happy,' Meryl asserts.

'Hmm.'

I only realise my error after the sound leaves my lips, but by then it's too late. Meryl's face has lit up in rapture at the realisation that I can make noise, and she launches into a diatribe on my beauty, intellect and kindness. This is accompanied by the desire to jump up and down on her toes and display her breasts to me. Lloyd chooses this moment for a visit.

'Oh God!' he declares on coming face to face with Meryl's not-insignificant chest. He covers his face and staggers off down the corridor groaning, 'My eyes...'

Meryl calms down once I have ignored her for ten minutes and lies back down on the mattress with her clothes on. I now get my first phone-call of the night, from my voicemail service.

'Yes, hello, PC Bloggs, it's Mr Carson here.'

I sigh.

'I am calling about my diary which I need urgently from Blandmore Police Station. I have gone into the police station twice now and you were not there. Please call me as a matter of immediacy.'

He leaves no phone number and I put away the pen I had scrabbled for to note it down. It may surprise my readers to know that police officers do not hold the phone numbers of everyone they have *ever* met in their memory banks (though, in Mr Carson's case, I do not recall ever being given a telephone number or address for him since he moved out of the county). I mentally replay the start of the message and realise that it was left ten days ago, which is one of the benefits of having an automated voicemail service. If this sounds implausible, it isn't. I'm not talking about a simple civilian voicemail service, as provided by Vodafone or Orange - you know, where someone calls, you miss them, they leave a message and your phone alerts you immediately. Oh no, I'm talking about a *police* voicemail system, set up by the force and artificially linked to an officer's mobile number. Your punter rings the nick and the operator transfers him through, without checking whether you are on duty, in the country or even still alive. When you don't pick up, the punter leaves a message on the force system and it can take days before the system thinks to forward this to you. It's a work of genius, almost designed to enrage both officers and Mops.

My second voicemail is from Enid Pimento, the Scrutineer. 'PC Bloggs, it's about this job on Ratchet Path. We really need some more information on this one, and you will have to inform the aggrieved that we are filing it. Give me a call when you're next working a day shift.'

I take out my diary and discover that my next day shift is Friday, when I will be in court. Enid's role is so vital that there is no need for her to come into work between 3pm on Friday and 8am on Monday, by which time I will once more be on my rest days. I make a note in the diary to phone Enid in twelve days' time when I will be on duty at the same time as her. If you're wondering which of my investigations her message refers to, me too.

While I have my phone out, I try sending some texts to various members of the team, to see if any of them can bring me a cappuccino or some conversation, but not even Will replies. I shove my phone into my pocket and vow never to text him again.

Meryl is now rolling back and forth from one side of the mattress to the other, grabbing a tissue from the row each time she is in range and lining them all up on the other side of the cell. After half an hour of this, I am again distracted by some arrivals in custody. I hear Becks saying, 'He's been arrested on warrant.'

The Long Dark Tea-Time of the Cells

When someone is arrested, charged and forwarded to court, there is a fifty percent chance that they will not show up on the day of their trial. This can be for one of many reasons: forgetfulness, being stoned/drunk, being in prison, fearing they will go to prison, legal advice not to or simply not being bovvered. In the unlikely event that the trial is not binned, a 'warrant' will be issued by the court for the arrest of that person. If it is at Crown Court, quite often the police will be asked to go straight out and try and bring the person in. At Magistrates, the trial will simply be adjourned for eight months to give the victim and witnesses a chance to consider whether they will bovver to show up next time and to allow the defendant more time in which to intimidate them out of doing so.

In either case, the warrant will be sent across to the local police station where, at Blandmore, it is filed in the Warrants Drawer. This is a place of mystical energy and ancient cases from times when people could be arrested for 'Breaking and Entering' and 'Indecency'.

Every now and again, someone will stick a pin in the relevant letter of the alphabet, and a warrant will be dredged up by a keen officer with nothing to do on a night shift. The officer will go to an address where the offender has not lived for a year and knock on the door until they wake up all the neighbours. The warrant will then be reinserted into the drawer where it will remain until the wrongdoer is arrested five years down the line, probably when they are stopped for having a brake light out.

This archaic system has recently been thoroughly computerised, which means that it now works in exactly the same way, except without the use of a stapler.

There's a pause, while Sergeant Hayes taps away at her PC. 'OK. And what is the warrant for?'

I can almost hear Becks swelling with importance. 'It's for murder, sergeant.'

At the word 'murder', or 'Murr-dah', as it should always be known, a thrill of excitement canters up and down my spine; arresting someone for murder is just about the most exciting thing that can happen to a young PC like myself. We hear of fewer than one a month in my part of the force and if you get involved further than just standing on a street corner with your tie and hat on for two days, you are lucky.

In light of this, I send a person-to-person call to Becks to congratulate her on the arrest. She receives the call on her radio and pokes her head down the corridor to wave at me. I see Guy standing behind her and beckon her down to talk more easily.

'How did you get him?' I say.

'Just stopped a car with a brake light out and did a check on his name.'

I shake my head. 'Did he try and run?'

'No. When the result came through we were told to withdraw and contain him in an alley, which was a bit daft given that he'd been chatting to us happily for ten minutes. The helicopter came out and the ARVs. They were Level 1 authorised, and then his family turned up and kicked off.'

A Level 1 authorisation. The helicopter. A mass brawl. I shudder with pleasure. (Level 1 is when firearms officers are authorised to fire at will, just spray people down with their guns set to automatic. Well, technically, they're just authorised to draw them out, but that doesn't sound as impressive.)

Meryl's eyes are closed, and she may have dozed off. I risk tiptoeing up the corridor a few feet to get a view of the villain.

He's standing at the custody desk protesting his innocence in a thick Scottish accent. 'I havnae done it, ma'am! I know nothin' aboot any murr-dah.'

Becks speaks out of the corner of her mouth. 'He's been saying he's the wrong guy since he was nicked. I almost believe him.'

It seems Sergeant Hayes is starting to feel the same way. She looks the male in the eyes and says, 'You are Peter Robson? Date of birth 28th of the first, 1984?'

'Aye, yes ma'am,' he says.

'That's the name he gave at the roadside,' says Becks, going back to show the sergeant her pocket notebook.

'Hmm.'

Hayes fiddles with the computer for a minute, and then produces a sheet of paper from the printer. 'Well, here's a photograph of the Peter Robson who is wanted for murder.' She passes it over and I see Becks staring at it in confusion.

'This isn't him.'

There is a flurry of confusion, and the prisoner is escorted by Guy to the fingerprint scanner, Livescan, to confirm, once and for all, who he really is. While they await the result, Becks wanders down to the cell doorway - I'm back on my chair - for a chat; we agree that it's all most confusing.

I check for nosey listeners and gesture towards the Livescan room where Guy is with the murderer. 'Has he said anything about Jo?'

Becks smiles. 'Yes. I don't think much happened. More to the point, you haven't said anything about Will.'

'That's because there's nothing to say about Will.'

Becks is most dissatisfied with this. 'If neither of you will tell us anything, how are we supposed to gossip?'

It takes ten minutes to get the Livescan result and Sergeant Hayes summons Becks back to the desk.

'He isn't Peter Robson.'

'Oh.' Her disappointment is palpable.

'Livescan says he is a Jack Lyngrove, 12th of the sixth, 1985.'

Mr Lyngrove is returned to the desk and he hangs his head mournfully. 'I did give a false name, ma'am, that's true,' he says.

'But why?'

'Cos I'm wanted for theft in Carlisle, ma'am.'

'So let me get this straight. Because you were wanted on warrant for theft, you gave the details of someone who was wanted on warrant for murder?'

'Well, I didnae know he was wanted for murr-dah!'

The unfortunate Mr Lyngrove is carted back to his cell to await court in the morning, albeit for a rather less exciting offence, and I focus on the reclining Meryl. Dare I say it, she's dozed off.

By midnight I have missed out on three High Street brawls and an arson. Rich and Becks are both dealing with prisoners in custody and pass me fleetingly every few minutes with exciting batches of papers in their hands. I watch, longingly. Lloyd has been sent to Charl nick to deal with a drink-driver and Guy is 'sorting out his docket'. Bongo is in court the next day, so went off-duty at eleven. Judging by the scarcity of voices on the radio, the sergeant is tucked up in the station reviewing important burglary investigations that cannot wait until Monday morning. That leaves the one hundred thousand residents of Blandmore safely under the control of both Nick and Will, which might explain why Will hasn't replied to any of the texts I have sent him. It is something of a luxury to have a whole two officers on hand to receive the mass of club-goers due to flood onto the streets in a couple of hours.

At 1am, I hear the sergeant on the radio asking for some Friendly Neighbourhood Officers to stay on past their allotted home-time to assist with the deteriorating situation out on the streets. The controller has no authority to pay people overtime, so there is a pause as she relays the request to the Duty Inspector. Bainbridge is not in the mood for jokes and his 'No' is uncompromising. His idea is to put Rich, Becks' and Lloyd's prisoners to sleep for the night, to release those officers back onto the streets. This creative solution is virtually without fault: the number of officers on patrol have more than doubled, and we will also get to detain a load of people for many more hours than we need to.

I'm sure Inspector Bainbridge has nothing in principle against people being paid money for the time they work. And it's not as though the cash comes from his own pocket. However, should he have set his gaze on a cushioned armchair in a top floor office somewhere, he must excel at the lofty police skill of budgeting. To be honest, I couldn't tell you what Blandshire Constabulary's budget is. I have no idea how much it costs to buy my yearly four shirts or fix the pandas my shift have wrecked. I don't know how much we spend on litigation, or printing out those little glossy leaflets you get through your door when your neighbour is burgled. I have no idea of the value of an extra gaoler, nor how big the bill is when our Incident Control System goes down. Half the time, I'm not even sure what figure is going to be on my next payslip.

I have, however, grasped some basic essentials of police budgeting, which will stand me in good stead when I have all my babies and get promoted into the Finance Department to manage their spreadsheets.

The first rule of police budgeting is simple: the cheapest option is the best. A Chief Constable will rarely stay in post for more than a couple of years before either resigning for failing to prevent crime or being seconded to the Home Office for succeeding. This means there will never be any repercussions for choosing cheap solutions because when the time comes to replace them, the Chief will be away somewhere typing up a report that shows how he/she was able to save money during troubled times.

The Long Dark Tea-Time of the Cells

The second rule of budgeting is: why replace something when you can cobble it back together with duct tape? This applies to IT systems and panda cars as much as it does to office furniture. It also applies to forms and documents, and systems of filing. Indeed, the rule is so universal that you can even form your national policing strategies around it and apply it to local community problems.

Thirdly: if you have a choice between doing things right or producing reports that show you are doing things right, always choose the latter. There is no point doing anything right if no one gets to read about it, and writing about it rather than doing it is cheaper.

Fourthly, and finally: civilians cost less and are easier to fire. If you remember nothing else, these golden rules will get you through.

Inspector Bainbridge is fully aware of all of the above. He is also aware that you can't actually measure the effects of pressure and stress on individual officers, which as good as means it has no effect. It is knowledge like this that makes Bainbridge a good inspector.

Apparently, it's the ability to sit on my backside until it gets pins and needles that makes me a good PC. By 1.30am, I fish my sodden Guide from the plastic bag and gingerly peel apart the pages to pass the time. By 1.45am, it's given me a headache, so I put it down again. It flips open, the cover smacks into the floor and - horror of horrors - Meryl wakes up.

Her hair is now a tangled mess covering much of her face; her eyes stare out like those of a roused tiger and she staggers to her feet. Her knees lean inwards against each other for support. She emits an animal roar and lurches towards me.

'Go back inside!' I say.

She blinks a few times, and shovels her hair out of her eyes. 'Who are you?'

The boredom is by now so immense that I start talking to her. 'I'm PC Bloggs,' I say. 'I've been here for the last four hours.'

She takes in the rancid state of her cell and sits down on the row of tissues she laid out earlier. She's not daft; there are now several splashes of that unpleasant yellow liquid on the floor. 'Are you a lesbian?' she says.

'Not the last time I checked.'

'You look like one.'

'Thanks.'

There's a pause of a minute or two, during which time Meryl stares at me with a sort of strange fascination. At length, she clears her throat. 'I'm not really mad,' she says.

I nod. 'I'm sure you're not.'

'It's only when I haven't taken my medication.'

'Just a wild guess, but I'd imagine you haven't taken it for some time?'

'A couple of weeks.' She pauses and then lets out a snorting laugh. She shakes her head. 'I know.'

'You know what?'

'No... sorry, that was Beverley.'

'What was Beverley?'

'Just then, talking to me. She thinks you're a lesbian too.'

I sit back slightly in my seat to consider the alternatives. I can ask, and take the consequences, or I can spend the rest of the night wondering. I decide to ask.

'Who is Beverley?'

Meryl smiles, secretly, almost to herself. 'The Devil.'

Oh good. I wriggle my toe across the floor until it touches the cell door again, ready to boot it shut in her face if she makes a dash for me.

'Does Beverley talk to you a lot?'

'Oh yes. She isn't real though.'

I take my toe off the door. 'She's not?'

'No, I only hear her cos I'm schizophrenic. I know she isn't real, but I still hear her. She sings when I'm in bed so I can't sleep.'

'Right.'

After that, Meryl lightens right up. We spend the next two hours filling in the crossword of the custody sergeant's newspaper with some hilarity. It turns out that Meryl went to university and studied International Relations, before she married an abusive drunk and started overdosing on amphetamines. She gets far more of the answers than I do, and her general knowledge is impressive. Mind you, Beverley gives her the answer to one in five of the questions, which must be cheating.

I am relieved from the cell watch just ten minutes late and am on my way home when I remember something important. I turn back to the nick and collect the weed killer and handwriting exhibits to ferry them up to Scenes of Crime with the two ten-page documents I prepared the other day.

I then head off home feeling rather less tiredness and rather more bum-numbness than is usual for that time of the morning.

I would not go so far as to say that I have had a good night, but dealing with Meryl has made a nice change from the truly mad things in this world, such as Crime Management.

11

Race, Hate and Precrime

BLANDMORE MAGISTRATES Court: that most hallowed of recreation spots for all manner of reprobates. It is the one place in Blandmore where offenders of any age and race can hang out together with absolutely no fear of the legal system interfering with their fun.

I jog up the stairs between rows of be-hoodied figures, holding my jacket around myself to hide my uniform. The police and prosecution room is full of people: three officers from Charl, two from another team at Blandmore, and four or five civilians sitting nervously on their hands and waiting for their cases to be called. As I squeeze onto a seat, I see Jamie Lewis, the kid I arrested last year for criminal damage, gawking through the glass at us. He is trying to catch the gaze of a girl in the corner, but she is studiously staring at her hands.

The Witness Care lady takes down my name and the case I am there for, then ticks her sheet with a flourish. 'We're still waiting for the victim at the moment.'

The victim is Lisa Perril.

If you know anything about the Criminal Justice System, you are now hurling this book into the nearest bin and describing it to your friends as pure fiction, for the mere suggestion that a case could get to court within three months of the incident.

Unfortunately, your reaction has been premature: I am not in court for the beating of Lisa Perril on 18th February, nor for her stabbing on the 25th of that same month. I am here to give evidence in the case of R v Wayne Perril from 3rd April 2005, which is apparently some kind of common assault. I have no idea what my involvement might have been in the case, but I close my eyes and wait patiently to find out.

By 10.30am, there should be five trials getting underway. This is quite some feat, given that Blandmore Magistrates only has three courtrooms.

It is this issue that has caused a delay and the ushers and lawyers have been yo-yoing between rooms for over half an hour. I have been told twice that I can go home, only to be told that they are giving Lisa ten more minutes. Finally, it is decided that the Charl case will go ahead and I should return this afternoon having established whether or not Lisa intends to come.

'I hate to be negative, but I don't think she will,' I say to the CPS lawyer. 'She was arrested last week with Wayne and they're still very much together.'

The lawyer sighs, and prepares to convey this news back to court. Meanwhile, one of the Charl officers points out that two of their three witnesses have not arrived either, and that the Officer in the Case, who was supposed to bring a quantity of drugs and weaponry with him, has been taken ill. No-one else knows where the exhibits are.

The lawyer frowns deeply and looks at the other two Blandmore officers. 'How about your case? Which one is it?'

'R v Roister and Cox.'

'Ah yes.' The lawyer looks down at his file, 'I think they'll probably change their plea to guilty.'

'When will we know?'

'They won't change their plea until they know whether or not the trial is going to go ahead. At the moment it's listed for four hours, so we probably won't fit it in.'

'But if they plead guilty, it'll take five minutes and we can go home. And him.' The PC gestures to one of the civilians, an older man clutching a few sheets of statement paper and some photographs.

'Their legal advisor won't recommend a guilty plea if there's a chance to adjourn the trial, because a later trial means some of the witnesses might not show up.'

'Even if they've told him they're guilty?'

The lawyer just shrugs and goes to re-negotiate the day's work, leaving the room thick with frustration.

By 11.30am, one of the trials has been adjourned as no witnesses at all have appeared, and a second has been put back to the afternoon and its witnesses sent out shopping for a few hours. A trial actually begins in Court 2, and one lucky civilian gets called in to give evidence. Still I wait. I have now read all of the magazines on offer. I read most of them six months ago.

Finally, 12pm ticks around and the lawyer reappears. 'Right,' he says. 'We've decided not to summons Lisa Perril against her will, so the case is going to be dropped.'

I've already zipped up my coat, and I wend my way home gloomily. This farce will undoubtedly be repeated later in the year when Wayne appears over the stabbing and the robbery for which I've also arrested him. On the plus side, maybe the cases will fall when I should be working a night shift, and I'll effectively get two days off for each of them.

* * * * *

On Saturday I'm the Crap Car. My first duty for the day is to call up the Crap Assignment Officer and obtain my missions for the day.

The Crap Assignment Officer works in the Quality Service Department, and he is the person who actually sends police officers to the Crap jobs.

Today the CAO is James. I know nothing more about James than the fact that he saw fit to apply to a civilian department in the police force, or possibly was head-hunted for the job, but I hate him all the same.

'Good morning, PC Bloggs,' he says, cheerfully. 'I have a lovely Racist Incident for you today.'

It has come to my attention over the years that some police officers hate attending racist incidents. I cannot understand this attitude. Race hate crime is a serious business.

To place this in context, the Stephen Lawrence Inquiry defined a racist incident as, 'Any incident which is perceived to be racist by the victim or any other person.' This definition has now been adopted by all police forces to prove that they aren't sweeping racism under the carpet.

This means that if anyone mentions Racism when I attend their report, the crime is elevated from just requiring a crime reference number to needing a full statement from the victim, a Racist Incident Form, a checklist, and a signature from a supervising officer.

A racist incident can be identified as such by anyone, and frequently is. This is a good thing because, whilst we police officers love to do all the extra paperwork brought on by the naming of a Racist Incident, we are not always very good at identifying them, and we have to be helped out by others. For example, the control room operator. It may appear that he is just a civilian sitting in a room 48 miles from where a given incident took place, but in fact he is capable of sensing Racism through the telephone line. Other parties who are excellent at spotting Racism are random passers-by with no connection to the incident. Sometimes we police get too immersed in the fact that an incident is merely a criminal offence, and it helps to have it pointed out to us that one or other of the parties is not white.

Likewise, the attitude of groaning when sent to a Racist Incident is misplaced. Now that the police force is no longer full of the Ku Klux Klan and has wiped bigotry out of its staff, we can go about our work with a happy heart. We should jump at the chance to fill in a checklist which is going to eradicate prejudice and hate. When I see an officer taking a five page statement for a job which should never have been a police matter, I thrill with the anticipation of world peace. And yet some of my colleagues have no faith in the methods used to tackle this scourge of society! It's as if they somehow feel that these important procedures and forms bear no relation to the deep-seated grudges and bad feeling circulating in the souls of the masses!

The only thing I can put it down to is that Racism just isn't talked about enough in our training. More about training shortly.

Having considered the mighty ramifications of the incident I am about to attend, I say, 'Oh good.'

'It's just a few days old...'

James goes onto explain that over a week ago an Indian lady was racially abused and nobody has yet managed to go and see her. She is now feeling justifiably aggrieved and is on the verge of making a complaint to my inspector. This is because, apparently, it is me who has failed to go and see her. It transpires that ten days ago, when I was the Crap Car, I irresponsibly blithered off and made an arrest. The three incidents I had been allocated to went unattended and I have consequently inherited two of them as my very own. It used to be that unless a police officer had actually set foot within the four walls of a victim's house it was not considered that the police had 'attended' and another officer would keep trying when you went off-duty. However, it was recognised earlier this year that it is Best Practice to assign every victim with a personal police officer, whether or not you tell either party that this has been done.

I meekly write down the details of Mrs Patel to call her later on, but first I screw my courage to the sticking place and open my docket.

Diary of an On-Call Girl

As a result of my cell watch, I now have a queue of victims to update with the news that I have done no work on their investigations. It's too early in the morning to phone already-angry members of public, so I make a list of phone numbers and put it to one side.

I now open my emails. The first informs me that the latest in a veritable blizzard of Acts of Parliament came into being as of midnight last night. The email explains what the Act is for and finishes with the exhortation, 'Do not forget to visit the Development Centre to complete your online training!'

I recall some strange references to this particular Act over recent weeks, with colleagues warning me that its advent would split asunder the very fabric of the police-crime continuum. It will no doubt mean that a number of offences I am used to arresting people for will not exist any more, and will be replaced by ones that have longer names. I am fully in favour of the barrowload of legislation brought in by recent governments and enjoy the daily task of trying not to do anything illegal by accident. With any luck, this one will involve the need to fill in a brand new colourful form of some description.

Dutifully, I click onto the icon for the Development Centre, but the server is down, so the continuum will have to continue as before for a while longer and I will just have to hope that I don't arrest anyone for an offence that doesn't exist any more before I manage to complete the training. I wonder if I am secretly very old indeed and just look young, or whether it is true that, within recent memory, training was delivered by a teacher in a classroom, and not by an online workbook?

I lean back in my seat with an odd sense of listlessness. It is still before 8am, which means there is absolutely no work to do, short of arresting someone on a warrant. A quick phone-call to custody confirms that not only are all the cells full, but the courts are on strike today and will not be accepting anyone on a warrant or anything else.

My eye falls on my pile of video-tapes. In short order, I am snug in Interview Room 2 with a cup of tea and images of a petrol station forecourt. A car draws in. A male gets out. He appears to fill up with petrol. He enters the shop. He returns. He drives away. End reel. It all seems strangely familiar. I insert the third video and watch exactly the same sequence again. It appears that my worst fears are confirmed: not only have I been sent ten copies of exactly the same footage, but the footage shown does not provide any evidence of any crime whatsoever.

Moreover, I am not investigating any incidents involving petrol station forecourts and have not done so for as long as I can remember.

The sack of videos comes with me to buy a chocolate bar and from there it is lugged across the back yard to my panda, as Lloyd and Rich have just been tasked to attend a car accident and it sounds too good to miss. Wearily, I look at the space between the shovel and the first aid kit in the boot: can I be bothered to move them aside to make space for the tapes? No. I drop the nine superfluous ones into the car park bin, and spin my wheels out onto the street after my team-mates.

The cyclist is lying under his bicycle in the middle of the road. An anxious crowd gathers round, through which Lloyd strides with the gait of a hero.

'It's all right,' he booms, without discernible irony. 'The police are here.'

Our highly-trained first aid skills lead to the removal of the bicycle from the top of the stricken man. We are then able to see a semi-conscious chap with a gash in his head, mumbling something about the lights being green, or possibly red.

It is at this point that 'Traffic' are summoned. Apart from being experts at fining you for minor motoring transgressions, Traffic Officers are the gurus of all things accident-related and are able to tell merely by the sound of radio airwaves whether or not the person mown down is seriously injured (the theory being that if it is not a serious injury, they do not need to attend). Therefore, if you are the mower or mowee in an accident, it is probably not good news to see a Traffic car pull up.

By the way, nowadays we are not allowed to call these 'accidents', even though I just did. As we all know, no two cars can collide without the malicious intent of one or other driver. Most car drivers are latent murderers waiting for the opportunity to strike, and the terminology should reflect this. Therefore, the correct term for these outbreaks of malevolence is 'collisions'. As a police officer, I'm pleased to say that the government is gradually introducing measures to keep these homicidal maniacs in check. In the past, judges have shown themselves unwilling to jail people for momentary lapses in concentration, but this situation is gradually reversing itself. The next few years should see a raft of convictions for causing death by careless driving, among other new offences. If the offence is one that can attract a detection, and therefore boost our figures, this is a certainty.

Rich and I wave our arms at passing vehicles for about ten minutes, wondering where, exactly, our Traffic saviours are. We are instructed to change channels on our radios, whereupon we discover that the Traffic car en route to our accident has begun chasing a drunk driver and is now twenty miles away with the gap increasing rapidly.

There is also no sign of any ambulance; it turns out to have gone to the wrong North Street and is also twenty miles away with the gap increasing rapidly.

I listen to the pursuit for a few minutes. It appears the fleeing driver is circling a roundabout repeatedly with four pandas following him. Two minutes later a crash is announced and the sound of running Traffic Officers replaces the sirens.

By now the squashed businessman is starting to panic. 'Is there some delay, officer?' he says.

I go to reassure him that help is on its way, or at least, if it's not, that some police officers elsewhere in Blandshire are having a lot of fun.

At long last, we hand over the scene to Traffic and I am released to begin my mission of pacifying the victims I have let down over the last few days by being off-duty. First, I return to the station to collect my list of telephone numbers and inform James that I am on the way to the Racist Incident. As he has no other duties than to dispatch the Crap Car to jobs, it is only common courtesy to let him know when he has succeeded.

In passing the front counter, I am accosted by the clerk. 'That man was here to see you.'

'That man?'

'The one with dreadlocks. Parsons or something.'

'Mr Carson? Is he still here?' I dive out into the foyer in the hope of thrusting his diary into his hands before he leaves again.

'Oh no, he said just to tell you he was here and ask you to give him a call.'

'Did he leave a number?'

'No, he said you would have it.'

'Well, I don't.'

Affronted by my snappy tone, the clerk frosts over and stalks back towards her office.

'Sorry,' I say, massaging my temples. 'Just tell him to leave his number if he comes by again? His diary's going to be destroyed if he doesn't get it soon.'

'Very well.'

I head out with my list of victims to make Blandmore a happier, if not a safer, place. Unlike some of my colleagues, I have no fear as I make to the scene of a Racist Incident. This is because I have absolute faith in the training I received some years ago in DIVERSITY.

Our teacher at police school was known as Staff Donald Warmsley, a grasshopper of a man who was once a senior entity in a CID department somewhere and had since devoted every minute of his day to memorising the exact words of every law in Britain.

This is how Donald Warmsley taught us to be 'diverse':

Warmsley (laying out four pieces of flip-chart paper): 'In *this* corner I have written the words 'Non-Prejudiced Non-Discriminator'. In *this* corner the words 'Non-Prejudiced Discriminator'. In *this* corner 'Prejudiced Non-Discriminator', and in *this* corner 'Prejudiced Discriminator'. I am going to read out several types of person and I want you to go to the corner that describes the way in which you think you respond to them.'

The class shuffles uncomfortably.

Warmsley: 'Black people.'

Everyone surges to the Non-Prejudiced Non-discriminator corner. Phew. Relief that no one went wrong. There are so many of us in the corner that Paul, the blond jock with the pecs visible through his pockets, is being pushed ominously towards the Prejudiced Non-Discriminator corner. He holds his breath and balances on his toes to keep himself in position.

Warmsley: 'Women.'

Hesitation. Help! What now? Only Lena (the token black recruit) and I remain confidently still. Paul, Steve, Graham and, after a pause, Bill move into the Prejudiced Non-Discriminator corner. They think women are less good, but they've no intention of getting kicked out of the force over it.

After a moment of crisis, Prav (the token Asian guy) stays still. Nigel, Chris and Palmer follow the other guys, Roger stays still and Chris 2 bravely adopts a lone post in the Prejudiced Discriminator box. The final two guys remain with us in the safe zone, and after fluttering between all four corners, Shell finally takes up position in the Non-Prejudiced Discriminator corner.

Everyone stares at her.

'I think women are equal,' she explains. 'But I'm still sexist.'

Everyone stares some more.

'Well, I'm not sexist. I just like men to hold doors and carry stuff for me.'

'That's not discrimination,' says Lena.

'What is it then? I think women are weaker physically, and I like being looked after.'

Nigel and Palmer are looking at her with positively withering contempt.

'So you are prejudiced,' says Lena.

'Huh?'

'You think women are weaker.'

'We are.'

'Prejudiced!' Lena points fiercely at Chris 2's corner. 'Get over there, girl.'

Shell drifts that way, tears in her eyes.

'But she doesn't discriminate,' Prav pipes up. 'Just getting a man to hold a door isn't discriminating.' He propels Shell back towards the other corner. 'She's just a Prejudiced Non-Discriminator.'

Shell complies and stands between Graham and Bill, who tower over her like pillars.

'Hold on,' says Bill. 'Am I allowed to carry stuff for women without being discriminatory?'

Lena considers his point. 'I guess, as long as you basically don't have a problem with us.'

'So, where do I go, then?' Bill hovers in the middle and Lena yanks on his arm to bring him into our box.

The guys begin to break ranks and Nigel looks decidedly uncomfortable, but before chaos can ensue, we are interrupted by Warmsley.

'Travellers,' he says.

We pour into the Prejudiced Discriminator corner. When we realise everyone is there together, we all giggle and then a few of us have the decency to feel a bit uncomfortable.

Warmsley: 'Interesting. Most interesting.'

Staff Warmsley then does a survey of who in the class has ever been stopped and searched by the police. Only Prav and Lena put their hands up.

Race, Hate and Precrime

That is how the police teach DIVERSITY and, I think you will agree, it is pretty powerful stuff.

* * * * *

Feeling fully-equipped to deal with all the 'isms' the world can throw at me, I ring Fatima Patel's buzzer. There is no way to tell whether or not it works, so I buzz again.

'Come on up,' says a disembodied voice. 'It's the top floor.' (Have I mentioned that victims of crime always live on the top floor?)

The block is gargantuan and there are at least a hundred flats within it: most of them inhabited by people who cannot spell their own names and have to carry around details of how many children they have in case a head count is required. The journey to the top floor means fourteen flights of stairs, otherwise known as the lift. I press the call button and wait with my thumbs tucked into my stab vest in a very police-ish way. Eventually, it groans and lurches into sight, a metal box rocking slightly on its cable, the door jamming twice before there is a gap big enough for me to squeeze through. The door closes, and I take in the harsh yellow light and the smell of urine. I think it has started to move, although I can't be sure.

As I travel, I peruse the incident log in my hands. Most of the pages are covered with attempts by various controllers to dispatch officers to the address, followed by the reasons why no one is available. Page 3, however, makes my heart swallow. It appears that PC Ash actually attended Fatima's address three nights ago, however he never made it to the door. The code relating to his arrival is followed ominously by the update: 'Please call fire brigade, am stuck in lift.'

My eye falls on the red dots displayed above my head to denote what floor I am on. It takes me five seconds to establish that I am looking at half a 5 and half a 4. The situation remains this way for another thirty seconds and I feel my fear of having no one to talk to all night beginning to rear its head. I turn the pages of the log in desperation to establish how Ash got out of the situation, and find to my horror that the time of his release is shown as over an hour from the time he announced being trapped.

I press the transmit button on my radio, planning to call for help as early as possible. But I'm met with the cheerful two-tone bleep indicating no signal.

I suppose it's expecting a bit much of a piece of hyper-modern police-issue kit to work under these circumstances.

I fumble for my mobile. Of course, the advantage of the modern digital radio system is that if you have no reception on your radio you usually have no reception on your mobile either. This proves to be the case and I am left considering the alarm button in the elevator itself. Can I face the embarrassment of begging for assistance by speaker from someone I no doubt arrested last week?

Time passes. I feel tearful. Why, oh why, did it take two years for Will and me to get drunk and go home together?

As sweat runs into my eyes, I cast another tentative glance at the number display: 7! It is probably the happiest moment of my police career. The lift is simply moving more slowly than continental drift and if I just wait another five minutes I will have arrived.

Fatima is awaiting my arrival with the door half-open. 'Good morning,' I gasp, out of breath with relief. 'PC Bloggs.'

The tea is served in a cup with a saucer, on a tray. Next to it is a sugar-bowl, a spoon, and a plate of Hobnobs. I begin to feel self-conscious about the material of my trousers making contact with Fatima's immaculate white sofa, let alone the contents of the lift floor being dragged in on my boots.

'To be honest,' she begins, 'I'm surprised you came.'

'Yes, I'm sorry for the delay,' I say. 'It just isn't good enough.' I used to hedge around the issue of apologising for Blandshire Constabulary, but now the words positively flow from my tongue.

'I mean, it isn't as if anyone was hurt.'

'Well no, but this behaviour is not to be tolerated.' Gosh, I'm impressing even myself.

'I just reported it for information really. I know you'll never catch them.'

'Oh...' I shuffle through the pages of the printed incident log. 'It says here that you have been waiting to see us and have left me several messages.'

Her eyebrows draw together in confusion. 'I did call to say that if no one came by ten o'clock I'd be in bed, but I wasn't upset. I only really rang so I could get a crime number for the landlord.'

'Right... erggh?' It may not be professional, but sometimes indeterminate noises are the best way to elicit information.

'A crime number, for the damage - so the landlord can get it repaired on the insurance?'

I shuffle more papers. 'It says something about racist abuse here.'

She looks genuinely amazed. 'Goodness, no. I must say, the call-taker did keep asking me if it was racist incident. I thought it was odd at the time.'

'So what has actually happened?'

Fatima gets up and leads me to her door, which sports four little panes of stained glass. 'This panel, this one here, it was smashed the other morning. We've had a few problems with cannabis being smoked in the hallway and eggs being smeared on the door handle.'

I reopen the door and look up and down the corridor. Fatima's flat is at one end and benefits from a dual aspect area boasting a convenient ledge that could ideally double as a seating area for youths to congregate in, as an estate agent might put it. 'Why do you think they target you?'

She indicates the ledge. 'Just our location. All the end flats get kids smoking outside them.'

I nod sagely. 'Well, I'll give you a crime number and let the local Friendly Neighbourhood Officer know you're having some problems.'

Fatima shakes her head. 'Oh, don't worry,' she says. 'They actually gave me the crime number on the phone. They insisted on sending someone out, though I did say it wasn't necessary. But thank you for coming round, all the same.'

Somewhat perplexed, I make my way outside. Further examination of the incident log reveals that the Crime Centre has indeed already generated a crime number. A visit to the police station is in order to drum up some details of this mystery crime report. I can hardly bear the suspense - the way this case is going it has probably been classified as arson.

By 10am, I'm back at the nick with a bacon sandwich, poised to log into Crime Management. However, the report writing room is full of officers I have never seen before, all of whom are typing out statements, updating crime reports and swearing at the printer. There must be a team training day on.

I go in search of a free computer and finally try the front office. Will beckons me in quickly, gesturing for me to be quiet. I duck into the seat opposite him and whisper,

'What's going on?'

He gestures to the foyer, where the desk clerk is busy informing a line of Mops that there are no police officers available to deal with their complaints and they will have to go home and wait there.

'If they see us, we'll have to go and talk to them.' He's right. Mops never seem to understand that we can be just as busy sitting at a computer as we can be attending incidents.

I power up the computer. As I log in, I notice a familiar-looking, lumpy brown envelope on the desk.

I get into my account and discover that an email has been circulated advising whoever put the CCTV tapes in the outdoor bin to collect them from the front office and dispose of them, in line with force policy for confidential waste. I delete the email and deposit the parcel of videos in the confidential waste bin in front of me.

The Crime Management System informs me that Fatima's phone-call has indeed been listed as a Racist Incident. As explained, this means I should have taken a statement from her, filled out a special form, a checklist and informed my sergeant. Instead, I am struggling to remember if I even took out my pen.

It's time for another email to the Scrutineer, this time requesting a reclassification to criminal damage, and a removal of the reference to racism. The email is sent with a fair amount of nervousness: I have learned not to be complacent as to my ability to define the incidents I attend. I simply have too much training and hands-on experience to fully understand the concept of a criminal offence. These matters are far better dealt with by the Crime Centre or, as I like to refer to it, the Pre-Crime Centre.

In the 21st Century police service, there exist unique beings with powers beyond those of ordinary mortals. These beings are drawn to jobs in the public sector and many ultimately end up in positions of power within the police forces of our nation. As well as the ability to act without hesitation on the outpouring of instructions from the Home Office, these beings are able to visualise and recreate criminal acts as told to them down the telephone.

Hence the establishment of Pre-Crime.

No longer can police officers be allowed to arrive blind to reports of fights, disputes and accidents, using the limited tools of speech and hearing to seek understanding. Instead, if you open the incident control system for any area in Blandshire Constabulary, you will probably find a list of incidents with crime reports already pre-generated and the reference numbers distributed to their callers.

This is both ethical and convenient, and I thoroughly support it.

I no longer need to think about whether there is a crime to investigate; I merely look at the system and it tells me the answer. To the untrained eye, some of the classifications might appear surprising, or, dare I say it, nonsensical. You might even think that they had been chosen at random by someone who has no knowledge of the law. You are probably MISSING THE POINT.

I have already described the role of Crime Compliance, there to rein in officers who attempt to sweep under the carpet those incidents where the police are neither wanted, needed nor helpful. Couple this worthy department with the great notion of Pre-Crime and you have yourself a completely foolproof crime recording system.

A demonstration of this arrives within minutes of my email to Enid Pimento, when my mobile rings. It is the Scrutineer Herself.

'Hello, PC Bloggs? About this racist incident?'

'Yes?'

'We can't just reclassify it.'

'Why not?'

'Well, how do you know it wasn't racist?'

'The victim doesn't think it was.'

'Well, how does she know it wasn't?'

She's got me there. I mean, just because Mrs Patel doesn't think it was racist doesn't mean it wasn't, I suppose. But I recover like lightning. 'Um... well, how do *you* know it *was*?'

There's a momentary silence, and it sounds like an irritated one. Then she replies. 'I will change it to a criminal damage, but unless you can provide verifiable evidence that it was not racist, the classification will have to stand.'

Will is now watching me with his head on one side, looking thoroughly amused. That's the problem with more experienced officers: they treat all this Crime Managing stuff as a joke and just go along with what the Scrutineer wants.

I swivel my chair to face away from him and refuse to succumb. 'Verifiable evidence that it was not racist? Like what?'

'Perhaps if we knew the motives of the offender?' Said as though talking to a small child, or an idiot.

'Perhaps if we knew who the offender *was*, I could arrest him or her and find out. Do *you* know who the offender was?'

'Now, now, PC Bloggs, I know it seems pernickety, but we have to abide by ethical crime recording rules.'

'But if it's racist, I have to do a report to the Hate Crime Unit. I can't do that because the victim doesn't think it's racist. So the report will just say that it isn't racist, in which case why am I sending it to them?'

'Well, I'm afraid that's just the way it is.'

'But...' I am starting to doubt my sanity. 'How did it become a racist incident in the first place? The victim doesn't think it is, for goodness' sake.'

'If someone perceives it to be racist, then it is.'

'It looks like the only person who perceives it to be racist is the Crime Centre.'

'Well, that is 'someone'.'

'Look, this is just some kids chucking stuff at a door. It's antisocial, it's annoying and I'd love to arrest the little blighters if I knew who they were, but it isn't racist.'

'That's your view.'

'Fine... can we just file it then?'

'Not without the report to the Hate Crime Unit. It won't get through Crime Compliance.'

'Fine, I'll do the report.' The call ends.

Will chuckles to himself and I give him a violent glare.

'Don't take it so seriously, Bloggsy.'

'It *is* serious,' I say. 'It's so, so serious.'

Will puts his hands up in surrender and we carry on Crime Managing in silence.

In Great Britain there are people who think crime is spiralling out of control. Who think that police forces and officers are fiddling the figures to reduce the appearance of violence and racism.

For those people I have some good news: Blandshire Constabulary is doing the exact opposite.

12

Missing .

ON 7TH JULY 2005, I worked a night shift. I came home and briefly switched on the news to see that the London Underground had come to a jarring halt over some kind of faulty fuse.

When I woke up, the faulty fuse turned out to have been a team of suicide bombers.

For the next three months, people came up to me and said, 'You must be awfully busy at the moment, with all the troubles.'

I would nod sagely and agree that I was, indeed, awfully busy. Blandmore town centre being the United Kingdom's hub of international trade and politics, we were hit with an outbreak of Terror in the form of flour smeared on post-boxes and children's backpacks left in restaurants. Every other town in the country was the same.

In actual fact, I contributed in no way whatsoever to the investigation into the London Bombings. I may even have hindered it, by continuing to attend robberies, assaults and shopliftings without any regard for the magnitude of worldwide events.

One positive thing that came out of the Bombings was emails like this:

From: Jack Bauer, Counter-Terrorist Unit, Blandshire Constabulary
To: All officers and staff, Blandshire Constabulary
Subject: Terrorism
Officers attending incidents involving suspicious packages should adhere rigidly to force policy: on receiving a call, Operation Sapper should be informed (if there really is an Op Sapper anywhere in the UK, sorry - I made this name up).

Operation Sapper will advise the officer of the protocol. In most cases, the caller should be advised that the police are taking no action and it is really up to them to deal with the problem.

On occasions when an officer does attend, the package should be examined. If the package contains white powder, this is a possible ANTHRAX attack. In which case the officer should forensically seal the item and isolate it from public contact. (An example of this might be wrapping it in Clingfilm and putting it in the bin.)

If the item turns out to be suspicious, the officer should inform Operation Sapper who will send a specialist unit to assess the scene.

Officers should bear in mind that it might be an idea to move away from the package before using their personal radio to transmit a signal. Operation Sapper can provide no guidance on how far away it might be an idea to move.

OK, you had to read between the lines a bit, but that was the gist. I can safely say that this sort of advice has saved my life on no less than zero occasions.

It is now Monday. In my job, this brings no more groans than any other day of the week. Indeed, the day begins sweetly enough with my being wrapped up in a big fluorescent ribbon and sent forth into the town to Reassure the Public.

We have to go out of the side door, as the front counter is closed with police tape across the doors. The sergeant informs me that someone walked in and slit her wrists in the centre of the foyer yesterday. It is being investigated as a possible complaint against police.

An hour of foot patrol later, Will and I are in full Reassurance mode, just in time for the shops to actually open at 10am. We have traversed the pedestrian zone four times and seen absolutely nobody in fear of crime, which is surely a sign that we are doing our job well. In fact, we have seen absolutely nobody whatsoever, which is an even better sign.

'I hate foot patrol,' I moan.

'But why?' He is genuinely amazed. 'It's real police work.'

'That's fine and dandy, but I have twelve jobs in my docket and could do with some time to go and do the enquiries for them all.'

He shrugs. 'Yes, but if you go back inside you'll be sent out to another incident, and you'll collect another investigation.'

His logic is infallible.

'So you think we should go out on foot all the time?'

'Oh no,' he says. 'If we did that, there wouldn't be enough people to go to all the fights and murders. They'd have to do something drastic, like recruiting more police officers.'

'Now you're just being silly.'

We walk on with an air of friendly amusement.

You may find it hard to believe, but despite recent developments in our personal lives, Will and I actually manage to make our way about town without diving into doorways to feel each other up. That's just how professional we are. I have cast the occasional sneaky glance at him, though, and for that I am ashamed.

At 10.05am, however, our rambling is interrupted by a flustered young woman.

'Have you seen my son?' she gasps.

As I have seen no-one, this doesn't take much considering. 'No, why?'

'He's missing.'

'How old is he?'

'Four. He's called Ali.'

This calls for my pocketbook. I record a description of the toddler and broadcast it over my radio for everyone to be aware of.

'Where did you last see him?' I say.

'By the train station.' She waves her arm in that general direction. 'He was right behind me. We walked down from the Porle on the way to his nursery school. Then I turned around and he was gone.'

'Can you show us where exactly?' I begin to tread towards the station, but the woman is hovering.

'Well...'

'Yes?'

'Well, I need to get on, really.'

'*Get on?*'

'I'm late for the hairdressers.'

My confusion must show on my face, for she produces a mobile phone and elaborates. 'I'll just be round the corner at Chanterelle's Hair and Beauty. If I give you my number, can you tell me if you find him?'

I dumbly record the woman's name and phone number and I'm so taken aback that I don't even ask for her address. I watch as she strides away. Even Will is speechless and there is silence on the airwaves when I update Control. The two of us linger, bemusedly, in the centre of the High Street, and then I shrug.

'I suppose we'd better look for him.'

We split up and perform spiral arcs from the train station, thinking that it would help if we had some idea where the child had been coming from and where exactly he was last seen. As I walk, my phone bleeps and I discover that I have a voicemail. I listen to it and find that Mr Carson is again requesting his diary back; he's polite enough, but he sounds like a man struggling to hold back a tide of anger and frustration. Once again, he leaves no contact details whatsoever, giving me no choice but to delete the message without doing anything. I make a mental note to put a sign up in the front office for staff to chain him to a pipe and run to get me if he surfaces.

At 11.30am, the sergeant sends me to re-contact the child's mother to see whether she has gone for layers or a bob. I locate Chanterelle's and find three apprentices leaning on the counter and absolutely nobody having their hair done, nor any sign that they have been recently. Enquiries reveal that the woman left an hour ago and didn't mention a missing child.

I'm starting to wonder whether she was having us on, when suddenly the controller directs me to Lisson Park Zoo where a Mop has found a small child trying to get into the giraffe enclosure.

Ali is a pretty little boy, with tight curls and big eyes, and is unaware that he is missing when I pick him up. I set off towards the police station in the unfamiliar condition of having a toddler sitting on my hip. Passers-by are entranced, CCTV is monitoring, and Ali is starting to cry.

We arrive at the nick and I set about trying to find his mum. Cursing myself for failing to take her address, I telephone the number she gave me. It rings out. A check on her name fails to elicit an address or landline number. What am I going to do? It finally occurs to me that the boy himself might be able to shed some light on his identity. By now, he's sobbing pitiably.

'Hey, mate,' I begin.

He stops crying and blinks at me.

'Where do you live?' I say.

He chews his fist contemplatively and then points to my shoulder.

'No, you don't live there. What's your address?'

Again he points fiercely at my shoulder and I suddenly twig that he means the '3' on my epaulette badge number.

'You live at number 3?'

He nods.

'Which road?'

The answer is an expressive shrug.

'Well, that's a start, I suppose.'

I sit bouncing him on my knee and trying to work out what to do next, when out of the window I suddenly spot his mother. She's sauntering in the direction of the police station with a couple of bags of shopping. There's no noticeable change to her hair. I dash out and walk towards her, her son on my hip again.

'Mrs Bell?' I say, as she almost walks right past me.

'Oh, Ali.' She takes the proffered child from me and sets him down on the floor. 'Thanks, officer,' she says. And off she goes.

'Whooah, hold on a second,' I say. I'm not passing up the opportunity to give her the dressing-down I've prepared for her.

She stops. We establish that the root of the problem was that Ali had been complaining about her walking too fast, so she stomped off ahead of him and only realised he had not followed half a mile later when she was entering the town centre. Words of advice and a letter to Social Services later, I am relieved of my Reassuring duties and make my first sortie into the report writing room for some car-keys. I hear on the radio that Nick has arrested Warren Bond, our friendly neighbourhood shoplifter, so I wander into custody to find out how many joints of lamb he has stolen this time.

* * * * *

I am still in custody, waiting for Will to find me, when the radio pipes up once more.

'Could you attend the Benucci Foundation. Colin Roach has gone missing again.'

The Benucci Foundation is a Care Home, providing twenty-four hour supervision of troubled under-16s, and the name of Colin Roach is more familiar to me than my own. He goes for a jaunt two or three times a week, and the staff at the home do little to prevent it.

One of the rules of the twenty-four hour supervision is that it is the police's responsibility to keep track of the youngsters who live under it. Thus, when a Missing Person is reported, a police officer will be dispatched to the relevant home, where a five-page description and Risk Assessment will be completed. This is actually the most crucial part of the whole process, as without knowing whether the Person is classified as High, Medium or Low Risk we are unable to determine which rank of officer will be fired if they are found dead. Luckily, we are proficient at finding them alive. Not only do we have the ability to telephone their family members and ask if they've seen them, but we're also good at driving to their favourite haunts or texting them on their mobiles to ask them where they are. These skills take many years to master and should not be attempted by civilians.

Most Missing Persons are regulars. They are usually in care or foster homes, and have poor criminal or behavioural records. They are between 13 and 16, they drink, smoke and do drugs, and they ain't scared of no Feds. All of these factors mean that their carer is under a legal responsibility to inform the police when the Person goes Missing, even if Missing just happens to be going down the shop for a Mars bar. No matter: the police delight in spending hours on pointless tasks, so we are more than happy to cruise the streets of Blandmore searching for these youngsters, and, when we find them, it's always a joy to spend half an hour trying to persuade them to go home without any actual power to make them do so.

Colin is 13 and I have located him three times already this year. On each occasion I found him in the same place: back at the Foundation sitting in front of the television.

This time, we are shown in by Carlita, one of the live-in carers. She makes me a cup of tea and apologises for having to call us out.

'So,' I say. 'Why did he go this time?'

'He went for some fags. We usually let him have one after doing his homework, but he wanted one now. So he just left.'

I look at the front door, a sturdy-looking PVC thing with two bolts. 'How did he get out?'

'He opened the door.'

'Did anyone try to stop him?'

'We aren't allowed to do that!' She looks horrified at the suggestion. 'If they become violent, we retreat.'

'But couldn't you just lock the door?'

'We don't lock them in,' she says. 'That might make them violent.'

Perhaps I have misunderstood the nature of the Foundation. I ask for a recap. 'Why are kids here again?'

'High risk offenders. Most of them have committed rapes or sexual assaults on younger kids. Colin raped a younger boy last year.'

'And they aren't in prison because... ?'

'Well, most of them were also abused as kids,' Carlita explains. 'They're not even sixteen, so it wouldn't be fair to just chuck them in jail and throw away the key. They're mixed-up kids.'

Missing

'So let me get this straight: you have a house full of boys who have been victims of sexual assault, living in a house with boys who have committed sexual assaults?'

'Well, they aren't allowed in each others' rooms.'

Colin is under a Supervision Order from the court and Carlita shows me the Order. It lays down in no uncertain terms that Colin is to stay indoors at the Benucci Foundation all day, except when escorted to school and back by staff or taken on outings authorised by staff. He is to abide by the rules of the house and is not allowed to be rude or threatening or to assault anyone.

'So he breaks this Order every time he goes storming out?' I ask.

She nods. 'If he does it again he'll be put in a high security home.'

Will takes out the paperwork. 'He's done it… let's see… 30 times in the last three months.'

Sadly, this is no exaggeration. Colin and others like him really exist, as do their records of going 'missing'.

She shrugs. 'Well, like I say. One of these days he'll be put in high security.'

I shake my head, and go to look for the little ragamuffin. First stop, the park. As we drive into the park our car is surrounded by a gaggle of ten-year-old boys in school uniform and we chat to them for five minutes. On leaving, I look in my mirror and see some parents pull up to collect the kids. I wonder what those parents would say if they knew that a thirteen-year-old child rapist wanders through that park two or three times a week, untroubled by the court order designed to protect their children from him.

Yes, Colin Roach was abused horribly when he was young. But it seems to me that now he is no longer a small child, the courts are giving him a chance to get his own back on someone else's. Blandmore's only real hope is that Colin turns to petty crime when he goes on his escapades, whereupon we will at least be able to cart him off to custody for a few hours.

I inform the local CCTV operators to look out for him, and begin a half-hearted sweep of the town centre. I know he'll end up back at the Benucci Foundation by the end of the day, but in the back of my mind is the thought that he just might attack somebody before then.

We haven't spotted him by 1pm, and, bafflingly, we're otherwise not especially busy, so we pop into the police station for a lunch-break. Will goes to the sandwich machine with instructions not to buy anything with egg, cheese or tomato in it, while I go to check my docket - and in it I find an oddly familiar brown package.

Once again the stream of video tapes bounces off my left boot and I bend to pick up the hand-written note that came out with them. '*You cannot dispose of hard items in the confidential waste basket.*'

I stand still frowning for a few minutes. I realise that I was naïve to think that a complex task such as disposing of video-tapes could be accomplished without problems arising. I'm not allowed to throw them in the outside bin, and now I cannot throw them in the inside bin either.

The videos squashed back in my tray, I fire off a few emails to some specialist departments. If you're not in touch with these departments on the few occasions that you do work a week-day between 9am and 5pm, they will accuse you of not being at work at all. In the course of justifying my presence, I discover another message from the Scrutineer and remember that I am due to phone her back about the mystery domestic in my virtual docket.

Will enters in time to hear me say, 'Hi Enid, it's PC Bloggs here.'

He tries to hide a grin, puts down my sandwiches and leaves the room again.

'Ah, PC Bloggs.' Her tone is that of a woman pulling up a chair for a long chat.

'I got your message about this Ratchet Path job. You'll have to jog my memory.'

Enid taps at her keyboard for a minute. 'Domestic... caller reporting drunken fight between her neighbours. It says here that you attended and classified it as assault.'

I scour my memory. 'I don't think I went to that one.'

Enid logs into another few systems as I wait patiently. While I sit there, Will comes back in with Lloyd and Becks in tow.

'Bloggsy's on the phone to the Scrutineer,' he says. 'Always good for a laugh.'

I glower as they all sit down around me to listen.

'Here we are,' says Enid, after a minute or two. 'You went with PC Mitchum.'

'Guy...' A distant image of a brass dog, a stained glass porch and a pair of torn trousers begins to surface. 'Ah... yes.'

'Oh, good,' says Enid, clearly expecting an admission of guilt.

'But it wasn't a domestic,' I say. 'I updated the crime report to say that the occupants of the address had no knowledge of any incident.'

'Then why did it go down as assault?'

'I have no idea. I certainly didn't put it down as assault.'

'So what you are saying is that this is a no-crime.'

'Well, in the sense that no crime whatsoever has happened, yes.'

'Can you update the crime report to reflect that?'

I open it up myself. 'I have, here where it says, '*Officer has attended and no domestic had taken place.*''

There's a triumphant silence on the end of the phone which lasts about three seconds. 'Ah! That won't do I'm afraid,' says Enid. 'Put in a fuller update explaining exactly what did happened and why you believe no crime has taken place, and forward the paperwork to me.'

'There is no paperwork, because no crime took place.'

'What about the Domestic Risk Assessment?'

'There isn't one, because there was no domestic.'

'So... are you saying that no offences have taken place at all, not even a domestic?'

'Yes.' I mean, is it me?

'Right, well forward the paperwork to me and I will get it sent up to Headquarters for no-criming.'

'Did you not hear me just say that there is no paperwork?'

Lloyd, Becks and Will are listening avidly, with encouraging grins on their faces.

Enid is stumped. 'Well, I can't no-crime it without anything... let's see, did you get a pocketbook entry signed by the caller, to say that there was no domestic after all?'

'No, because the caller was anonymous.'

'So how do we know there was no domestic?'

'Because the people who were meant to be having one said nothing had happened and were obviously fine.'

'Well we will need something in writing from them.'

'Something in writing?'

'A signature, to confirm that they don't wish to make a complaint.'

I gasp for breath, for several seconds. 'Right, fine.'

Once again a conversation with Enid ends in my hanging up the receiver in a manner far too abrupt to be representative of a professional 21st Century Police Officer.

It's all down to my naïvety, again: I had not realised that part of the police's job is to knock on people's doors and get signatures from them to confirm that they have not called the police.

I stare at my computer screen, trying to think of a way to make this crime report go away without disturbing the poor occupants of 42 Ratchet Path for a second time in a month.

Becks pats me on the back, 'Never mind, Bloggsy, you'll win one day.'

My team-mates all depart with commiserations.

As I sit there, a woman pokes her head into the report writing room.

'Ah, brilliant! PC Bloggs!'

Vague recognition stirs but only to the extent that I identify the female as either one of the front office clerks, or possibly our Assistant Chief Constable.

'Yes?'

'I'm DC Hudson; I'm dealing with the sexual assault on Anne-Marie Culhart which you attended back in February.'

Phew. It's not the ACC. I recall the lanky girl and her fateful taxi journey. 'Oh, right.'

'I read in your statement that you took swabs from her neck for possible saliva.'

I nod. 'Yes, I hope I took them right.'

'Not sure, because I can't find them.'

I sieve my brain. 'I think I booked them into the freezer.'

'Can you come and have a look with me?'

We enter the walk-in shelving unit on the first floor and I open up the freezer. The problem is immediately apparent. It's empty. Just one lone packet of DNA adorns the centre shelf of the freezer.

I shrug. 'Well, I'm afraid I can't help you. I put it in here, along with a DNA sample from the girl.'

DC Hudson wanders off down the corridor with a deep frown on her face, muttering something about seeing the Property Manager. I am about to follow when a commotion starts up on the radio.

'Making off!' shouts a voice, then cuts out.

I run out of the police station, power up my panda and screech to the back gates.

'A prisoner's escaped from custody,' the voice elaborates. 'All units, Warren Bond has escaped!'

Missing

He can't have got far, so I abandon my car at the back gates and race onto the High Street. In the distance, I can see Lloyd and Sergeant Woodcock careering into the shopping centre, so I run the other way, into the underpass, and head for the Porle.

Sergeant Hayes is on the radio giving a description of Warren's clothing, then police officers I never knew existed begin to pour out of Blandmore nick and down the road. I even catch a glimpse of a detective running, which is an image worth remembering.

Apart from a police officer in trouble, an escaped prisoner is probably the number one thing that will get everyone out of the station. On occasion, even a superintendent might break sweat. Though this will usually be due to the effort of shouting at the PC who lost the prisoner in the first place.

Before I've even begun to pant in earnest, it's all over. Someone has recaptured the escapee and I fall in with PC Champney from the Being Nice to Criminals Department to walk back to Blandmore in jocular conversation. I park my car up and return to my computer screen, now Crime-Managing with a film of warm perspiration under my uniform.

Will slumps into a chair next to me and throws his tie onto the desk. 'Cor, that was a moment of panic.' With his top button undone and a film of sweat around his throat, I'm suddenly not thinking much about the escaped prisoner.

I jolt myself back to business. 'What happened?'

'I was just booking someone else in when he slipped out. There were builders in and I think one of them actually held the door for him.'

'Who nabbed him?'

'I don't know. He only got as far as the front office.'

'Really? I thought he'd be away on his toes.'

'He didn't know about the scene closure.'

I suddenly recall the police tape across the front door of the station, and the suicide attempt that had caused it. 'You're kidding, so what happened?'

'Well, he couldn't get out the front and the internal door had closed behind him. Someone found him hiding in the disabled toilet.'

The rest of the team enter now in varying states of perspiration and we chuckle for a few minutes about poor Warren's brush with freedom.

While the sergeant is there, I trick him into signing his name on my Missing Person paperwork; that means it is now he who will be fired if

Colin Roach is not found. Even as he realises what he has done, the radio controller interrupts us to inform me that Colin is now back at the Foundation and could I please go and lay eyes on him so the incident log can be closed.

* * * * *

I lay eyes on Colin from about fifty metres away: he is standing on the roof-top outside his bedroom and when he sees me he screams that he will jump. I race out of sight and inform Sergeant Woodcock by telephone that he is about to be fired after all. Fortunately, Colin is coaxed down from the roof by Carlita and a packet of Marlboro Lights, whereupon he kindly informs me that if he ever sees me again he will smack my pretty face in.

It is one of the more complimentary threats I have received, so I thank him and record this on the Missing Person report for the officer who will be carrying out the same procedure again on Wednesday. Carlita apologises once again and I depart with the satisfaction of someone in possession of paperwork that is ready for filing.

I re-enter the police station to file it before it is spontaneously lost, and on passing the property store I see DC Hudson inside, remonstrating with the Property Manager.

'But, Max,' she's saying, 'how can someone just throw away important exhibits without checking they're not needed?'

'The freezer was too full,' he is responding. 'Talk to DI Lucas, he told me to do it. He was fed up of people just stuffing things in there and leaving them for months.'

'But some court cases take bloody months...'

I hover in the corridor, but it's coming up to 3pm and I have time for one more lost soul before going off-duty. I deposit the Roach paperwork before Will and I are dispatched to the Lucien Estate, in South Blandmore, where a woman is locked in a telephone kiosk screaming for help.

We are halfway there with blue lights blazing when we are passed a further update: 'The female is saying that there is a man trying to get into the phone booth.' Pause. 'He is... er... he is described as seven foot tall, with hair on fire and bleeding hands.' Another pause, slightly longer. Then the controller finishes. 'So, if you could look out for someone like that?'

Missing

We arrive, and I'm not especially surprised to see the deranged figure of Meryl Chance inside the old style red phone box. She's holding the edge of the door and pulling it as tightly shut as she can, to the point where the tips of her fingers, just visible in the crack, are white. She is barely recognisable even as the grubby figure I cell-watched in custody just a week ago, and I suspect she has been living rough since then. I am slightly disappointed to find that there is no flaming giant in sight.

As I approach, I hear Meryl speaking into the receiver. 'They're here,' she says. 'I said they'd get me. They're coming for me.' She begins to sob.

I knock politely on the door to the booth. 'Meryl, it's PC Bloggs. Do you remember me?'

Her eyes do not focus. She whispers, 'It's the police. They've come for me at last.'

'Meryl, can you open the door?'

She uncurls her fingers from the door and squeezes herself against the back wall as it swings outwards. The person on the other end of the telephone appears to be saying something, for she suddenly thrusts the receiver towards me. 'They want to speak to you.'

I pick it up. 'Hello?'

A male voice answers, 'Yes, hello, it's the police here.'

I reply, 'It's the police here, too.'

'Ah good. I suppose it's over to you then.'

'I suppose so.'

'Just to let you know, Meryl is currently under section at Brookmead Hospital, Ward 4.' Ward 4 being the secure unit for psychiatric patients.

'Thank you.'

I conclude the rather surreal conversation and look at Meryl, who is now shuddering on the floor in the corner of the booth.

'Come on, Meryl,' I say, in my kindest voice. 'We'd better get you back to hospital.'

She nods in relief and shuffles out after me. 'I am an alien,' she wails. 'I've come here to kill you all.' Her hands float towards my throat in a peculiarly unterrifying manner.

'Right,' I say, sidestepping her half-hearted attack equally half-heartedly. I guide her into the back of the police car.

'I don't want to do it,' she suddenly exclaims. 'I don't want to kill you all, but I have to.' She covers her face and begins to cry.

I install Will in the back of the car with instructions to propel her hands gently away from anyone's throat, and drive her back to the relative safety of Ward 4. On arrival, a bustling nurse grasps her by the wrist and erupts in recriminations.

'You know it isn't safe for you out there, Meryl,' she says. 'What were you thinking, running off like that?'

The alien is tugged back inside, sobbing her apologies, and the highly secure door half-closes behind her.

I reflect that it must be just awful to live set apart from humankind, feeling forced on an unwanted mission of destruction and terror. I reflect further that I have some experience in the area myself.

I log off-duty just half an hour late and consider the day's work. There seems to be a lot of terror going around these days. Terror of bombs and white powder. Terror of sad, harmless, lunatics like Meryl. The government has tried to legislate the terror away, but somewhere along the way they left common sense behind. Now the sense is missing, missing from the legislation, missing from our lives, missing from policing.

So now we're searching, scouring our old haunts and hoping it will turn up somewhere. We should stop assuming that it will.

13

The 'S' Word

I HAVE A recurring dream.

I dream that I'm working as a clerk and living in a cupboard under the stairs.

My wealthy aunt and uncle keep giving all their cash to a fat civilian, whose job is to make sure that the people whose job it is to make sure other people are doing their jobs properly, are doing their jobs properly.

Then, one day, a letter arrives from Superintendent Dumbledore and I am spirited off into a parallel reality, where people in society respect one other, school discipline works, I am trained to investigate crime and information only needs to be recorded once, by one person.

In my dream, I have become a *Police Officer*.

Unfortunately, I then wake up and am back in the cupboard under the stairs.

For some, this could be quite a stressful experience; not so for the highly-trained, 21st Century Police officer. You will be pleased to hear that STRESS is not a problem because the police nowadays have PROCEDURES and POLICIES in place to deal with Stress; indeed, they are on the verge of stamping it out completely.

When you feel the onset of Stress, you inform your 'line manager'. In my case, that's my sergeant. He or she immediately informs an Occupational Health nurse, who has training in handling the unique pressures that a police career can put on a person. Occ Health will use this training to send you an email advising you to see your doctor.

Doctors, too, have special training in handling police officers. Their training tells them that a police career can put unique pressures on a person. Therefore, if a police officer turns up telling their doctor they are stressed, they most probably are and should be signed off work indefinitely.

Occupational Health is diligent in tending to the off-work officer. You will receive weekly emails to your work address as you languish at home. You will still receive all the necessary voicemails from members of public and phone-calls from sergeants on other teams asking why you are not present to charge your bail prisoner. You will by no means miss out on overtime while Off With Stress, as the Duties department will blithely continue to call you and offer you rest-day-working with no knowledge of your ailment.

When you do make it back to work, you should expect to work whatever shifts you wish for the first month, whereafter everyone will forget that you have ever been ill at all. Indeed, there is not even a stigma attached to stress any more: the force intranet says so. As long as you do not apply for promotion or a specialist department for two years, you can put the whole nasty episode behind you.

Our training tells us that Stress can be brought on by attending deaths, seeing blood, dealing with sexual offences, or being attacked.

The training does not say anything about the Scrutineer.

Today - the sodding Exposure.

I've been ignoring it for over three weeks now, in the hope that it would go away, but on coming into work this afternoon I notice it still showing as 'undetected' with still no update as to why. This prompts me to search through my various email folders and discover an old - and deleted - message from Enid Pimento.

Enid advises me that if I want to claim the credit for charging the kid with Exposure, I really need to inform the victim that the kid was charged. As the victim has now been to court and given evidence against the kid, I had foolishly assumed that this meant the victim had been fully informed. However, the Crime Management System has not been informed in the slightest and, as you may have gathered by now, if the Crime Management System has not been informed, no one has. This is called Accountability and is a Good Thing.

I now have a dilemma. Should I just record the fact that the victim has been informed, and dishonestly back-date it six months? Or should I call the victim up again in a display of police moronicism and inform her for a second time?

Before I can make a decision, I am interrupted by the arrival of my post. This is normally handed out in briefing, but today it has come at 3pm and Becks struggles into the report writing room carrying a milk crate full of envelopes. One envelope is taking up most of the crate and this, it turns out, is for me. So are five of the other six envelopes in there. I really must stop dealing with crimes.

I empty out the contents of the envelope and out falls a stack of handwritten reports in plastic bags, followed by two ten-page documents sporting my signature on the front.

I read the attached note: *'PC Bloggs, you have not filled in p.5 of the Scenes of Crime forms correctly. Your handwriting exhibits have been returned to you for re-submission, and as the weed killer was too bulky to put in the internal mail, we have returned it to the property store.'*

I scan through the documents and find that page five relates to the serial numbers on the exhibit bags. I squint at them for several minutes until I ascertain that both the seal numbers and the exhibit numbers have been recorded correctly, but a big red question mark has been inserted into the column titled 'bar code'. My blood pressure raises a notch: none of my exhibits were drugs or DNA, so there was no bar code to record.

A phone-call to Scenes of Crime is in order. It takes a few minutes to locate the person who wrote the note. I'm cross, and it probably shows. 'About this bar code business,' I say. 'My exhibits don't have one.'

'Well, then you just need to score through the box.'

'So you've sent the form back to me so I can score through a box? I don't mean to be rude, but can't you just do that?'

'We can't handwrite on the forms. You will have to score it through on the computer and print them out again.'

'Right, so if I just score through this, print it and submit it again, it should be fine?'

'Yes, absolutely. If you bring them up to me in the next two minutes, I'll book them in now. After that the office is shut for the weekend.'

My computer has been commandeered by Becks, so I charge to another and log in. By the time I have loaded MS Word, four minutes have passed, and by the time I have found paper and punched the printer the requisite five times, it is half an hour past my time limit.

On the other side of Blandmore, a shoplifter has just made off with a 12-pack of Stella.

On this side of Blandmore, I am standing in front of the Scenes of Crime office, which is shut. For the weekend.

'Sodding sod.'

I trudge to the temporary holding store for property and am about to chuck the handwriting exhibits in there for the weekend when a thought occurs to me. I pull out the note attached to my paperwork and scan down to where it says that the weed killer has been returned to the property store.

I catch the Property Manager on his way out of the nick.

'Max, what would happen to an exhibit booked into the store at another station, if it got accidentally put in your store?'

Max pushes his spectacles up his nose. 'Well, I would find that the reference numbers didn't tally, and I would send it back to the correct station.'

'So my exhibit from Nutcorn Property Store, that it took me three weeks to get brought over, would have gone all the way back to Nutcorn?'

'Are you talking about some weed killer?'

'Yes... please say you've seen it!'

'I have indeed.'

My heart leaps.

'Yes, I received it this morning and I put it in the dispatch to Nutcorn just now. Just caught the post lady on her way out!' He grins cheerily. 'Have a good weekend - oh and by the way I finally destroyed that diary for the guy who never came to pick it up.'

I stand for a few futile moments in the door to the report writing room and then attempt to insert my head into my metal docket and close it. Unfortunately it is full of video tapes and I can only just get my forehead in. I make a mental note to re-re-bail Neville Saunderson.

Then I remember the Stella shoplifting, and pounce on a set of car-keys. A few minutes circling the streets around Tesco will cheer me up. Before I can fire up the ignition, however, I am summoned back to the front counter where a Domestic Harassment is taking priority over a few stolen beers.

It takes me twenty minutes to establish that the harassment consists of the victim's estranged daughter-in-law phoning at the ungodly hour of 10am to ask after the welfare of her children, who were staying with their granny.

'And how were they?' I say.

'They were fine,' she replies. 'Obviously.'

The 'S' Word

I don't know if she was as tart with the daughter-in-law as she is with me, but whatever she said seems to have led to a tirade of telephonic abuse. I tell the good lady that I have recorded the incident and she toddles off happy enough.

Now, how about that shoplifter.

* * * * *

As I pass the sergeants' office, Chris Woodcock pops his head round the door and brandishes a wad of paper at me. He used to scare me with this sort of thing, but I've long since realised that brandishing paper is actually his main responsibility; it is Nothing Personal.

'Bloggs,' he says. 'Could you go and deal with two prisoners, please? Team 3 arrested them at 2pm and they've just completed the paperwork. It's for assault. Fairly straightforward, I think.'

I hang my car-keys back up on the board where they are devoured by two waiting officers, and enter custody to check on the status of my prisoners. You might think that a police officer could be pretty sure a person in custody was available to be interviewed at any time, but in fact any number of delays might prevent this. The prisoner could be sleeping, eating, smoking, waiting to see a doctor, solicitor or parent. They might not have the medication they require and I will have to courier it in for them. They might be pregnant, mad or old, and therefore simply not fit to detain or interview.

With all this in mind, I am still unprepared for the crowd of gaolers and sergeants clustered around the CCTV monitors behind the desk, their cameras trained on a prisoner.

'Is that Charlie Dune?' I say, staring at the pile of blubber stretched out on its back in Cell 4. Charlie is one of the prisoners I am supposed to deal with.

'Yup, he keeled over eight minutes ago,' says the sergeant.

'Um, shouldn't someone be doing something?'

'They are.' The sergeant gestures at the ambulance in our back yard. 'We're watching the replay.'

She winds back the camera for me and I watch with interest as great fat Charlie Dune looks furtively over his shoulder, then crumples to the floor with his hands out to break the fall. He lies still for a minute or so before opening one eye and glancing around surreptitiously, before Mickey the gaoler happens to pass by and races to his aid.

The paramedics take all of five minutes to give their verdict. 'He's faking.'

Charlie is most unhappy to be told that his ploy has failed, and that his solicitor is en route. While he continues to feign laboured breathing, I go and check on his other half. Judy Dune is in Cell 9 and has been craning her neck to peer out of her porthole at the activity around her husband's door.

Still, she doesn't seem all that worried about him. 'Come on, then,' she says. 'I don't want a brief, so can I be interviewed now?'

Sounds good to me. I locate a set of keys and escort Judy down to the custody desk. Before taking her to interview, I am required to sign her out on her custody record. This is so if she dies later on I can prove that it was not my fault, since hand-writing and signatures are impossible to refute in court.

I wait by the sign warning me that I must wait there to speak to a gaoler and by no means attempt to cross into the custody area where the records are stored. It is not acceptable for a police officer to walk into the office and write on a record. If we all started doing it, custody would rapidly descend into chaos, with everyone working quickly and quietly to get the job done in a flagrant breach of force policy. As police officers are incapable of obeying typed signs, no matter what font is used, Blandshire has recently gone live with a state-of-the-art computer system that keeps renegades in line.

NSPIS - pronounced Enz-piss by us - is our new toy. The brilliance of the system is that it is PAPER-FREE. This means that, at the touch of a button, you can generate a paper-free paper printout of the custody record and hand it to whomever you want. Not only this, but due to the brand new concept of passwords, you can ensure that rogue PCs cannot get their grubby, wandering mitts on anything they should not.

I wait for ten minutes before I even see a gaoler, whereupon he tells me he has locked himself out of the system and cannot help me. Sergeant Hayes now notices me waiting and tells me there is actually a queue of people waiting to access the custody system and I will have to return Judy to her cell and join the back of the queue.

I look around. 'Where is the queue, sarge?'

The 'S' Word

She points at a couple of detectives lounging by the doctor's room. 'They're waiting to run their job past me. Then I have two to book in, then the doctor is seeing Dune again.'

'I just want to go to interview, sarge.'

'Well, I only have one gaoler and he's locked out of the system, so it has to be me marking up all the records. Just wait.'

And she walks past me and out of the suite, much to the consternation of all five officers waiting in line.

Have I mentioned that I am a woman? Well, I am, and after a minute of waiting I begin to froth. The only thing keeping me from leaping over the desk and screaming for someone to just type a few words into the bloody screen so I can get on and interview my prisoner is the fact that it would make not the blindest bit of difference. As a result, I merely rest my elbows and head on the surface in front of me and content myself with some quiet teeth-grinding. You have to hand it to the police: where else could you learn this kind of self-restraint?

Sergeant Hayes returns, smelling of smoke and self-satisfaction, and begins to see to the needs of the impatient. After 45 minutes, it's my turn, whereupon she decides that it might be a good idea to get on the phone to IT Services and get the gaoler's password unlocked. This involves 15 minutes of holding on the line, and then the system begins to flow again. A delay of an hour simply to take a prisoner ten yards along the corridor is a fact of 21st Century Policing and I feel only resignation as I finally get settled in Interview Room 1.

Judy is a delight. She is a petite black woman with perfectly-manicured fingernails. In interview, she is quiet, soft-spoken, talkative and lying through her teeth. She spends 20 minutes telling me that all the witnesses who saw her punch the other woman are wrong, and that they must be liars conspiring to get her and Charlie out of the neighbourhood.

'But none of them know who you are,' I say.

This revelation does nothing to dent her denial.

'Right, well, I guess I'll leave it there, then,' I say, with a shrug. 'Are you completely happy with the account you've given me? You definitely didn't punch her?'

Judy's response is to take off her glasses and spread her fingers out on the edge of the table. The next things I see are two flailing fists as she launches herself over the interview table and tries to slap me across the face. I stand up, my hands flying up to protect myself, and her perfectly-manicured fingernails rake the backs of my knuckles. Blood forms in the scrape marks on my hands.

For some reason, the first thing I shout is, 'Sit down!'

Amazingly, Judy sits. Her glasses go back on, her arms fold, and she sits there as if nothing has happened.

I face her in shock for a good ten seconds. 'Well,' I say, eventually. 'Well, you're under arrest for that now, too. Aren't you?'

I switch off the tape and escort the disgraced woman back down to the custody suite where I announce her misdemeanour. As I do so, I think that it was so bizarre and unprovoked that I'm not quite sure whether it really happened.

This is the third time I have been assaulted in my career. The other times were in the throes of fighting, once in the street and once in an arrestee's house. This time is different: someone has just gone for me without preamble, motive nor any likelihood of getting away with it. I am not at all ashamed to say that I am rather shaky as I put Judy back in her cell. I even phone Becks up to tell her what has happened, and she comes rushing back to the police station with chocolate for me.

Will arrives shortly after and comforts me with the less effective method of standing by the stack of dockets and looking like he wants to hug me.

Fortunately, the CCTV shows the incident beautifully, as otherwise my bleeding knuckles would have left me open to accusations of having twatted her. And there's more good news; as the victim of an assault, I can no longer deal with Judy as a prisoner, so the paperwork is passed onto Will and I make my way back out into the bright lights of the report writing room. If only all my prisoners assaulted me! Nothing serious, you understand, just a light slapping, a hair pulling or a twist of the ear. It would be heavenly.

I am searching for the telephone number of the Exposure victim when Inspector Bainbridge pokes his head in. He is fully 'stabbied' up, the body armour an unusual garment to see the governor in.

'You almost look like a police officer in that getup, sir,' I say.

'Ha, ha,' he says, entering and checking that the room is empty. 'Good, I need to speak to you about a complaint.'

The 'S' Word

I feel a sinking feeling and sink into the corner chair. Whilst numerous Mops have phoned my sergeant to rail about my inadequacies, I have received very few formal complaints. This is due to my innate 21st Century abilities in the fields of report-writing and Arse-Covering.

'Yes, guv?' I say.

'Does the name 'Mr Carson' ring any bells?' He sits down opposite me.

I sigh in relief. 'Oh, him.'

'What's the story?'

'I dealt with this guy over a year ago and didn't even know the case was over. He came in a month ago wanting his diary back. We'd seized it to check his handwriting. I released it and he never came in to get it.'

'And what attempts have you made to contact him?'

'I can't make any - I have no contact details for him. I keep getting voicemails from him but he never leaves a number.'

'Well, we need to get his diary back to him.'

'It's been destroyed, sir. We're talking a 2003 diary. He took forever to come and get it. Max – you know, the Property Manager? He said they couldn't keep it indefinitely.'

Bainbridge nods slowly, and I can almost see the complaint-deflecting cogs grinding into gear. Inspectors have two modes: 'Shaft' and 'Deflect'. Fortunately, I haven't put too many backs up in my short career and I normally benefit from the Deflect mode.

'Look,' he says. 'Can you write a report of all your contacts with him and what happened, and I'll try and make him see reason?'

'I'll try, sir, but I didn't keep a record of all his voicemails.'

'Probably a good idea to keep a record of everything you do, Bloggs.'

'Does that include noting down the times I note things down, sir?'

Bainbridge is not without personality, and I see a slight smile at the corners of his mouth. He leaves me to produce a vague account of my dealings with Mr Carson. I have the upsetting feeling that he is disappointed in this lapse of my Arse-Covering skills, and determine that I will dredge up every email and note made regarding Mr Carson and the fateful diary, in the hope that I will consequently never hear from the man again. As I generate the requisite preliminary cup of tea, I find myself wondering if some kind of laser could be used to trace my writing on the front office's whiteboard last week.

I am putting the finishing touches to my report when I hear the whine of an ambulance pulling up outside the report writing room's window. Pushing the window open, I find myself staring at the lumpy shape of Charlie Dune being ferried from the door of the Magistrates' Court by stretcher.

This calls for nosiness. It takes all of five minutes to establish that after Will charged him, Dune was transferred to court for immediate disposal. On waiting down in the court cells for his case to be heard, he pulled off a second miracle collapse. Unfortunately, this time the gaolers fell for it and the court decided to postpone his hearing to allow him to be rushed on blue lights to hospital. Yet another whale slipping the fine mesh of summary justice.

The Carson report safely placed on Inspector Bainbridge's desk, I manage to find five minutes to telephone the victim of the Exposure job to inform her that the person she just gave evidence against in court has been charged. There is no answer, which means I am required to log into two applications and record the fact that there was no answer, and the time at which the no-answering occurred.

The weekend passes in a blur of logging in, arresting drunk people and queuing with them in custody for up to two hours at a time. If only Mops would get into fights *one at a time* there might be some hope of efficiency, but the bastards always feel the need to kick off at someone who is kicking off back at them. The result is that Friday and Saturday nights generally go in waves of three or four prisoners being arrested within minutes of each other, taking eight officers off the streets all at once to queue up to book them in. I can almost hear your gasps of disbelief, but yes: sometimes we do have eight officers on duty at the same time.

If you're wondering why we don't introduce a system whereby officers can deposit prisoners at the station in minutes and go back out on patrol, you might want to turn back to page one of this book and start again.

At the end of the weekend, Sergeant Woodcock entrusts me with a mission. I have been freed up for the entire night for one purpose and one purpose alone: Drive to Nutcorn, collect the weed killer and bring it back to Blandmore, where I will destroy all evidence of it ever having been in Nutcorn at all. It will then be booked into Blandmore property, and I will never have to speak to another sergeant with a rural accent again.

The foundations are laid for my journey. A special car has been booked - a Ford Fiesta, no less. The item has been laid out for me in the report writing room at Nutcorn, courtesy of a few phone-calls made by Inspector Bainbridge in return for my report on Mr Carson. I have even taken off my stab vest and kit-belt and put them in the boot.

I think it's safe to say that I have never performed a duty so zealously. I do not even stop off for a free meal at the motorway services. It would be more accurate to say that I do stop off but the restaurant is closed, but still.

The weed killer travels well and by 5am is comfortably installed in its new home, making friends with the bag of ecstasy pills and screwdriver that have been lying behind the cabinet in the holding store for over a year now. I staple my sparkling new Scenes of Crime submission form to it and put the whole nasty business from my mind.

Let's forget the couple of hours spent waiting for recovery at the roadside when I accidentally put petrol in my diesel Fiesta.

The following night, I'm reviewing the case file of a job I am going to court for in two days. The witness list consists of five civilians and me, and I vaguely recall interviewing a man about lightly beating two neighbours with a sports racquet of some kind. As far as I'm aware, the two victims and the friends who witnessed it have all moved out of the area and just want to forget about the incident, but a year down the line the Criminal Justice System is doing its best to keep it fresh in their memories.

I haven't slept all day, and I'm struggling to remember much about the case. I discover from a memo within the file that I am apparently the subject of a complaint by the defendant's father, which is news to me, but I do not worry unduly. It is quite normal to receive letters from the Professional Standards Department informing me that some allegations against me have been disproved/dropped, and this will very often be the first I have heard of their existence. Sometimes, I'll even receive two or three identical letters about the same case over a two-year period, each reassuring me that various appeals have been crushed and my job is safe.

As I peruse the file, I become aware of Will groaning softly to himself at the next computer. He hasn't slept all day either. Whoever said dating another police officer was a good idea?

'What's up?'

He has pushed all his forehead skin down into one giant crease at the top of his nose and is staring at an email in great distress. 'I'm trying to get the CCTV of that woman attacking you.'

'Get it how? Isn't it down in custody?'

'Apparently not. I have to fill in a form and email it to Headquarters. In a week or so I can expect a technician to appear to download the clip onto a DVD, which will then be sent to me. I can then send it back to Headquarters to get a videotape made so that the court can view it.'

'It sounds an ordeal. Can't we just burn it to disc at the touch of a button?'

Will shrugs. 'It says here that I'd need a budget code to do that, as it would mean installing a DVD-burner in custody.'

I feel certain that modern computers generally come with DVD-burners as standard, but what would a female know about such technical matters?

I hover beside Will, my fingers curled over the back of his chair so they just brush the nape of his neck. We try to locate the correct email address for the form to go to, but in the end we just print it out and fax it. At this stage I notice my inbox. The latest email is addressed to my sergeant and has been forwarded to me, and it bears the dreaded signature of the Auditors. I uncurl my fingers from Will's chair.

'Sergeant Woodcock, please see crime report BX411999, relating to an ongoing investigation by PC Bloggs. You will notice that this assault occurred on 21st March at Ratchet Path and is still outstanding. This is not only a breach of the force's domestic violence policy but is counter to the new Victim Codes which are legally binding. Moreover, PC Bloggs has not updated the crime report with the victim's ethnic background which must be done to comply with Home Office Ethical Crime Recording rules. Please can you look into this and advise the officer accordingly.'

I think I might actually be leaving a trail of flames as I blaze into the sergeants' office. Chris Woodcock is on the phone, and I wait, seething, in the doorway, until he informs the person at the other end of the line to 'Write to the Chief Constable if you want to take it further.'

Then he swivels his chair to face me. 'Bloggs?'

'Fucking Auditing fucking bastards!' I announce.

'You got it then.'

'It's a no-crime. The arsing Crime Centre declared it an assault when it was just some nosey neighbour getting the wrong end of the stick on hearing a woman shout at the dog.'

Chris nods slowly. 'Yes, I know, I've read your updates. Unfortunately, somebody has stated that a crime has occurred, and unless we can get confirmation that one has not, we cannot do anything.'

'But I have confirmation. Do you really want me to disturb them again just to sign a form to say there was no assault?'

He sighs. 'I suppose not. Let's just file it, shall we?'

'But then we have an assault recorded when there wasn't one.'

'It's just easier to file it than argue with the Auditors, Bloggs.'

'Well don't blame me if my detection rate suffers. Half of my undetected crimes weren't even crimes to start with.'

'Bloggs,' he says with his chin resting on the heel of his palm. 'I don't give a monkey's uncle about your detection rate. I only dream of a day where I can delete emails from Headquarters faster than they arrive.'

So we file the bastard and Blandmore's violent crime figures edge one step closer towards proving the decline of society and the incompetence of the police.

* * * * *

The day of my vaguely-remembered court case dawns and, to my astonishment, all five civilians troop into the witness room decked out in suits and ties. They have been summonsed against their will by the Crown Prosecution Service, who felt it was unacceptable for victims to lose interest in their court case after a mere 14 month delay.

The standard couple of hours pass as the court determines how many trials they can hear today, and which witnesses will be disappointed. As it takes up to an hour per witness, and there are six to give evidence in my trial, this means we have run out of time and the case is adjourned for another five months, to a date in September when the same thing will probably happen again. With any luck, a new lawyer will review the case by then and conclude that it is a bit unfair to prosecute someone after all this time.

I return to Blandmore nick and sit listlessly at a computer. I am considering putting in a few more hours' work to justify the eight I will be paid for. As I wait for the system to power up, I rest my hands on the keyboard and examine the crusted scabs forming on the knuckles of my right hand. I hold out little faith of any punishment or comeback on Judy Dune. I'll be surprised if there's even a court case about the whole affair.

I am feeling sweaty for no reason and also somewhat sick. I sometimes find our shift pattern hard going, which is an unfortunate side effect of being a frail and delicate female. Psychiatrists and sociologists have spent a great deal of time assessing different kinds of shift patterns, and the one we work is rated highly in terms of health and comfort. The theory is that if you group together shifts of the same type, your body can cope better. Of course, it's fine to stick a court date in the middle of a row of nights, because the scientists didn't expect that and so there is no system for measuring it or introducing a target. Which means it can officially have no effect on us.

The situation probably hasn't been improved by the fact that if Will or I want to spend any time together outside work, we have to do it when we should be sleeping.

I open my inbox, which makes me feel sicker, because the Auditors have sent me another email - this time about the bloody Exposure case. PC Bloggs really must get a grip on her docket and learn not to attend incidents in the first place.

As I grind my teeth to myself, Charles Hammond comes in. The Crime Management, Investigation and Detection Supervisor has been doing his rounds for several days now, trying to wrap up some paperwork in time for tonight's Detection Target announcement. On this occasion, he makes a beeline for my docket without noticing me, and is perplexed to find his searching fingers barred by a great sack of video-tapes.

I turn my chair to watch him, one of my ankles resting on the other knee.

Suddenly, he notices me. 'PC Bloggs,' he says. 'You can't have your docket in this state. Look at it, I can't find the file I'm after. I mean, what on earth are these videos for?'

The 'S' Word

I can't quite describe the hot flare that fills me up from my toes to my eyebrows as I stare at the man. I plant both feet down, rise and approach the offending docket. 'Fine.'

Charles looks at me in horror as I snatch the parcel of tapes and blast out of the nick. I storm to the corner of the High Street and down to McDonalds, where I shovel the tapes into the bin, to the amazement of two burger-devouring children on a bench. For a moment, I stand there, looking down the street of chattering shoppers, and wonder what Blandshire Constabulary would do if I sat down on the bench with the children and stayed there for the rest of the day.

They would probably send me home with Stress.

I go back into the police station and discover an email from the Property Manager at Nutcorn: *'PC Bloggs. Thank you for your note regarding exhibit LED/1, the weed killer. I am surprised to hear that you drove all this way simply to collect an item. Next time perhaps you'd like to give me a call and I can just pop it in the internal mail.'*

14

The Great British Public

IT'S FRIDAY, AND Caitlin, our front counter clerk, has not come into work. Apparently she's off with stress, and PCs will have to cover her absence until a temp can be brought in.

Today, I'm in the hot seat. And so I spend the first three hours dealing with a line of irate Mops, getting steadily more and more irate myself. For some reason, Members of the Public seem to think that if they've been waiting at home for four days to see a police officer, one will immediately be available if they turn up at the police station.

What they do not realise is that in actual fact their chances of being seen promptly are pretty much the same no matter where they are; they increase marginally if they are lying in the road bleeding from the head, or wielding a heavy axe in a shopping centre.

It is a competitive world for the Mop who desires police presence NOW. In this day and age of performance monitoring, you have to make it worth our while to attend your incident. Try to make your call sound more appealing by elaborating on the truth. Here are some day-to-day incidents you might experience, followed by the phrase that will get the police rushing to your door straight away:

You get home and have been broken into. *'I think the burglar is still here.'*

You see a scrap between drunks. *'There's a fight and both parties have knives.'*

You have detained a shoplifter who is sitting quietly in the security office. *'He's kicking off!'*

A minor car accident has occurred and you want the police to see it to help your insurance claim. *'The other driver is refusing to give his details, is drunk and about to drive off. Plus, the road is blocked and a child might be hurt.'*

You've had an argument with your partner. *'My partner is trying to kill me.'*

Your garden wall has been vandalised by an unknown offender. *There are kids outside with weapons threatening to break into my house.'*

You are lost, drunk, and want a ride home. *'I'm being followed by a stranger down a dark alley.'*

You kicked your football through a neighbour's window after repeated warnings not to bounce it off the glass, and now she/he won't give it back. *'The old woman next door hit me!'*

You are going through a bad breakup and don't want your ex-partner's new boyfriend anywhere near your children. *'My daughter said she was sexually abused at her mother's house.'*

You just had a fight with an equally drunk friend of yours and warned him you'd call the police, so you are doing. *'I've just been stabbed.'*

Like all PCs, I attend calls like these on a daily basis, and invariably the first bit, not in quotes, is what I find when I arrive. With competition like this, the public cannot expect the police to attend incidents described, *'There is a car with no tax on my road'*, or *'There are kids doing something kid-like in the school grounds'*, or *'I was burgled some time in the last week'*.

If you are not prepared to compete with the mountain of exaggerated 'urgent' calls we get each day, I personally wouldn't bother to pick up the phone. We won't attend anyway, and whose fault is that? Yours, for not making your crime sound exciting enough.

My first whiff of such exaggeration today comes when Wayne and Lisa Perril burst through the door to the police station announcing that They've Been Fookin Robbed.

Turns out that in fact it's just Lisa who has been fookin robbed, while she pushed her buggy through the pedestrianised area.

Fookin robberies are currently a Priority Crime, which means they are investigated to the best of our ability and resources pulled away from other tasks to help. In other words, we have a force policy in place and a special four-hour pack to fill in. It is worth mentioning that the pack includes a checklist. *That* is how seriously we take it.

'How come you had a buggy?' I say by way of starting, while mentally checking the date to make sure it's not nine months since my tussle with Lisa in the street.

'You know, just preparing,' she replies, patting her anorexically-flat stomach.

I lean over the counter and can make out some bags in the seat of the pushchair. 'Been shopping?'

She snorts. 'Yeah, sort of.'

I think she means the sort of shopping which doesn't require money. 'So, how were you robbed?'

'Well, they come from behind and shoved me over and took my benefit money. I just picked it up. They took the benefit book, too.'

Of course they did.

'Did you see who did it?'

'Er… a white guy. In a hoodie.'

As I am on the front desk, I do not count as a police officer today. The joy I feel as I call Sergeant Woodcock and tell him to dispatch someone else to deal with this matter is something I cherish. I put down the phone to find Lisa Perril beckoning me over.

'Oi.'

'Yes, Madam?' I prop my elbows on the desk in a manner which I hope emphasises that I am about three feet above her.

'Look, I don't want to give no statement. I just need a crime number.'

In case you're wondering what is going on here, let me explain. There was no robbery; Lisa just wants to screw more money out of the benefits system, and to do this she needs to make an official claim, which requires a crime number. Ten years ago, this incident would have been classified as Benefit Fraud, which is what it really is. Lisa would have been civilly informed that if she was not willing to put pen to paper in a sworn statement there would be no crime number. Recently, though, the Home Office introduced a set of rules relating to 'Ethical Crime Recording'. The basic premise of Ethical Crime Recording is that if a victim *says* there has been a crime, there *has*. Thus, even though we know there's been no robbery, there has. Officially. What's more, it will require all of the time and resources (the aforementioned pack, complete with checklist) which would be applied to a real robbery. (You must be getting the hang of this policing malarkey by now, surely?)

As Wayne and Lisa bicker in the foyer over the pros and cons of making a false statement, I take the opportunity to check how my filing is going. Of the now eight open crime reports in my name, I am satisfied to see that three are not crimes, two have prisoners on bail, and three are nothing to do with me and I therefore have no intention of updating them.

The Great British Public

One of these three catches my eye, however. It is a Domestic Harassment by telephone, and the description of the circumstances reads, *The offender has made numerous abusive phone-calls to the victim.'* Further investigation reveals that I am now expected to arrest the offender and 'Detect' the offence to the benefit of all parties, especially Blandshire Constabulary.

As I wait for the personal details of the parties to load, my mind is turning over slowly and I delete the words, *'I have no knowledge of...'* which I've typed into the update screen moments earlier. Sadly, I do recall a brief encounter on the front desk last week - the one where the victim's daughter-in-law had made one phone-call which only turned abusive when she was not allowed to speak with her children. Bugger. Brought down to earth once more, I try to find out who has set me the task of arresting the daughter-in-law. It is the Investigation Supervisor. Whoever this new character is, he or she apparently has access to the darkest secrets of the Crime Management System and can therefore set plans of action for every PC in Blandmore, without the need for direct contact with the PC or even any knowledge of the investigation. Some power indeed.

I'm pleased to discover that it is now a criminal offence to be rude to your mother-in-law. For one thing, it will certainly make it easier to get detections. While I am pondering this development, I hear a polite tapping at the front counter.

'Good morning, officer?'

It's a promising start. I make my way back out into public view.

'Yes, officer, I am very concerned about a lady who shops in my store...'

It transpires that Mr Singh runs the newsagents on Boskin Square. Every day without fail, an elderly Scottish lady wends her way through his door and purchases two packets of Bensons and some Tunes.

'She used to buy Wrigleys Extras too, but now her teeth have gone.'

'And what is the trouble today?'

'I have not seen her for three days now. It is most concerning.'

Mr Singh describes how he once assisted the lady in walking home with some groceries, which is how he knows that she lives in the house on the corner of the Square. He has been past each morning and knocked on the door, and the curtains have been closed for three days. I take down all the details and send Mr Singh on his way with thanks.

The old lady is probably away with family or in hospital, but sergeants are paid to say things like that, not PCs, so I duly report it one level higher. Sergeant Woodcock decides that someone should attend and assess things. As the flow of front counter dramas has slowed to a trickle and another desk clerk is due in an hour, I am dispatched to the address with the sergeant himself.

* * * * *

On the way, we drive down the bus lane of the High Street. Since we're doing it for the sake of a few seconds' high visibility patrol, I don't feel too cheeky seeing the queue of motorists having to detour round the one-way system.

Just as McDonalds looms into view, I catch some activity in my rearview mirror and slow down to a crawl to have a closer look. There's a commotion on the pavement outside the DSS office. That in itself is not unusual for Blandmore, but the lurching figure at the centre of the action is oddly familiar. I decide to investigate.

I park in the bus-stop and on dismounting the vehicle I make out the distant figure of Wayne Perril, in the process of removing his trousers. A small crowd of teenagers is watching, and giggling. I saw him not 45 minutes ago, and he was sober then. It is hard to believe that he could have become drunk in the interim, but it appears I have underestimated him.

Chris and I wander towards Wayne. I generally don't break into a run unless life is at risk, as it seldom solves anything faster than walking does. Indeed, it can mean that I arrive in time to take a complaint of a crime, whereas a measured stroll can sometimes allow both offender and victim to disperse well before I get there.

In this case, unfortunately, Wayne is still present and still undressing when we get within earshot of him. He is showing off some kind of wound on his thigh to anyone who will look. He is doing so in front of a sign informing the neighbourhood that Blandshire Constabulary is Taking a Stand Against Crime.

'Wayne,' sighs Chris. 'Put your trousers back on.'

Wayne gazes crookedly past the sergeant. 'Huh?'

'Your trousers. Put. Them. On.'

Wayne adopts an expression of disappointment. Then he leers at me.

'Wanna see my scar?'

I exchange some head-shaking with two passing Mops. When I turn back, Wayne says, 'I know what you're thinking, PC Bloggs.'

'I doubt it.'

'I know what you're thinking: ASBO.'

I'd actually been wondering whether to eat my peanut butter sandwiches for lunch, or whether to get some chips from the van behind me. But now that he mentions it.

'Now that you mention it, Wayne,' I say, 'you could do with an ASBO.'

'Yeah.' He thinks this is hysterical, I'm not sure why. Anyway, he gets dressed and staggers away, so who cares?

Inside the DSS, I can see Lisa crying at the front counter and gesturing to the buggy at her feet. Wayne has staggered in a wide circle and he now arrives at the door. He bumps into the glass, and can't quite work out how to open it. Eventually, someone comes out, so he holds the door open and belches loudly at Lisa. She abruptly breaks off her crying, makes a few remarks under her breath to the woman behind the counter, and leaves. And off they stagger up the High Street. It seems they have completely forgotten the trauma of the fookin robbery just an hour or so ago.

I turn to the sergeant. 'Do you think we'd get an ASBO on them?' I ask. 'Ban them from drinking alcohol or owning knives?'

'Even if we did,' shrugs Chris, 'they'd just buy scissors.'

Antisocial Behaviour Orders are the 21st Century equivalent of chain gangs. Except without the chains, or the gangs. Or any work. If you are unfortunate enough to have been born with the name Kyle you will, at some stage in life, experience an ASBO firsthand. You will have been throwing stones at your neighbours since you were eight and stealing their garden furniture from ten. You were probably suspended from school three times before you reached twelve and were arrested for shoplifting and criminal damage at thirteen. You have reached your fourth benefit-of-the-doubt and your ninth second-chance. Enter the ASBO. No more will your truculent truancy be tolerated. You will no longer enter the town centre where you steal and break things. You will not be drunk or abusive in public, nor will you beat people up for cigarettes. In short, an ASBO prevents you from committing crime.

Woe betide the youth who breaches the terms of his ASBO. The local police will immediately be made aware of the breach by telepathy, or a neighbour. They will rush out and collar your ass, at a reasonable hour and not on a school day, whereupon you will be put before the next available court. If you cannot explain yourself, you face a five-year prison sentence or a telling-off from a very scary judge, whichever you choose.

Repeated breaches will be dealt with harshly. The judge may raise his or her voice and - if you show no signs of changing your ways - you could even face a loud reiteration of your ASBO!

These panaceas of crime-fighting are not only used on miscreant children. Last year, Blandmore achieved an ASBO against a local rebel who liked doing DIY at 3am and then threatened to drill holes in the heads of his neighbours when they complained. He was fully banned from threatening to kill people. On his twenty-seventh breach, he was given three weeks in prison and the judge even called him a 'bad person' in court.

So as you can see, ASBOs are not to be trifled with. If only an ASBO could be put on every person in the country we could stamp out crime overnight!

We return to our car, where I find that we have been given a parking ticket.

Before we can once more proceed to Boskin Square, I receive a phone-call.

'PC Bloggs? It's Andrea James, here.'

'Yes?'

'I am The Monitor.'

My chest tightens, my blood runs cold. Who is this 'Monitor', and how has she found me?

'I am calling about Neville Saunderson. Apparently he is answering his police bail for you tomorrow.'

'Um, yes...'

'I was just calling to see what the state of play is?'

Internally, I'm wondering why on earth someone called Andrea James should care about the state of play of Neville Saunderson. Externally, I say, 'Well, I'm still waiting on Scenes of Crime at the moment, so he'll probably be re-bailed.'

'Probably?'

'There's a small chance the evidence will come through tomorrow.' I hear the sound of keys being tapped.

Chris is now mouthing at me, trying to find out who I'm talking to; I mouth back the word, 'Monitor'. He shrugs, puzzledly. It appears to mean as much to him as it does to me.

'When will he be re-bailed to exactly?' says Andrea.

'I'm not sure yet. I've been a bit busy.'

This doesn't upset her, which leads me to believe that whatever she is Monitoring, she's not emotionally involved in it and possibly may not even have targets.

'Right,' she says. 'That's fine.'

'Anything else?'

'Nope, that's all.' She rings off.

I recount the conversation to Sergeant Woodcock, who nods with enlightenment. It turns out that the role of 'Monitor' is there to monitor people on bail and make sure they are being dealt with properly. This includes monitoring the PCs who are monitoring the person's bail, and also monitoring the sergeant whose job it is to monitor the PC. The information I gave will have been entered into a spreadsheet on Andrea's computer and at the end of the month will be compiled into a larger spreadsheet. If all goes to plan, Andrea's inspector should soon be promoted.

Without further ado, we pull into the car park in front of our destination. The pigeonhole for 11 Boskin Square reads 'Mrs Nigella Abbotsbury'. The sergeant and I peer through what windows we can, banging a few times on the door and calling Mrs Abbotsbury's name.

At last, I have a brainwave: the letterbox. I poke my finger into it, only to find an inner flap blocking my view. I am loath to put my finger all the way in, for fear a terrier lives there, so I bring out my trusty hitting-stick and insert that instead. I've never actually hit anyone with it, but it's invaluable for breaking windows and poking things.

Inside I can see a vestibule. Two tatty umbrellas are leaning against the door, one with a good old-fashioned ivory handle. Further in, the inner door has been left ajar. On the floor I can see a pair of stiff white legs poking out from the kitchen, and a piece of half-eaten toast on a plate on the table.

There's a clue here somewhere.

Of course, the toast.

Sometimes words are unnecessary, and I merely jerk my chin at Sergeant Woodcock to get him crouching beside me and scratching his eyebrows.

'I think we'd better go in,' he says.

'Shall I call for the Big Key, sarge?'

Chris eyes the wooden panels of the door. Like most men, my sergeant likes to lower his head and charge at doors like a bull wherever he can, so he declines the great metal enforcer and instead takes out his own baton.

'No, no,' he says. 'We'll get this open.'

Forty minutes later we are both sweating like boars, alternately shaking, kicking and shoving the door with little effect. My contributions thus far have led to a jarred knee and bruised shoulder, and having far less pride in myself than the sergeant, I press the button to radio for help.

Just as Bongo pipes up to offer gleeful assistance (door-boshing being one of his many fields of expertise), I hear an even more gleeful shriek and Sergeant Woodcock blasts through the door. He has even managed to do it heel-first, like in the movies.

Now we're presented with the stiff white legs close up. The old lady has obviously been lying in her crumpled position for some time, probably after falling down the stairs. Her night-dress is pulled up to her thighs and there's a small patch of dried blood on one knee.

For at least ten seconds, both Chris and I discuss how sad it is that the only person who noticed she had died was the guy who owns the corner-shop. At which point the corpse raises its head and moans. 'Help.'

A further one and a half seconds are spent discussing how it would be even sadder if she died while two police officers stood over her shaking their heads, after which we both burst to action. I cover the lady's icy legs with my coat while the sergeant roars back outside with ambulance requests spilling from his lips. He has just begun his transmission when the half-opened door blows shut, catching him smack in the middle of his forehead. He crashes to the floor on his back, unmoving.

As usual, it's down to the woman to sort things out. Chris rises slowly, mopping blood from his eyes, while I summon an ambulance for the both of them.

The day ends with my waiting in A&E for the results of the sergeant's head x-ray, watching Mrs Nigella Abbotsbury being coaxed from death by a veritable army of doctors and nurses. A week later I phone the hospital to find out whether she made it or not. No one knows. Or, it seems, cares.

I cannot count how many flats and houses like this I've been into since joining the police. There are usually tobacco stains on the curtains. Three generations of possessions are piled up against the front door. The upstairs could be rented out without the occupant's knowledge, providing the tenants are willing to live in a sea of family photos and five inches of fluff. They are the homes of people who still vote, if the bus comes on time. People who think Les Dennis is 'such a handsome fellow'. People who say 'bless you' and mean it. They are the homes of the Old.

They call us a lot, the Old. Whether barking mad or just lonely, they know that while their family can ignore the phone, the police can't.

I think I've been burgled but I don't know when, how, or what's been taken.

I've fallen out of my bed/chair.

My last light bulb has blown.

It's them kids again.

I'm old - help me.

These people have every right to call us and PC Bloggs is more than happy to attend and sit between two stacks of books dating from the turn of the last century, while Mrs Dora Biddles recounts tales of her war-time marriage. Dora lives in a ground floor flat and has not technically been 'Mrs' for thirty-five years since her husband died of alcoholism but in her heart she always will be, as the mean gold ring on her finger shows.

'John had a nasty temper,' she will tell me. 'He wasn't a nice man. Or handsome. In fact, you could say he was one of the ugliest people you could find.'

She will now rise, declining all offers to pass whatever it is she needs or help her up, and totter around the living room searching through a metre-thick perimeter of ornaments to produce a battered old photo of Major John Biddles. I note that he was indeed a hideous specimen. 'But then, we loved each other, you know.' Now Dora will cry for a few minutes while I locate some tissues.

I stay for half an hour and make Dora a cup of tea. By the time I leave, she has usually forgotten why she called the police and thinks I am her daughter Marjorie. I will be the only visitor she will have until the home-care woman drops in the following morning to put some milk in the fridge. Dora has family - three daughters in fact - but they prefer to leave the job of providing comfort and companionship to specially-trained crime-fighters in stab-proof vests.

A general rule of thumb for old people's houses is that the area of free floor space decreases with each year that passes, as if each square metre represents the number of years the person has left to live. In the end, the useable space in the room consists of a single armchair, adorned with a squashed floral cushion and next to a side-table covered in cigarette packets, medication and the TV controller.

That is where the old person lives, in that chair.

One day, their possessions and memorabilia will become too numerous and demand the final space on the cushion. The 999 call will be made, I will come, and I will break down the door, eventually, to find them dead and alone under a heap of unpaid electricity bills.

15

The Bloggs Inquiry

MANDY RICHARDSON'S rapist is in Crown Court on Thursday. He has been held in custody since his charge, which means even if he is acquitted he has served a good four months for the offence - a sentence of which any police officer should be proud.

I do not sleep well the night before, which is unlike me. I keep waking up thinking I hear a chugging diesel engine outside my window and am engulfed with a sense of impending doom. Fed up of my smacking him in the face with the back of my hand, Will resorted to the sofa about five hours ago.

It's 8am and daylight is pouring into my room. Muddy-headed, I realise I've forgotten to put my bin out, which explains the diesel and the doom.

Mandy's rapist is due in Crown Court today: I expect more tears, and a great deal more mascara.

In a startling display of efficiency, I am told from the offset that I will not be required to give evidence, so I install myself in the back of the court and decide to watch the case.

DC Barnes arrives and, in fairness to him, he is holding an impressively thick file. After the usual pre-trial negotiations between lawyers to make a last-ditch effort to halt proceedings, or at least ensure they finish in time for the football, the jury is sworn in and we are away.

Mandy's testimony is pretty horrendous stuff. She sobs for the bulk of it and is three times given a break to compose herself.

Despite several helpful questions by the prosecution barrister, she seems unable to recall half of the incident and departs drastically from her original statement when pressed on points by the defence. When she is taken to task on this, she merely shrugs and says it was a long time ago, before bursting into tears again.

From the back of the courtroom, I am absolutely disgusted that an abused single mother of three, living on welfare and suffering from depression and substance abuse, is unable to give a professional speech in front of a room full of highly-educated people in wigs. It is almost as if she has made no effort to continually re-live the day of her rape until now.

Outside the courtroom, once she has been released, Mandy cries on the arm of the friend who accompanied her. She is apologetic to the point of hysteria about her poor performance. In the end she leaves without waiting to know the outcome of the case.

The case drags on; witnesses who saw and heard nothing are produced to give evidence; the barristers give their impassioned speeches; and the members of the jury blink furiously to try and keep themselves awake.

It drags on into a second day. At 4pm on Friday, the jury announces that, based on the evidence it has heard, it just cannot decide. I can't even blame it. How can anyone decide anything, based on the evidence of a closed door and two people shouting opposite stories about what happened behind it? Especially when one of the two people is barely able to string a sentence together?

A retrial is booked for three months' time, when Mandy will have to go through her testimony all again. The accused is sent back to prison to accrue a few more zeroes on his compensation claim for when he is, probably unavoidably and possibly quite rightly, acquitted. I couldn't be more vociferous in support of long sentences for rapists, but even I can't quite accept that this situation is fair.

Perhaps it would have been better for us all, including Mandy, if we had been more realistic with her and just dropped it at the start. She wouldn't have been getting justice, but she might at least have had a chance of getting over it.

I take myself home. Will and the rest of the team started work half an hour ago, so I nestle into the space on the sofa where he was and watch Ellen Macarthur arriving back in England and giving a speech about overcoming adversity. Now really depressed, I spend my last few minutes before bed stamping down the excess rubbish in my wheelie bin.

* * * * *

Neville Saunderson is not amused. It appears my mental note to send him a letter with his new bail date got wiped off my internal mental whiteboard before I did anything about it.

'I had to drive for two hours to get here today, and now you're sending me away again,' he says.

'I am sorry, Mr Saunderson, it just is not good enough,' I agree.

'All this over a stupid lawn.'

'Well that isn't exactly fair, Mr Saunderson.'

'You're right, it was hardly a lawn.'

'What I mean is, this isn't just about grass, it's about detecting crime.'

'Crime? You mean your figures. Shouldn't you be after burglars and things?'

I consider this seriously. Maybe I should be after burglars and things. The problem with burglars and things, however, is that they are very hard to catch. Catching a burglar means infiltrating local criminal groups to gather intelligence, dressing up in plain clothes and hiding down alleyways, and possibly a good bit of running. It just is not the efficient way to work in the 21st Century. After all, a detection for criminal damage to a lawn is worth the same amount as one for burglary as far as my targets are concerned.

So surely we are better off focusing our energies on the people who are easy to catch? For example, I caught Mr Saunderson by sending a fax. I therefore conclude that instead of going after burglars and things, I should be sending more faxes.

Mr Saunderson snatches his new bail sheet from my hand and I weather a short telling-off from Sergeant Hayes for not informing the prisoner a few days in advance that he would not be needed. While she is talking, I internally formulate a to-do list for the day. I have been assigned to clear up my docket once again and first on the agenda is the Exposure.

It is with some satisfaction that I update the system that the victim has been well and truly informed of our success six months ago. I update the Crime Centre that the report has been updated, so that they can in turn update it with the detection. A good morning's work so far.

Second on my list is the Mysterious Case of the Offensive Daughter-in-law. I take this one to the sergeant.

Chris peruses my updates and nods. 'This will take some jigging, but I think I can get rid of it.' He takes the paperwork from me.

'Sarge,' I say, 'do you sometimes find we spend longer filing paperwork that should never have existed than dealing with real crime?'

'There's no such thing as real crime, Bloggs. There is just Accountability.'

Sergeant Woodcock goes on to elaborate. It appears that it does not matter how many burglaries, robberies or murders an area suffers, nor how much graffiti is on the walls or cyclists are run down each year. What matters is how much of this gets recorded. Similarly, it is not important how many crimes I actually solve, but how well I can explain why I did not solve the remaining ones.

You will be pleased to hear that I do not share Sergeant Woodcock's dim, cynical view of Law Enforcement. It has become clear to me after my time in the police that it is not the System that is to blame: it is people.

People are the bane of modern society. Without them, the cogs of the British police service would turn smoothly. Detections would be generated, crime figures reduced, meetings attended and laws enforced. But in spite of all the new and improved legislation that has aided us miraculously in the fight against crime, we have not yet discovered a way to eradicate the plague that is People.

People are unpredictable, prejudiced, selfish things. Worse, people are different. They want different things. They react in different ways. This causes a serious problem for the police service of this country, which relies on everything running according to fixed rules and procedures.

We are gradually developing a way to deal with this most pernicious of problems. The key to it is catering to the loudest voice, depending on the situation. The loudest voice is not always the one you would expect. For example, when it comes to something like murders and car crashes, the loudest voice is, of course, that of the victim or his family.

But for antisocial behaviour, the loudest voice is the newspapers'.

For burglary, it is the burglar's (they are just 'youngsters', and always deserve a few more chances).

By discovering what this voice is calling for and implementing it, the quieter voices will be drowned out and brute force will win the day. This is known as Democracy.

* * * * *

Before I can dart out onto the streets of Blandmore, Lloyd and Rich arrive in custody with a familiar woman.

'Lisa,' I say. 'Is Wayne with you?'

'Nah,' she says. She seems fairly jovial for the time of day.

Lisa Perril has been arrested for shoplifting expensive perfumes, and is apparently suicidal. Sergeant Hayes, Lloyd, Rich and I exchange glances as she reiterates her intention to hang herself as soon as she gets to the cell, an announcement which is made between pops of her chewing gum. There is no mention of her imminent childbirth.

'Well, you'd better go on a cell watch, then,' sighs the sergeant. 'Lloyd, perhaps you would oblige?'

'Nah, I want a woman,' says Lisa.

'You will be watched by whoever is assigned.'

There are moments when Sergeant Hayes' rigid adherence to policy is a delight.

'I'll kick off if you put me with a guy. It's embarrassing.'

We all stand there in dismay that things have deteriorated this far, to the point where a completely unsuicidal woman can dictate how the police spend their time simply so that she can have someone to chat to about girly subjects while she is stuck in her cell.

In the end I pipe up. 'I'll do it, if it makes things easier.'

Five minutes later, I'm installed on my favourite chair with my favourite Blandmore resident reading a gossip magazine on her stomach in front of me. Her clothes have been replaced with overalls made out of grey paper - a fair response to her threats to strangle herself with her T-shirt. Just as I get comfortable, Lisa requires a cigarette, so I escort her to the smoking yard where we find our way blocked by another prisoner and his entourage.

The two detectives with the male decide that Lisa looks harmless enough and she is permitted to stand on the opposite side of the yard. While we wait for our respective charges to finish their fags, I nod at one of the DCs. 'What's your guy in for?'

He doesn't answer, but the prisoner clears his throat. I notice that he is an odd-looking man. About forty years old, short, round and sweaty, his eyes flick unnaturally up and down and his tongue keeps flashing out like a lizard's.

'I stabbed my mother,' he advises me. 'I stabbed her good.' He lets out a sound which can only be described as a cachinnation.

The detectives both produce pocketbooks and furiously scribble down the man's words as he continues.

'Twelve times, with a big knife, I did.'

An awkward silence ensues. I hate awkward silences, so I decide to fill it. 'So... nice weather we've been having.'

No one agrees, and the man adds, 'I'm going down for murder.'

Once he is taken back to his cell, a detective informs me that the suspect was taken into care at the age of twelve and made up his mind to avenge the act that morning in the manner confessed. It's thought that he had an 'inappropriate' relationship with his mother which was destined to end either with a murder or the tearing out of his eyes, or possibly both.

As there has been a Domestic Homicide, all the top brass are milling around. I say 'sir' at least five times on the way back to Lisa's cell, and another three after sitting down. Then the doctors start to arrive. When someone has murdered their mother, the police only really consider two motives: madness or devil worship. As devil worship is hard to prove in court, we put our energies into identifying the former.

The first doctor is the police surgeon. It's his job to confirm that the man cackling to himself and rubbing his blood-stained hands together in the corner of his cell is not quite right in his mind and should really get some help. Next comes a psychiatrist, equipped with a mental health worker, and they disappear into the doctor's room together for nearly an hour.

I have turned my radio volume down to shield my ears from the wonders of the outside world, but as I settle down for some further ignoring of Lisa Perril, I catch the words, *'Major Incident.'*

Police officers do not bandy the word 'major' around without careful thought. If it is spoken even in jest over the airwaves, all kinds of systems kick in. A policy appears on the computer screen of the radio controller, several sergeants no one knew worked here will appear in Blandmore, and half of the team on duty will be stuffed into a Transit van with yellow jackets and driven fast across the force area. More dramatically still, the Assistant Chief Constable will be woken up.

I therefore turn up my volume and discover that there has been a train crash. I have never heard of the place where it has crashed, which is usually the way with these incidents, and cannot even be sure it is part of Blandshire Constabulary. Nonetheless, helicopters, DayGlo clothing and firemen are about to converge on a little-known village in the English countryside.

In 2006, a marvellous scheme was introduced to reduce congestion on the roads. During particularly busy times, drivers would be directed to use the hard shoulder, the spare lane usually reserved for emergency vehicles and breakdowns. Someone, somewhere high up in Blandshire Constabulary must have been watching. It occurred to them that if traffic flowed slightly better during busy times by using the hard shoulder, it would flow even faster at ordinary times of the day. The question was asked, *Why not use the hard shoulder all the time?*

The Senior Management Team do not get where they are without considerable transferable skills. They therefore transferred the idea of the hard shoulder into day-to-day policing. The police have all kinds of systems in place that kick in during times of emergency such as terrorist attack or demonstration against fuel prices. Officers can be called in from rest days, the army can take over certain tasks, police areas are reduced to minimum manpower and the extras sent to deal with the disaster.

The idea of 'hard shoulder policing' is that you start using these emergency measures in times of non-emergency, such as when things get a little bit tricky. Instead of just phoning off-duty PCs to make them come into work when a plane blows up, they can now be phoned any time there is an unattended domestic harassment. Instead of waiting for a death in custody to bring in shifts from other areas, they can be brought in when there is someone waiting at the front counter with driving documents. In this way, there is no need to recruit extra officers because you can simply double the workload of those you have.

The calling in of off-duty officers is, of course, done with their welfare in mind. An automated system prioritises first those who are due to start work later, those who have just finished work, those on rest days, those on annual leave, compassionate leave, sick leave, and finally those who are off with stress. Officers sitting doing nothing at court should never be called into work, and on no account should officers who have transferred into 'squads' and 'units' be torn away from their strategies, emailing and spreadsheet-compiling to help out, either.

At this stage you might be wondering, if emergency measures are in use during times of non-emergency, what happens when there is a genuine emergency? I do not think this kind of nit-picking is helpful.

I await the call to arms with some trepidation. Ten minutes later, Rich, Will and Becks have been Transited up and three Friendly Neighbourhood Officers have been called into work early to cover for the losses. As Lisa Perril's unsuicide attempts take precedence over a mere train wreck, I remain seated where I am.

An hour later, my eyes flash open to find Lisa knocking on the door in front of my face. As the door is wide open, this means she is standing outside the cell within inches from me.

'Hello, officer,' she bawls.

'Can I help you?'

'When am I gonna be interviewed, cos I'm bored?'

It occurs to me that Lloyd is frantically trying to do the job of four officers on the streets and is unlikely to have remembered about the unsuicidal shoplifter he arrested two hours ago.

'There's been a train crash, you'll have to wait.'

She sits back down in the doorway and reaches once more for her magazine. Behind me, the doctors start to pour from the medical room. One of them is clutching a computer printout; the others are shaking their heads. As they go to squeeze past me, they are accosted by an important-looking fellow wearing a red tie. I identify him as a Detective Inspector, the ultimate of all detectives.

In every TV police drama, there's a rugged, gritty figure walking round with his top button undone; he swears a bit, sleeps with the female uniformed officers and mysteriously goes AWOL in the middle of the big investigation before solving everything single-handedly just before the adverts. He is the DI. He has a flagrant disregard for rules, he 'gets things done' and he is smoulderingly sexy. Or, at the very least, he has stubble.

Not so DI Greene. He is a distinguished, balding chap who wouldn't dream of leaving home with stubble. He spends time in his office, signing authorities to invade people's privacy and complying with force policy in relation to serious crimes. Or, more specifically, ensuring that the PCs on his area are complying with force policy by sending them helpful emails pointing out where they are going wrong.

I have no idea whether DI Greene knew that would be his job when he applied for it. Perhaps, somewhere underneath the partially shiny head and combed sideburns, there really is a rugged, gritty, top-button-undone heart that lusts after me and longs to go AWOL on a daily basis. If there is, it must be a long way down.

As luck would have it, DI Greene is there to speak to the doctor. 'Is he mad?' he says.

It falls to the mental health worker to announce, timidly, 'Well, he's on our system.'

A strained look lurches into the DI's eyes. The murderer is On The System. For some reason, this perturbs him.

He takes out his mobile. 'Get the ACC on the phone.'

I am confused. Surely it can only be described as a Good Thing if the murderer has been dealt with before by the police or Mental Health Team? Rather than having to focus our sole efforts on locking one person up for life, we can now include a number of other parties in our investigation.

For example, any police officer who has ever put name to paper regarding the murderer is now eligible for disciplinary proceedings.

Any mental health worker who said the guy should not be sectioned can be fired.

Any judge who previously failed to sentence him to an adequate time in prison or a secure hospital can be pilloried by the tabloids.

A whole glut of BLAME opportunities have come to light by this one discovery.

Blame is a useful tool in any 21st Century police investigation. It stems from one basic fact: crime must be someone's responsibility, and it's not the criminal's. If your name is Lewis or Wayne, and you were born on the Porle, it's hardly your fault that you started burgling houses at the age of eight. However, if your name is Ellie Bloggs and you left school at eighteen, or have a degree, you have absolutely no excuse for not preventing any and all crimes before they occur. Thus, if I go to a domestic incident where a guy has sent his ex-girlfriend a dozen text messages, I should be ensuring that that guy is in no position to murder her for the rest of his life. If he goes into Top Shop three weeks later and blasts her head off with a shotgun, it's only right that I should be held personally accountable for her death.

Likewise, when officers attend an address to deal with a couple rowing, they should be using powers of divination to locate the areas in the house where children will later be starved, beaten and killed. They must then invoke spirit guides to lead them to the right decision to prevent these dreadful acts. If they are in any doubt, all children should be removed from any home visited by the police and kept in the care of the local authority until we can be certain they are not about to be murdered.

In any case of child neglect or murder, I would hope to see at least three police officers and an entire Social Services department dismissed. It is the only way to stop these tragedies.

Maybe, one day, we'll reach the happy stage where officers are able to knock on any door on any day and remove all persons from within for their own protection.

* * * * *

There is a lull in custody. With a murderer in the traps and a train crash nearby, there will be no more prisoners today, and the ones who are there already will be lucky to get dealt with before next morning. Staring at Lisa Perril, I am reminded of an article I once read about a girl arrested for racially abusing her teacher.

'She had her jewellery taken off her and her fingerprints taken,' said her outraged mother. *'Then she was kept in a cell for over three hours.'*

I can't actually remember the last time I dealt with a prisoner within three hours of their arrest. I tell a lie, I once got a guy processed inside two hours, but then it turned out I'd done something wrong and I had to run after him and arrest him again. In Lisa's case, I estimate she will be in custody for between four and eight hours, by which time it will be the end of my tour of duty. With me sitting watching her, and Lloyd gathering evidence against her out on the streets, it appears the government has hit its target of supplying two police officers for every criminal (the victims can generally cope on their own).

A gaoler relieves me for a few minutes and I wander up to the desk. Being the rebellious type, I have now reached the stage where signs reading, 'Do NOT Enter' just encourage me, and I pop into the custody office to use the telephone. Lloyd is at the shop, viewing the CCTV of Lisa's mischief, but he thinks he will have to attend a robbery before returning to interview her. The three Friendly Neighbourhood Officers who were called into work to help have now been sent to the scene of the train crash.

I log into a computer. It appears that even at a time of almost national emergency, someone has come into work at the Department of Critical Emailing. I delete the two emails telling me that I have erroneously ticked a box on a form three months ago and instead open one from DC Hudson. *Just to let you know that the swabs you took from Anne-Marie Culhart have been found and an offender has been identified from the DNA. He will be arrested this week.'*

I push back my swivel chair in a state of disbelief. Not only have I successfully carried out a complex police task, but it now looks likely to result in someone going to prison, or at least sitting in a room with a jury of his peers for a few hours. No amount of train crashes can dampen my spirits.

'Can I use that?'

I turn my head to find DI Greene leaning across me to pick up the phone.

Now if that's not repressed desire, I don't know what is.

Being the complete professional that I am, I do not eavesdrop on the DI's phone-call, which is why I have no idea that it's about how to handle the media interest in the murder. Or that he mentions the words 'Public Inquiry' twice. It's at times like these that I don't begrudge the higher ranks their pay cheques. I may be the focal point for email after email about un-ticked boxes and my bad attitude, but my lowliness in the world of 21st Century Policing can sometimes work to my advantage. No matter how many errors I commit, no matter how chronic my decisions out on the street, I am very small fry when it comes to the media and any talk of Public Inquiries.

Occasionally, the focus of an Inquiry is to generate a report on something that was supposed to save money, but has not. More often, the Inquiry is to highlight flaws in a system or a decision. These are worst of all when they follow a death, near-death or complaint by someone important. It is not my place to comment on the validity of these Inquiries that dog our lives. They are rightly campaigned for, and will no doubt help a lot of people to understand how the police and other agencies cocked up on a previous occasion. The Inquiry can then be turned into a Recommendation and the police can add sentences to their policies such as, 'we will search more white people'. There can then be a further Inquiry into whether the Recommendation is being followed, and this makes for lots of jobs for undercover reporters and embarrassing stories for chief constables. You can never have too many of those.

These Inquiries take up an impressive amount of paper. The Macpherson Report costs £26 for the average Mop to buy, and consists of forty-seven chapters and over 335 pages. Macpherson could just have written, *You are all racist pigs. Change your ways'*, but that would never have fit with the essential principle: the more paper, the better the Inquiry. I agree with that principle, naturally.

Take the 3,000-page report generated into murders possibly committed by a guy who had already died of a brain haemorrhage.

Or the Inquiry into the wasting of £1.2m on an investigation where the suspect was acquitted, which also came to several thousand pages.

We should hold an Inquiry into every case where a police officer wasted his or her time investigating a pointless crime; it is the Only Way We Will Learn.

The other use for the Inquiry is to get senior ranking officers fired. There is no other procedure for achieving this, unless a senior ranking officer is kind enough to be caught sending dirty pictures of himself in uniform to random horrified strangers.

The DI finishes his phone call, hangs up and sighs.

'Do you think there will be an Inquiry, sir?' I ask.

'Probably...' he tails off as he either stares at my right breast or tries to make out the name on my badge.

'PC Bloggs, sir.'

'Ah yes, Bloggs.' He snaps his fingers. 'You had a good result with some swabs for us.'

'Yes, sir.' I gesture at my open email. 'I just read about it.'

'Good stuff, good stuff.'

I suppose, in the scheme of things, it is fairly good, so I nod along affably.

The Bloggs Inquiry

DI Greene heads back out of custody and into the world of detecting, and I sink back into my seat outside Lisa's door. I am even in a pleasant enough mood to impart to her the good news about her sister's near-enforced blow job and the imminent arrest of the attempted blowee. Every now and again, it is me, and only me, who turns up at a crime scene and does something right, and it's a very nice feeling, thanks very much. (I did say 'now and again'.)

As I chat to Lisa about the likely sentence for Anne-Marie's attacker, I consider launching my own Inquiry. It appears the qualifications for doing so are wide-ranging, and I am sure with a few promotions and a knighthood I could find myself a cause. Perhaps my investigation would recommend legislation compelling forces to monitor how well they are monitoring things, as a first step towards a new and better Britain.

Of course, I may well have forgotten what it was I wanted to Inquire about by that time, or be so far removed from the problem that my recommendations appear idealistic or unworkable. I can only hope.

By turning up my radio for a few minutes, I discover that Lloyd has indeed been dispatched to deal with a robbery.

I come up with the genius suggestion that he relay the facts of the shoplifting to me over the phone and I can interview Lisa for him, but Sergeant Hayes puts paid to that idea as it is in direct contravention of Best Practice. Lloyd says he will fax the statements through as soon as he nears a fax machine, and I settle down to wait.

While I sit, the mother-murderer is charged and put back in his cell. I doubt the morning magistrates will even look twice at his file before dispatching him to prison to await trial. I will be surprised if the same magistrates even look once at Lisa Perril's file before dispatching her home to await her next fight with Wayne.

Two hours later, Lloyd wakes me up subtly enough for it not to be obvious on the CCTV. Together, we interview Lisa Perril and she is charged to appear in court some time next week. In a fit of rage at having had a murderer in custody all day, Sergeant Hayes puts bail conditions on Lisa that prevent her from entering the county of Blandshire.

While Lloyd completes the file, I watch Lisa walk out of the police station and into the waiting arms of her beloved. Wayne is leaning against the railings with what looks like a joint of cannabis in his lips and he shoves his darling away by the shoulder when she tries to kiss him. This prompts Lisa to retaliate and their voices raised in bickering can be heard as they slouch into the High Street and out of my sight.

Before logging out for the day, I find myself staring at a newly-arrived email: *'PC Bloggs, I have today entered the detection for the Exposure of 01/12/06. You might be pleased to note that because this was first detected back in January, and again in March, it has now been counted three times. There is no way to alter this. Enid.'*

Lloyd deposits his file in the out-tray and we both shut down our computers.

Somehow it has become 7pm and there is no sign of the rest of our shift, who have been swallowed up into the deep jaws of the Major Incident.

Due to said train crash, no one is allowed to book off-duty without the say-so of a designated senior officer. While the control room try to locate him, Lloyd and I tread the little-travelled path to the third floor and enter that most sacred of all places - the TV room. Brushing a few millimetres of dust from the cushions, we install ourselves in front of the evening news and entertain ourselves trying to spot members of our team at the crash site.

At last, we spot Will and Becks standing on a cordon with a newscaster talking to the camera in front of them. I immediately phone Will and giggle to see him answering it on screen.

'How's my hair?' he asks, managing a surreptitious wave.

'Under your hat.'

'Just where I like it.' He wanders off slightly, away from Becks. 'You finished?' he asks.

'Waiting to be allowed home.'

He lowers his voice a little. 'Cheer up, we've got three days off once this is over, and I have no plans to leave the house for anything.'

I sigh happily and ring off. Perhaps there are plus sides to dating someone working the same shift pattern as me.

Lloyd has been listening with a slight smile, but says nothing, and we watch the rest of the news report in a tired silence. The shot changes to an aerial view, with dozens of yellow figures clambering in and out of the debris, sometimes bearing little orange stretchers between them.

From that height, you cannot tell the difference between black and white, male and female.

The voiceover to the pictures is saying that there are fewer fatalities than had been feared, and that the train line should be open again in a couple of days.

It seems that the emergency services are fairly good at dealing with emergencies.

It's all the other crap that brings us down.

Glossary

Accountability: There is a lot of talk nowadays about Accountability. The government says it is improving the accountability of the police by things like National Crime Recording Standards and Detection rates. In actual fact, this is only improving the accountability of the police to the government, as it is only the government who gives two hoots about NCRS and performance figures.

The public don't care about NCRS. They don't care what their average local detection rate is. They don't care how many ticky-boxes are ticked. They only want to feel safe, not to be burgled and to have a police officer smile at them when they come round and, later, to have a fair stab at catching the people responsible.

Most complaints from Mops are to do with crime in their area, the 'attitude' of the police officers who come to see them, the fact that they can't get hold of the right police officer who is dealing with their case, or the fact that they have been 'beaten up' by the police officer who arrested them. Absolutely none of these concerns are addressed by NCRS or performance figures.

They should be addressed by local sergeants, inspectors and area commanders. Unfortunately all these people are too busy accounting for themselves to the government.

Arse-Covering: In this 21st Century culture of blame, everything is someone's fault. As the police have responsibility for just about everything, from crime to social issues, this means everything is the police's fault. If the government can possibly hang someone out to dry as a result of a murder, bomb or flood, they will.

The only way to avoid falling prey to blame is to Cover your Arse everywhere you go. This involves making audit trails of every contact you have with every victim. You should record it every time you use handcuffs or shout at someone. You should follow Best Practice rigidly, even lunatic corners are begging to sensible high heaven to be cut. Hence the phrase, 'I'm sorry, I'm just doing my job.'

This extends to the field of prosecution, where police and lawyers are faced with the decision whether or not to charge someone based on the evidence. If they fail to prosecute, and the person later murders their victim, or goes out and rapes a child, someone, somewhere, will dig out the decision not to prosecute and fire the person who made it. This means that, nine times out of ten, it is better to prosecute in cases of domestic violence or sexual offence, despite the fact that everyone knows the case will be discontinued on the day of court. This isn't necessarily a bad thing. I have nothing against guilty wife-beaters, rapists and muggers getting hauled through the legal process, even if they are never likely to be convicted. But it does waste a lot of money and makes for low conviction rates, which makes for low confidence in the legal system and less genuine victims coming forwards. Plus it does mean innocent people get dragged through, too.

That *is* a bad thing.

Auditors: Auditors check the work of Crime Compliance (see below), to make sure it is being done properly. They are just about the last checkpoint before the paperwork is permanently inserted into a shelving unit. If you get your file past the Auditors, the only thing that can resurrect it is a complaint from the victim.

Best Practice: There are policies for most eventualities in the police. These are documents drawn up explaining how the police force will deal with a variety of circumstances, ranging from sickness levels, under-performing officers, to firearms incidents, missing persons and bomb threats. 'Best Practice' is when the policies are followed to the letter. Following Best Practice is the best way of ensuring that you cannot be criticised for your actions, and that your Arse is fully Covered.

Crap Assignment Officer: This person works in the Quality Service Department and it is their responsibility to send police officers to see the callers. This is another thing that used to be the job of police sergeants, who would often phone the caller and say the magic words, 'We're not coming'. The CAO is not a police sergeant, and has no authority to tell anyone that we're not coming.

It is also the CAO's job to phone up Mops who have been waiting to see a police officer for two weeks and stoke them into a small fury by apologising for how long it has taken for us to get there. This can usually be achieved by using the words, 'There've been a lot of far more important calls this week.'

In an ideal world, the police officers allocated to the Crap jobs would do nothing else, and would probably work their way through all these calls within the space of each day. In reality, the officers are constantly being dragged away from the Crap jobs to go to emergencies. This is because there aren't enough response officers to go to all the emergencies, let alone all these other jobs.

Crime Centre: When a member of the public phones to report just about anything, whether it constitutes an offence or not, they will be put through to the Crime Centre. Here a civilian will use a series of drop-down menus to identify what crime has taken place, and will generate a crime report accordingly.

This is just marvellous: if only I had been shown these drop-down menus when I first joined the police, I would not have had to study law for fifteen weeks at training school.

Crime Compliance: Sometimes, police officers attend incidents where a crime has not actually taken place (such as my non-existent domestic at Ratchet Path). Our bureaucracy requires that a crime report be created for each of these incidents, with the crime recorded as whichever crime is as close as possible to the crime that it would have been, if it had been a crime. These crimes are obviously undetectable (because they have not happened), so they will then be 'filed', which means they remain undetected.

Police officers dislike filing jobs, because we're judged on our percentage of detected crime. We therefore try not to create crime reports when no crime has occurred. This outrageous practice is wholly irresponsible, and Crime Compliance is there to stop it.

The classic example of the system in action is the Domestic Argument i.e. one stage ahead of Ratchet Path, where the couple weren't even arguing.

We attend. No crime has been committed; one party has simply called us to sort out an argument over the telly. Because our force and the Home Office know that individual police officers do not care about women being beaten up and want them all to die, they do not trust us just to use our discretion, separate the warring parties for a moment and decide that they should watch ITV. Oh no. They would much rather we created a crime report of assault as soon as the word 'He' is mentioned by our caller.

On the one hand, this does make it easier for the police officer to arrest someone rather than bother trying to explain why they're not going to. On the other hand, is it really the right thing to do?

Anyway, Crime Compliance pore over everything we do and write in an attempt to find a box unticked, an arrest not made, a lead not followed.

This successful system is now pushing the honest coppers underground where they belong: whereas before they used to be able to say there had been a bit of a scuffle but both parties were equally to blame, now it is better just to lie and say that no physical contact took place whatsoever. I think you will all agree that this is the best outcome for society and the victims of crime.

Crime Desk: When the Mop has finished on the phone to the Crime Centre, the resulting crime report is forwarded to the Crime Desk. The daily crime reports are reviewed and some are given out to police officers to investigate, while others are taken on by civilians. The process for deciding who will get what is to fold the crime reports up into lottery balls and whirl them round in a big machine.

Crime Management, Investigation and Detections Supervisor: There are numerous people described in this book whose job it is to check other people's work and do it all over again for them. The CMID Supervisor is yet another of these. He has one goal and one goal alone: to make sure that if a police officer 'detects' a crime, that detection is added to the force's statistics. It may be surprising to think that detections can be 'lost' in the system, but amid the morass of Home Office rules about crime-recording and Blandshire's own numerous computer systems, this happens a lot.

For example, the custody system is not linked to the crime recording system. Which means if I charge a prisoner on the custody computer I have manually to input the details of the charge into the Crime Management System and then tell a more senior person I have done this so that the crime report can be marked up as 'detected'. The CMID Supervisor goes through each charge each day on the custody computer and makes sure that the CMS has been updated with it.

Glossary

There is a multitude of other ways to 'find' detections, but you need five or ten years of front-line experience and a promotion to sergeant before you could hope to understand them.

Crime Management System: This is the computer application that contains the database of all crime reports. The CMS is continually modernised and upgraded with new ticky-boxes and checklists to complete, all completely compliant with NCRS (see above). This creates exhaustive audit trails for all our investigations and has the added bonus that we require re-training each time a new ticky-box is introduced.

The important of these tick-boxes should not be under-estimated. Without the correct combination of ticks, no crime report can be filed, 'cleared up' or re-classified. It isn't a case of anyone trying to be difficult; the System simply WILL NOT WORK unless the right boxes are ticked.

There is a hierarchy of access to the CMS. PCs like myself are permitted to make phone-calls requesting updates to our crime reports, and we are even allowed access to tick one or two of the boxes. Above us is a plethora of sergeants, scrutineers, auditors and senior managers who are all able to tick a varying number of boxes. Only the scrutineers have the power to 'file' crime reports (see below).

Department of Critical Emailing: There is no actual, single Department for sending out critical emails - the title is IRONIC. This is in fact the job of *all* departments from CID to Senior Management. You can guarantee that no matter how many things you have done right, it will be the one you have done wrong that generates an email.

Department of Being Nice to Criminals: This department exists in all forces and is usually known as 'Restorative Justice' or 'Youth Offending'. It reviews all cases involving young offenders.

It works on the premise that, in the modern age, it is the police's job to make children apologise to people when they do something wrong. The Department of Being Nice to Criminals can set up these apologies and arbitrate to make sure neither side's parents have a fight.

The way this works is: a child steals a car or hits someone. If they have never been in trouble before, they are given a couple of second chances before they go to court for it. This means they are given the chance to admit what they have done, and are then asked to return to the police station on another day to speak to someone in this special Department. On the day they return they get a 'warning' on their criminal record and a lecture from a wise older police officer.

I don't have a problem with the concept of a few chances for kids. But the lecture used to be given out by the custody sergeant on the day the child was arrested, and I have no idea why we need special people to do this for them.

Detections: The corner-stone of modern policing, Detections drive our world these days. A Detection is awarded when someone is charged, reported or formally warned for an offence. When this happens, the offence is said to have been 'detected' or 'cleared up'. Chief Constables are judged on their percentage of 'cleared up' crime.

For anyone who has not grasped the concept of percentages, this gives two ways for police forces to improve their Detection rate: they can obtain more Detections, or they can reduce crime overall (so that the Detected crime rate rises).

The easiest kind of crime to reduce is that being committed by people we know about, who we can put in prison for a short period. While they are in prison, our recorded crime rate will fall. But so, unfortunately, will our Detection rates - as these people were accounting for the majority of our Detected crimes.

It is therefore far better to concentrate on *increasing* the overall number of Detections, even if that means the number of recorded crimes goes up. To this end we are given monthly targets for Detections. The targets vary depending on the current fad, so one month we will be encouraged to give out penalty notices for shoplifting and the next month it will be formal warnings for cannabis.

This keeps us on our toes and is no doubt good for morale.

Detective Chief Inspector Responsible for Informative Emails: Detective Chief Inspector is a seriously high rank. It is about as high as you can go in the realms of detective-hood before you start investigating things like the London Bombings. The DCI is pretty much held responsible for how well his area's detectives are investigating murders, rapes, serious assaults etc. This puts a lot of pressure and media attention on the DCI.

Glossary

The DCI therefore spends his days dreaming up ways of ensuring that murders, rapes and serious assaults are investigated well in his area. Since uniformed response officers are usually the first on scene to most of these offences, the DCI takes a keen interest in how the response officers deal with the incidents. He cares very little about how many other jobs the same response officers are going to each day, or how many other pressures they have.

As a result, we are blessed with 'round robin' emails and letters from the DCI telling us how to do our job better. The emails and letters make a lot of sense. It's just that we know it all already and most of us are doing our best.

Ethical Crime Recording: This is just another way of saying that a police force is recording crime in line with NCRS. The word 'ethical' suggests that people think the police dishonestly try and make crime figures look lower.

The effect of Ethical Crime Recording is that police forces are nervous about telling anyone that the crime they say happened, didn't happen. We are forced to record a crime anyway. Which has the effect of dishonestly making the crime figures look *higher*.

Go figure.

File (as in, the investigation is 'filed'): This is when police have given up hope of catching somebody and the paperwork is sent to the Archives for storage. It is actually checked by several other departments first, but if everyone agrees it can be filed away for good, it is.

It used to be that police officers would discuss all investigations with their sergeants and together decide when it was no longer worth pursuing. The sergeant could then 'file' the paperwork and no more work would be done on it.

Nowadays, however, sergeants have to send the paperwork to another department where it will be checked and filed by them. More on this below.

FNO (Friendly Neighbourhood Officer): In the 21st Century, all police forces have been instructed to promote 'Neighbourhood Policing'. This means bobbies on foot patrol on every street corner, ready to spring on wrongdoers. Neighbourhood Officers (I added the

'Friendly' myself) are usually recruited from response teams and are supposed to deal with any incidents that occur in their area. This should relieve some of the pressure on response teams and please the public at the same time. In reality, Neighbourhood Officers are inundated with ongoing problems in their areas such as antisocial behaviour or burglary, and spend all their time attending community meetings or patrolling on foot in yellow jackets, and can't actually take much pressure off the response teams at all. The result: fewer officers to respond to incidents and a lot of officers walking around not responding to incidents.

I'm in favour of Neighbourhood Officers, in theory, and there's no doubt this is what the public wants. I just have this crazy idea that if we don't have enough police to respond to emergencies, perhaps we ought to sort that out first.

Inspector Responsible for Being Responsible: Every day a Duty Inspector is in charge of Blandmore. His or her job is to make daily decisions about events that are unfolding and people in custody.

If this sounds important, it is. If someone dies as a result of something the police do, it is the Inspector Responsible for Being Responsible who will be responsible. In other words, the inspector on duty at the time it happened will ultimately take the rap for anything he/she did or didn't tell his/her troops to do.

Each inspector is also in charge of his/her own response teams. This means it is the inspector who gets blamed for any shortfall in the monthly targets of the police officers in those teams. As you can imagine, the inspector cares a great deal about how well his/her teams are doing, to the extent that most of the pressure on PCs to perform well in the monthly figures comes from the inspector. It isn't their fault; they are just handing down the pressure put on them from above.

Investigation Supervisor: This person's job is to review the work of police sergeants. Police sergeants have responsibility for five or ten PCs whose investigations they oversee and send for filing when necessary. The system for overseeing investigations is for the sergeant to review them every few weeks and give advice on how to proceed to the officer in charge of the case.

Glossary

As police sergeants are also busy sending police officers out to fight with people, Blandshire Constabulary kindly provides the 'Investigation Supervisor'. This will be a police constable installed in an office who has nothing to do all day other than review the reviews made by police sergeants and point out how they have gone wrong.

The Investigation Supervisor can then carry out their own reviews and give the PCs contradictory instructions to those from their sergeant, which is tremendously helpful all round.

What this reflects is the fact that nobody trusts police sergeants to do their job any more. Instead of improving the training of sergeants, or having a different promotion system, it is considered easier just to employ someone to do their job for them after they've already done it themselves once.

Livescan: I think I can safely say that this is the only piece of technology introduced to the police in the last five years that has actually made my job easier. No longer do we have to cover ourselves with ink taking fingerprints from the people we arrest, but we now stand them in front of a red laser and their prints are scanned onto a computer screen. It is ink-free, takes half the time, and because the prints are downloaded straight onto the national database, they are almost never lost in transit. The other brilliant feature of the machine is that if you think someone is lying to you about their identity, you can send off their prints to compare them against the name they are giving you. If there are prints for that person on the database you can find out immediately who you have arrested and what they are wanted for. Plus there's a Gucci red laser involved, which is always a good thing.

Major Incident: A major incident has an official definition: an incident involving more than one emergency service. What this means in practice is an incident that puts severe strain on resources. When a major incident is announced, a series of procedures and policies kick in that allow for overtime to be paid to all kinds of people who are never normally allowed to claim overtime.

Monitor, The: Sometimes, following an arrest, the police have more enquiries to do that will mean bailing the suspect to return to the police station at a specified date and time. When they turn up, they will be booked back into custody and then either re-interviewed, charged or released for good. One officer can quite easily end up with eight or ten people on bail at any one time, which puts a huge strain on that officer to carry out the relevant enquiries in time for the bail date, and strain on the police station to book in and deal with this amount of prisoners.

Blandshire Constabulary has therefore created the role of Bail Monitor. It is clearly not possible for police constables and sergeants to keep track of the people they have on bail, as that would involve organisational and supervisory skills. As explained, sergeants are no longer expected to supervise anyone without help. The Monitor therefore keeps track of who is on bail and whether the officer is ready to deal with them on the right day.

If the officer is *not* ready to deal with the prisoner, the Bail Monitor will record this fact in a spreadsheet. The hope is that if officers think someone is checking up on them, they will be ready in time. In reality, the reason the officer is not ready is that they have ten people on bail and absolutely no free time to carry out the enquiries. The fact that this is recorded by the Bail Monitor makes no difference.

What *might* make a difference is if the Bail Monitor was employed to go out and do the enquiries instead. But then who would compile the spreadsheet?

Mops: Members of the Public, otherwise known as Muggles.

National Crime Recording Standards: There is a general consensus that police forces do their best to show how crime rates are falling. This has, in the past, led to them dishonestly recording less crime than they should, or only recording the crimes that have been 'cleared up'.

There are now, therefore, strict rules about the recording of crime, handed down by the Home Office. The rules dictate how many crime reports should be created, how many should be 'cleared up', and how many can be justifiably 'binned' or 'filed'. I won't go into all the rules of NCRS now, because it's just too boring.

Each police force is left to implement the NCRS in their own way. Blandshire Constabulary has chosen to do it with the Crime Management System. Forces are even graded on their NCRS-compliance, which means if a force is unable to detect or reduce crime, they can still be regarded as 'excellent' in how they record it. Reassuring, no?

No-Crime: As explained above, the rules on recording crime are quite strict. One of them is that a crime should be recorded on the police computer system within 24 hours of it being reported to the police. Sometimes, therefore, crime reports are generated BEFORE any police officer has actually attended the incident.

The people who record these crimes are civilians with very little legal training, who essentially have to guess what offence might have been committed based on the meagre details they can obtain from the victim over the phone. So sometimes when a police officer actually visits the victim, it turns out that the reality is very different from what has been put on the crime report. On some occasions, as you know, no actual criminal offence has been committed at all.

You can't just delete a crime report as this could lead to accusations of the police 'losing' evidence in cases. The system actually will not allow anything to be deleted at all. Instead, you just change the classification of the crime to a 'No-Crime' and this means if anybody looks at it they will see your explanation and realise that no offence was committed. It will then not be counted towards crime figures, although it will remain on the computer system forever.

Positive Intervention: This all started when someone pointed out that whenever a victim of domestic violence didn't want to prosecute, the police were just leaving without doing anything. This led to all kinds of recriminations if one party (usually the female, let's face it) was murdered several months or years later.

Voila, Positive Intervention. Now it is up to the attending officers to make sure that somebody gets arrested every time they go to a domestic, even if for the most minor of offences.

Police officers used to be pretty good at judging which incidents to arrest someone from and which ones to leave without doing anything. But society has become litigious and someone is always held to account if there's a murder, so it's now just easier to go along with the policy and arrest everyone in sight. Of course, once they've been arrested for an offence, we might be in for a chance of a detection, so we go the whole hog and try to get a CPS lawyer to agree to charge them. The CPS is just as worried about recriminations, so they advise a charge and hey presto: a whole court case where offender and victim are still living together and there is zero chance of the victim showing up on the day.

As a woman, I couldn't be more against the idea of women being murdered by their partners. I just wonder if Positive Intervention is actually doing anything to prevent it, or if it's effectively numbing police officers to the truly nasty cases, when they come along.

Pregnancy: There is a glut of legislation surrounding employers' responsibilities to pregnant women. There are also a lot of government leaflets for pregnant women describing how to sue their employers for endangering them or their babies. The leaflets explain how the employer has a responsibility to find work for them to do that is not dangerous or stressful.

Anything involving the words 'woman' and 'sue' is terrifying to a police force. As soon as you fall pregnant, therefore, you are whisked off 'front-line' duties and planted somewhere 'safe'. For many forces, this means absolutely no public contact whatsoever. If you are young in service and still performing your mandatory period on the front-line, this can have a serious impact on your career. It's worth pointing out that there is a lot of good police work you can do without actually getting physical. Most of it does involve some kind of public contact, but no more than anyone in any job involved with customers.

I have searched long and hard, but I can't find any leaflets for pregnant women who want to continue with front-line work as long as possible, or who are prepared to meet with the odd Mop in the hope that they won't be spontaneously attacked. I can't find any legislation supporting those athletes who stay in competition for a good twenty weeks of their pregnancy and return to it straight after the birth. Believe it or not, I can't actually find a form for a woman to sign to say she understands the risks and has made her own decision.

Maybe I'm looking in the wrong place. Or maybe the sight of a pregnant police officer is just too much for society to stomach just yet.

Quality Service Department: It used to be that police sergeants and control room operators could filter through calls from the public and prioritise which ones to send police officers to first. Some callers' issues could be solved on the phone, others could be threatened with prosecution if they didn't stop calling.

We have moved on from these dark days into the bright era of customer service. There is now a whole department dedicated to sending police officers to incidents that are not police matters. This means that Mops get told to sod off personally, face-to-face, rather than by telephone which just wasn't good enough.

When someone calls the police regarding something that is not a police matter, they will be put through to the QSD and a civilian or pregnant officer will then spend their day trying to persuade response officers to go and speak to the caller. Most of these incidents should not even be recorded, least of all attended. But the idea is that if we let these people see a police officer, they might not make a complaint and Blandshire Constabulary will move up the ranks when it comes to 'customer satisfaction'. Take it from me, many of these Mops will never, ever, be satisfied, no matter how many times we go to see them. We will never stop these people from calling the police, and they have every right to try, but I really think that a robust call-taker explaining, 'We're not coming', might help things dramatically. That would free up the officers to attend the minority that *are* important.

Risk Assessment: This has a multitude of meanings in the police. One meaning is just the daily risk assessing we all do when determining whether to put our feet on the broken paving stone in front of us, or whether to walk around it.

The main meaning in the police though, is to do with Domestic Violence, and assessing how likely you think it is that someone is going to kill their partner in the near or distant future. Because this is the 21st Century, this process has been formalised into a checklist and questionnaire. So on attending Domestic Violence incidents, the police officer asks both parties a list of Yes/No questions about their relationship and hands the list to a sergeant to hand to the Domestic Violence Unit for checking. The case will then be graded High, Medium or Low Risk, which is important because it affects the colour of the folder used to file the paperwork.

Scrutineer: Essentially the Scrutineer fields requests from PCs and sergeants who want to file or no-crime their investigations. The Scrutineer will either reject the request, or re-type it in a format acceptable to the Auditors and forward it to them for re-checking.

The Scrutineer is a civilian, and is therefore not weighed down with any knowledge about the kinds of incidents police officers find themselves attending. This makes it easier for him or her to filter out the requests from officers who are dishonestly trying not to investigate crimes that haven't occurred. In a nutshell, the Scrutineer is employed solely to check that police officers are not trying to file or no-crime jobs that might otherwise result in a detection for Blandshire Constabulary. This is another thing that police sergeants used to be trusted to do.

Tactical Inspector: This inspector is trained in firearms, public order and siege tactics, and will run any incident involving any of these skills.

Victim Codes or the Victim's Charter: This dreamchild is the innovative solution to the problem of 'customer satisfaction' in the police. It has been long understood that while the police should work with the consent of the public, the public is probably never going to love them. A lot of our job involves making difficult decisions that are always going to piss someone off.

Well, pissed-off people don't vote for the government, hence the birth of the Victim's Charter. This sets down strict rules for how often victims of crime must be updated by the officer in the case, and forces are measured by the Home Office on how well they comply with it. Blandshire has chosen to introduce a system of checky-tick-boxes that monitor compliance.

Maybe I'm expecting too much of our world-weary sergeants, but I always thought that again it was their job to check how well the officers they supervise are doing their jobs.

OUT SOON FROM MONDAY BOOKS:

IN FOREIGN FIELDS: TRUE STORIES OF AMAZING BRAVERY FROM IRAQ AND AFGHANISTAN

by Dan Collins (Hardback - £17.99/ published October 2007)

The Iraq War has turned into a quagmire of hatred, violence and death. The bloody Afghanistan conflict is equally savage - a seething cauldron of roadside bombs, ambushes and constant danger. Day after day, our soldiers face implacable and ferocious enemy forces in the searing heat and choking dust of two faraway foreign lands. To make matters worse, many feel the public has turned its back on them.

But the young men and women of our armed forces do not have the luxury of deciding where they fight, and in the deserts and towns of Iraq and Afghanistan a new breed of hero is being born.

Blues and Royals Corporal of Horse Andrew Radford ran 70 metres through a hail of machine gun fire and RPGs to rescue a terribly injured colleague.

Royal Marine Sergeant Matt Tomlinson charged machine gun posts during a river ambush outside Fallujah, and saved the lives of the US Marines he was attached to. Parachute Regiment Lieutenant Hugo Farmer led his men in a desperate, three-hour fire-fight against the Taliban - in the same action for which Corporal Bryan Budd was awarded a posthumous Victoria Cross. This list goes on and on - and now, for the first time, they tell their own stories.

In Foreign Fields features 30 medal winners from Iraq and Afghanistan talking, in their own words, about the actions which led to their awards. Modestly, often reluctantly, they explain what it's like at the very sharp end, in the heat of battle with death staring you in the face. If you support our armed forces, you will want to read this modern classic of war reportage.

A PARAMEDIC'S DIARY
Life And Death In London

by Stuart Gray (Paperback - £7.99/ published September 2007)
Stuart Gray is a London Ambulance Service paramedic and this is
a diary of a year in his working life. It's a moving, funny and
absolutely gripping insight into the business of saving lives in the
world's most famous city.

CRYSTAL DEATH: An Undercover Warrior
And The World's Most Dangerous Drug

(Paperback - £7.99/ published November 2007)
Joe Clarke was the best methamphetamine 'cook' in the USA -
until he was busted. Then he became the FBI's best undercover
agent in the war on this terrible drug. His astonishing true story -
of one man's journey to hell and back - makes hair-raising,
fascinating reading.

ALREADY PUBLISHED BY
MONDAY BOOKS:

WASTING POLICE TIME...
THE CRAZY WORLD OF THE WAR ON CRIME
PC David Copperfield (£7.99)

PC DAVID COPPERFIELD is an ordinary bobby quietly waging
war on crime...when he's not drowning in a sea of paperwork,
government initiatives and bogus targets.
Wasting Police Time is his hilarious but shocking picture of life in
a modern British town, where teenage yobs terrorise the elderly,
drunken couples brawl in front of their children and drug-addicted
burglars and muggers roam free.
He reveals how crime is spiralling while millions of pounds in tax
is frittered away, and reveals a force which, crushed under mad
bureaucracy, is left desperately fiddling the figures.

His book has attracted rave reviews for its dry wit and insight from The Sunday Times, The Guardian, The Observer, The Daily Mail, The Mail on Sunday and The Daily Telegraph;.

'Being a policeman in modern England is not like appearing in an episode of The Sweeney, Inspector Morse or even The Bill, sadly,' says Copperfield. 'No, it's like standing banging your head against a wall, carrying a couple of hundredweight of paperwork on your shoulders, while the house around you burns to the ground.'

IT'S YOUR TIME YOU'RE WASTING

A Teacher's Tales Of Classroom Hell by Frank Chalk (£7.99)
The blackly humorous diary of a year in teacher's working life. Chalk confiscates porn, booze and trainers, fends off angry parents and worries about the few conscientious pupils he comes across, recording his experiences in a dry and very readable manner.
"Does for education what PC David Copperfield did for the police"

ROAD TRIP TO HELL:

Tabloid Tales Of Saddam, Iraq And A Bloody War (£7.99)
Tabloid journalist Chris Hughes records his many visits to Iraq pre- and post-war: he finds Saddam's underpants, is carjacked and almost dies and watches US Marines kill unarmed people in a crowd.
Visceral and brutal in parts, amusing in others, Hughes is very warm about the Iraqi people and scathing about the US invasion.